# LAW, LIFE AND LAUGHTER
## A PERSONAL VERDICT

'I look upon anecdotes as debts due to the public, which every man who has that kind of cash by him, ought to pay.'

Lord Orerry to Dr Birch, 1741

# LAW, LIFE AND LAUGHTER

## A PERSONAL VERDICT

Irvine Smith, QC

BLACK & WHITE PUBLISHING

First published 2011
This edition first published 2012
by Black & White Publishing Ltd
29 Ocean Drive, Edinburgh EH6 6JL

1 3 5 7 9 10 8 6 4 2    12 13 14 15

ISBN: 978 1 84502 441 3

Typeset by Ellipsis Digital Limited, Glasgow
Printed and bound by CPI Group (UK) Ltd, Croydon, CR0 4YY

# CONTENTS

# ACKNOWLEDGEMENTS

My thanks are due to the widow, Dr Jill MacDonald, and the children of the late Sheriff Alistair MacDonald for their permission to print two of his letters to me; to Mr John Black of Bexley Heath for permission to print his letter and to Jack Webster for permission to quote from his autobiography *Grains of Truth*.

My thanks are also due to Lord McEwan, Sheriff Kenneth Mitchell, Professor Charles Hennessy and Mr Paul Reid, Solicitor Advocate, who read and commented on the manuscript and, again, to Lord McEwan for accepting my invitation to contribute the foreword.

The publishers of the *Scots Law Times* gave me permission to quote from their Journals, reports of cases in which I was involved.

As the stage of publication was reached and communications between an anxious author and a schedule-conscious staff of the publishers became numerous, my lack of email literacy and practice presaged delays and difficulties, to which my uncertain health was already contributing. These difficulties have, I think and hope, been avoided by the intervention of Alison, my elder daughter, who has readily, willingly and inexhaustibly discharged throughout, the roles of inspired Personal Assistant and first-class secretary. Had it not been for her, supported by the patience and encouragement of her mother, I would not now be writing these acknowledgements.

# FOREWORD

by Lord McEwan

I first met James Irvine Smith (known to all as Irvine) when I was a law student at Glasgow University. He opened the door for me to the life of the Bar, the world of advocacy and legal learning. He encouraged me and others like me to pursue and attain excellence. It is a great privilege and pleasure to write this foreword.

The opening chapters are both stern and amusing. He has a good and detailed memory of his childhood, his early years and the privations suffered and cheerfully borne on 'holidays' in Ayrshire with some of the main characters in his life. On visits to Dailly, newspapers assumed a special importance as the reader will discover!

To Irvine his friends were valued and a source of pleasure. At the Bar those who are your friends are also your professional rivals. The present generation of advocates may just remember Ranald Sutherland but almost certainly never knew Sir Randall Philip, the great Manuel Kissen and Sheriff Alistair MacDonald. Mere names in dry legal text books now, come vividly alive in Irvine's pages.

The book takes on a dark mantle when the writer returns to the difficult days of Capital Murder trials. Irvine defended a number of men and one woman who faced the death penalty, and lost only one to the hangman, and he was but a boy. I know from my many communications with him about that case how the execution has never left his mind, and will haunt him for ever.

The author's mid life was spent and enjoyed as a sheriff-substitute in Glasgow and his insight abounds into the fun and subtleties of that 'holy city'. It was a large part of his life which changed when he went to another Sheriff Court, and not for the better. For the last quarter of the twentieth century Irvine was the best after dinner speaker in Scotland, and his reputation at Burns Suppers was international. The reader will find in the chapter 'The Cult of Speech' a veritable quarry of information about how to acquire these skills. Reading aloud, elocution, learning by rote and the value of poetry are all commended. To an older generation these were second nature. Today's generation should pay attention.

This book is a splendid work about a valuable and useful life well enjoyed and happily ongoing. It will be read and appreciated by the legal profession and layfolk alike, even, I venture to suggest, by the many miscreants who appeared in Irvine's court before being returned to 'secure accomodation'. I wish the book all success.

ROBIN G. McEWAN

# 1

# A THIRTIES CHILDHOOD

Falkirk, where I lived in or close to for fifty-seven years, is an ancient Scottish burgh with a long vivid and chequered history. It was the scene of two significant battles. One, at which the fortunes of William Wallace saw their first serious setback, and the other which did nothing to halt the retreat of Prince Charles Edward Stewart's army to its ultimate destruction at Culloden. In the eighteenth and nineteenth centuries, it was famous for its iron industries and annual autumnal 'cattle trysts', where all the drove roads of Scotland terminated.

In the 1930s, however, Falkirk was a town uncertain of its present, anxious about its future and nostalgic about its recent past. It was anxious because the decline of the industries, on which its prosperity had been built, was becoming all too obvious. That prosperity began with the founding of Carron Iron Works in 1759. Thereafter, with the rest of central Scotland, where iron and coal lay in abundance, it became a town of iron foundries. These foundries employed not just men, but generations of men from the same local families. My paternal grandfather, who died before 1914, was employed there. My father, too, worked there as a fitter all his working life, as did his brother, John.

Iron foundries and the Carron Company, in particular, were the major employers of men in the town in the 1930s but with the Depression, which only ended with the start of the Second World War, like the rest of the country, many a man had no job. My father was one of the lucky ones. He was never unemployed, although when the war started in 1939 his work changed from assembling iron grates to assembling implements of war, and he and his contemporaries, for the first time, earned significantly greater wages. The 'war work', as it was called was intense. He would start at 6 a.m. on a working day and I recall, as a boy of thirteen, walking the two miles or so from our home to Carron Foundry with his breakfast; a flask of tea and bacon rolls, the bacon being always my mother's choice, Wiltshire bacon. Between 12 and 1 p.m. he would come home for what was then the main meal of the day. He and his like lived their whole working lives to the sound of the factory whistles, which, in recollection, I can still hear.

In the 1930s, in Falkirk, like many Scottish industrial towns, you were never far from a foundry and never far from a church – a phenomenon by which an over-abundance of spiritual comfort was provided for the people of these towns. In Falkirk I recollect seven Church of Scotland Churches, one Roman Catholic Church and a substantial, well-attended Methodist Church. There were also meeting halls of Plymouth Brethren and the Salvation Army's Citadel to which throughout all my time in Falkirk, a substantial band marched every Sunday morning with banners flying, drum beating and brass sounding, all the way up the main road from Grahamston to the centre of the town.

They brought their music and with it their message and conviction to every class in that variegated community. It was an impressive custom and one which the sight and the sound of the marching band, gave me my first experience in concerted outdoor music making. The contributions of this by the other churches was less melodious but more historical. Every church had its own bell, each recognisable and distinguishable to its faithful. Each church, on Sunday mornings and on the Sunday evenings, called its individual congregations with 'the ding frae its iron moo', because in the 1930s many people still – even though it was then in decline – believed in the Scots and Victorian habit of belonging to a Kirk, whose attendance there was a duty. In the war which started in 1939 the Kirk bells were silent: to be rung only if the country was invaded. At Stenhouse Parish Church, which I attended, there were services at 11 a.m. and 6.30 p.m. Many children, like myself, were taken to church on Sunday mornings where we sat through the service and then went to Sunday school. I fear my early experience of sermons of twenty-five-minutes duration, sometimes more, did not encourage in me any enthusiasm for their institution. Sunday school attendance was not onerous, but it too could certainly be boring. I recall one Sunday school teacher who considered it essential that a class of nine or ten year olds should be able to recite by heart the names of all the books of The Bible in their proper order. The object of this, he claimed, was that we could then more easily look up the text when it had been quoted by the minister, without wasting time looking up the index. Now in my eighties I can still recite, in order, the books of the Old and New Testaments: the value of which, I confess, I have never been able to discover.

Attendance at Sunday school did, however, qualify you for the two highlights of the year: the summer Sunday school trip and the Christmas Parties. The trip in June usually set out from Stenhousemuir in buses, with streamers flying and a general excitement and noise, which the adults early abandoned all hope of trying to control. The favoured destinations were the Hillfoot villages such as Alva and Tillicoultry, with Doune, near Stirling, a special favourite. Once there, if the weather was good, there were races of all kinds and for all ages, ball games and walks to the neighbouring towns to purchase presents – very modest presents – for parents unable to be present. If it rained there was always a hall available. Alva Glen was, as I recall, the best equipped with this alternative, and there the adults did their best to occupy their excited but disappointed charges by organising games and running a concert in which every child was expected to volunteer to do their turn. This was an exercise productive of some unusual talents and results. If one of the objects of the 'trip' was to preserve the children's loyalty and encourage their attendance at Sunday school, it certainly succeeded. For the adults who came with the children – it was my Aunt Bella who always took me – the trips had the entirely laudable conclusion of exhausting their charges. There were very few streamers on the way home. The fathers, incidentally, rarely attended the Sunday school trips.

The Sunday school Christmas Parties were more sedate affairs. One such party for all the children was held in the church hall by the Sunday school organisers. Another, for the younger pupils, was held every year by a family of, I recall, three sisters, the Misses Bauchops, all unmarried and all comfortably off in their own large and comfortable home. The three, always in black, sat in the pew in front of ours in the church, and my attendance at church being something they were bound to notice, it invariably became more committed as Christmas approached. Their party for we children was one of the events of the year. The games we played in their sitting room were the traditional children's games of the day which generally involved holding hands and walking around in a circle singing to a piano accompaniment. The names of most of the games I have forgotten but I do remember the concluding line of one chorus 'And we are all children, And we must all die' – a proposition which at that particular stage did not much concern us, even if we had understood it.

At the end of one's youth, one was expected to be admitted to full membership of the Kirk and to be grateful for the privilege.

Attendance at and adherence to a particular church in these days did not just mean professing one's faith and practising a religion. It admitted one also to the many activities of which the individual church was then the centre. In particular, Stenhouse Parish Church, in my childhood, had an annual *Kinderspiel* – a form of musical which had the triple object of keeping the children occupied in practising, the adults occupied with rehearsals and preparation, and the parents and congregation, being entertained when the first night was reached. The context of the piece invariably carried a moral message and ended, of course, in the triumph of virtue. I recall one snatch: the chorus was sung by Robin Hood and a company of junior archers who were his 'men', who had somehow found their way into this unlikely scenario where fairies and goodwill abounded. It ran:-

4

Learn a lesson from the archers,
Take a hint from Robin Hood,
And whatever may befall you,
Ever let your aim be good.

Some of the more ambitious city churches in Glasgow at that time selected, rehearsed and presented a musical, such as *Chu, Chin Chow, The Girlfriend* or *Rose Marie.*

Church halls were the regular scenes of concerts at which local amateur singers, instrumentalists and elocutionists purported to entertain the congregation and raise money for some charity, usually a necessary church repair. The repertoire did not vary much: it was the old Scots songs, which then everyone knew, and the familiar Victorian and Edwardian ballads: 'Love's Old Sweet Song' and 'The Trumpeter', together with the more recent song 'Bless This House', which then everyone also knew.

In the 1930s, of course, there was another significant form of entertainment, which was not amateur and which was to find its apotheosis in the world's fixation with television from the 1950s onwards. I refer to the recently invented 'talking films.' We had a small theatre in Falkirk, then called 'The Electric', later 'The Roxy', which attempted to continue the tradition of the music hall but which declined in popularity before the films. The screens, silent and then talking, which were then to be found in no less than five cinemas within a half-mile radius of the centre of the town, and others in neighbouring communities were a weekly draw to the population. The number of churches and the number of cinemas seemed to be about equal.

Falkirk then was a town and a neighbourhood; not a village but a community that had many characteristics of a village. There was much familiarity with the comings and goings, the ups and downs of fellow citizens and their children. The academic, sporting, artistic and other successes of its children and youth were of interest, and, as a consequence, became the talk of the town. The successful graduates gave satisfaction, not only to their parents, but to fellow citizens. The departure of a minister and who should succeed him interested all who had a connection with any church. The birth of a child to what was called 'an old Falkirk family' evoked all the interest it would in a village community. We knew where most of our contemporaries went for their holidays, if they went anywhere: I knew only one family – the father was a prosperous grocer – who regularly went on cruises. This for most was still the golden age of the Costa Clyde.

It was into this town and in my parents' house that I was born on 26 November 1926, in a small three-storey tenement building in Grahams Road.

I was the only child my parents were to have. They were married comparatively late in life. My mother had me when she was forty-two, and, I am told, a sore time she had of it. She told me long after that, Chrissie, one of my father's sisters and a spinster, had once asked her if she had considered the whole experience had been 'worth it?' When they married, my parents bought their home which was rather special because it gave them a bathroom which had a toilet and a bath but, as an Edinburgh 'friend' once remarked disdainfully 'no wash hand basin at all'. It gave us, again for these days, more space than most. It cost £340 in 1924. They took out a mortgage, which must have been paid regularly since both were working. Our house was, I fear, a wholly unlovely building architecturally. It had been built, partly to house a successful herbalist business at the centre ground floor, with a small shop at either side and a close for entry to the three flatted houses above. The shop at the north end of the building was known to the local children as a sweetie shop or if more precision was required, 'Chrissie's shop' after the owner. The shop at the south end had a more varied mercantile history. Its stock changes included linoleum, electrical spares, and tropical fish and their food. This was to be my home until I married in 1958, at the age of thirty-two, and it was my father's home until the end of his life. He died there, aged seventy-four, by which time my mother was in hospital, a victim of senile dementia.

In later life, I have often been accused by affluent and public-school educated left-wingers of 'knowing nothing about the working classes'. I consider it my privilege and advantage that, in my origins, parental and local, there was to be found what I regard as the Scots working folk at their best. What my parents gave me was a more intimate experience of what the working man and woman were in the 1930s than those who challenged me. In addition, I could and can speak the language of the folk I came from, with the accents which I have never forgotten, and which did me no harm in what I did later in life.

Ugliness, inconvenience, and an entire lack of domestic coherency in the architecture characterised that house of my parents. There were many steps and what was called a 'lobby', but at the end of the lobby there was 'the front room' – it was never called a lounge because *lounging* was not an activity with which my parents were familiar – but they had a 'front room' with a piano, which neither of them could play, and a wind-up gramophone with about twenty records, mostly of the songs and singers of the day.

My mother's younger sister, Jean, also had a piano in her flat in Glasgow and she and her children were self-taught, amateur pianists. It was from our gramophone and the songs that I learnt at Aunt Jean's, where I went every summer for a fortnight's holiday, that music came into my life and I first tried to sing. From both sources I managed to acquire a modest repertoire which my father decided to put to a somewhat unusual use.

Immediately to the north of Stenhousemuir Tryst, separated by Bellsdyke Road, there was a mental hospital, built with all the size and confidence that characterised the Victorians in these things. I did not know how many patients it treated, but it seemed to be a considerable number. You saw them as gardeners keeping the grounds immaculate – though at a pace which would not impress a commercial enterprise of today. My father called them 'the speedies', but the leisurely approach they had to landscape gardening gave them ample opportunity to converse with any of the public who happened to be passing on Bellsdyke Road, or walking in the grounds of the hospital itself, which was not, as I recollect, regarded as a risk, even for the young. These patients came to know people, like my father, who, when he was not working, went back to Stenhousemuir and made his way to the Tryst Cricket Club pavilion – an unlovely but practical building to which the retired men of the village could not only take their daily walk, but could sit and talk there in all weathers and seasons for as long as they wanted. There was then a certain camaraderie between the habitués of the cricket club and the more nomadic patients of the mental hospital. The former learned from the latter all that was happening in the hospital – which it did not appear was very much. There was, however, a regular, possibly a weekly, concert for the patients to which some of their own number contributed, but also for variety, relied on amateur talent from the surrounding district. It was in this unconventional milieu that I had my first introduction to making public appearances.

The patients of that mental hospital were, fortunately, not a particularly critical audience though, sometimes, they could be a diverting one. Occasionally, in the course of the performance, one or other of them would, for no apparent reason, shout an inarticulate shout and then relapse into silence. It was never possible to determine what they were shouting about. Their shouts were wordless and certainly did not appear to be abuse, or disapproval of any of the performers. There was no quarrelling among themselves – they just felt like shouting wordless noises which, however innocently prompted, were not always conducive to concentration on the part of a teenage soprano who was making an attempt to sing some operatic aria. Such interruptions, however, did not deter the amateur singer and reciter from offering and giving their services at these hospital concerts.

My link here was my father. He would be told there was a concert coming up and he volunteered my services as a singer. I think this started when I was about the age of seven or eight and not averse to trying to sing. My father certainly thought I could sing or, perhaps, he thought I *should* sing.

8

I have mentioned our wind-up gramophone and its twenty or so records, with Harry Lauder, *Songs of the First War* and of the music hall and such sentimental gems as 'Granny's Highland Hame'. We boasted no opera in this modest collection and the only orchestral item that I can remember was Ketelby's 'In a Monastery Garden' and one 10-inch, 78 rpm record, which gave music for a polka, a barn dance and a waltz,. I learned the words of the songs fairly quickly, and by the age when I made my bow to the patients in Larbert asylum, I possessed a small repertoire of such songs.

For these concerts I would be appropriately dressed in a kilt of the Crawford tartan because I was told my father's mother was a Crawford. But this choice was not dictated by any clan or matrilineal sentiments: it was because my mother liked the Crawford tartan, and the only person the family knew with a name entitling them to take the tartan, was my paternal grandmother.

In this appropriate garb, I had the colossal juvenile impertinence to mount a platform and sing songs and invite the patients to join in the choruses, which they invariably did. Usually, there was a pianist present but I was unable to enlist his services because there had been no rehearsal and I had no music except in my head, and I was afraid the piano would put me off. These 'performances' went on for about three years. I have mentioned earlier the *Kinderspiel* produced in the church we attended, and for these I was also an enthusiastic participant. In short, it would seem this boy liked to be on stage.

# 2

# THE FOLK THAT BEGAT ME

I have often been addressed, to my embarrassment, as if my name was double-barrelled: Irvine-Smith. It certainly was not. I was christened James Irvine Smith, the 'James' from my late paternal grandfather, the 'Irvine' as a Christian name, after my mother's family, whose surname it was. The Irvines were a Border family which, in the past, made a significant and frequent contribution to the criminal statistics and criminal jurisprudence of that area. The antisocial reputation of our ancestors, however, was unknown to my parents and I am satisfied they named me as they did because they thought Irvine as good a Christian name as it was a surname.

## THE SMITHS

My father came from a large family. The Smith grandparents, both of whom died before 1914, had eight children: Madge, Elizabeth (Bett), Agnes, Christina (Chrissie), John, Isabella (Bella), my father (James) and another daughter, who died of consumption. It would appear to have been the custom in those days in working class families to have at least one child who died of that condition. John died suddenly in 1929. Madge, the eldest, emigrated to Australia before the turn of the century. I was brought up to know all the others; some better than others. They were, undoubtedly, an interesting group and their parents must have been a determined and formidable couple. The living my grandfather, his sons and their kind earned from the foundries was never generous. About the mid '30s I saw a payslip for my father showing a weekly wage of three pounds ten shillings but modest though their earnings were, my grandfather Smith was a house owner. He was one of the founding

10

members of the local building society which in the later nineteenth century built streets of modest but solid houses in Stenhousmuir where property-owning artisans ensured they had and kept a roof over their heads and in our case, to remain the family home until the last of my grandfather's daughters died in 1962. These Union Street houses gave permanence but they did not give convenience. They had a room and kitchen on the ground floor each with a bed and a stair to the upper floor which ran the length and breadth of the house. These cottages were built in blocks of three with an entry dividing each of the blocks. Each had a strip of garden at the back with a washhouse in which was the only toilet. To use this, the potential user had to leave the house by its front and only door and walk round the block to it. That location presented inconvenience at any time but on a winter's night it must have proved a positive deterrent to its use. How these grandparents brought up such a mixed family in the restricted overcrowding of their house in Union Street is, to me, inconceivable. Indeed, I would say they were very fortunate to have lost only one child from 'consumption'. When I knew that house, it had a bed in the kitchen, a bed in the parlour and, in the upstairs room two box beds – accommodation which would have been as familiar to many generations of Scots as it was to Robert Burns. Small wonder some of the more restless of these generations left home as soon as they could fend for themselves.

I had little contact with Madge and Bett, but the remaining aunts, Agnes, Chrissie and Bella, were not only very much part of my childhood, they were among the characters of my life. Agnes did what most girls of her station did before 1914, she went 'into service' – that is domestic service – at first, I think, with local gentry, and she nourished a lifelong and uncritical regard, indeed reverence, for the gentry. Theirs were the standards she admired and, in her eyes, they could do no wrong. If, as a child, I ever left food that had been put in front of me, her comment was, 'The gentry's weans aye cleaned their plates', which may have been explained by the cuisine of their public school, or by their hunger or their manners – or all three.

11

She had other 'places' but, before the First World War, she entered the service of the Houldsworths of Kirkbride House, Crosshill, Ayrshire, and became a respected and trusted member of their establishment and, as she told me many times, bitterly regretted the day she left them, as well as the reason for which she did so. As she put it: 'I would have been housekeeper at Kirkbride if I had stayed', and of life she would have asked no higher promotion. She left to marry an older man, James McCrindle, a widower, and regretted it for the rest of her life.

From about the age of eight, I used to spend part of the Easter and summer holidays there. She lived in what had been built as a substantial farm-type house on Dalquharran Estate, Dailly, about seven or eight miles from Kirkbride House, which had been built to house a grieve or cattleman. One small section of the ground floor was a separate dwelling consisting of an entry lobby, a kitchen-cum-living room to the right, and a mini-sized bedroom to the left, in which it was just possible to have a single bed with about two feet between it and the wall, and no other furniture. It had a small window at the foot of the bed, which never opened because it could not. It was in this unventilated and unheated room that my Aunt's ageing husband habitually slept – alone – in the single bed. She only ever joined him when visitors, like my parents, occupied the double bed in the kitchen.

Facing the door of McCrindle's little bedroom was another short corridor to the 'front room' in which room, in my day, it was impossible to move for the collection of memorabilia my aunt had brought from her various places of service – modest ornaments and a multitude of framed photographs of her various employers and their offspring. She regarded the lobby at the entrance to her front room as the coolest part of the house and any foodstuffs which were not for immediate consumption were stored there on two stools, under wire covers. These covers may have kept the flies out – I stress 'may' – but they did not keep in the smell of whatever was under them and, when I recall that lobby, I recall also the almost perpetual smell of Finnan haddock, which lay there until their smell made their consumption inevitable and urgent. The only attempt, indeed, to combat the flies, which, in summer were everywhere, were two flypapers, like ribbons coated with a caramel-coloured glue, which hung from either end of the pulley in the kitchen, above the kitchen table at which we ate.

The house floor was stone throughout, not like a cement floor, but earth covered with flat stones about 20 inches square, with the earth showing between them. Taking a bath was impossible – not only because there was no hot water – there was no bath. Even the conventional zinc hipbath was unknown there. I recollect only two rugs on the floor, one a patch rug, the other made of pack-sheet. The only running water to this house was an outside tap to the right of the only door. There you washed – if you did wash – in cold water. For me it was hands and face only.

It will be appreciated from the singular water supply that there was no toilet. There was, some forty or fifty yards from the house, a patch of wood in which was situated a wooden privy – a hut containing an unvarnished wooden seat with a twelve inch diameter hole cut in it and beneath it a pail. No money was ever spent on toilet paper, but the daily newspaper, which came with the milkman each day, eventually found its way to the privy, which was emptied when the pail became so full that there was no alternative but to empty it, for to abandon the privy, which, since it had served the house since it was built, was unthinkable.

Elementary sanitation, however, was but one of the inconveniences of a stay with Aunt Agnes. The kitchen housed one high double bed, entry to which was only possible by means of first climbing on to a chair. When Bella and I were there, the two sisters slept in the kitchen bed together. Since it had apparently been decided at an early stage that I would – with Bella – regularly spend part of the Easter and summer school holidays with Aunt Agnes, a camp bed had to be got for me, which was unfolded each night and folded up each morning. Much time was spent in bed by the occupants of that house. It offered an idea of what life must have been like for the majority before the invention of gas or

13

electricity, and assuredly there was neither gas nor electricity in Dalquharran Mains. The only lighting was by candle or by the ceremonial and – as I remember it – rare lighting of a paraffin lamp. The light given by this ancient lamp hardly justified the effort taken to light it. You certainly could not read by it. Later, in a cottage where a friend and I, as students, used to holiday at Crinan, they had a sophisticated paraffin lamp with a pump action which gave an admirable light by which we all could read. Agnes's one lamp knew no such sophistication and if you went from the kitchen to any other room it was by candlelight. Any reading or household activities depended on the kitchen being lit by the light of day. I was never there in the depths of winter but on my holidays there, as in the Middle Ages, the day was dawn till dusk – in winter a very short day, in summer a very long one, and bed the only quasi comfortable place in which to pass the hours of darkness.

Due to the inaccessibility of the village by virtue of distance and Agnes's rheumatism, the household foodstuffs were delivered by the Dailly grocer on his pony and trap once a week, except the milk, which came daily. Fresh bread was only available while the bread brought on Fridays lasted. Bread, however, here, was an irrelevance. Instead of bread, we ate Aunt Agnes' soda scones, baked on a girdle over the uncertain fire, which had been coaxed into some life especially for the occasion, but I still recall the first day I tasted these girdle scones.

In the 1930s, my Aunt Bella's and my journeys to and from Dailly were major and traumatic occasions. They certainly did not support Robert Louis Stevenson's view that 'it is better to travel hopefully than to arrive'. These journeys involved the carriage of much luggage, and seemed, in retrospect, to occupy a full day's journey by buses from Stenhousemuir to Dailly. The journey began with a bus from Falkirk to the then Glasgow Buchanan Street bus station. The bus for Ayr however, which was our second bus, left from another bus station in Glasgow, namely Waterloo Street, and to that terminal we walked. Bella who was a diabetic was unfit to carry the luggage she had and I carried as much as I could of my own. This luggage included not only clothing but also foodstuffs. Bella's solution to this problem was not a taxi, but to bargain with one of the men who then haunted the bus station, seeking jobs as porters. It was The Depression period. Her ideal price was 6d; our potential porters however, usually wanted 1s. There was usually a compromise at 9d whereby her luggage was carried as was part of mine, but the responsibility for the rest remained with me.

On arrival at Waterloo Street we had usually to wait sometimes half an hour or an hour for a bus for Ayr. Bella never seemed to know when the bus was to leave, so we had no planned and timed itinerary. Against such contingencies as these delays, my mother had provided sandwiches to sustain us in what I seemed to recall, was about a seven-hour journey in all. These were not the days of fast travel, as I remember. These journeys, on which I could not read for the jolting of the bus, seemed to me interminable. There was however yet another bus journey, this time from Ayr to Dailly, again starting after a wait, again a bus whose departure time we did not know and a journey even more interminable, since there were still stops and requests all the way throughout that countryside. Eventually we arrived at the Dalquharran Toll where we – and myself with a profound feeling of relief – alighted.

Arriving at Dalquharran Toll however was not the end of the travelling. We were now about a mile and a half from our destination and we walked that distance carrying our own luggage, though I recollect we sometimes left part of it at one of the cottages we passed and went back for it later when we were less encumbered. It was a road from this bus stop to my aunt's home which then knew little or no traffic and never once do I recall any passing van or lorry offering us, or our luggage, a lift.

By the time we arrived at the house, we were undoubtedly 'ready', as Agnes invariably said we would be, 'for our tea'. I certainly was so hungry that, the first day I encountered them, I had to be stopped from consuming the whole of the particular baking of girdle scones Agnes had prepared for our arrival. These scones were unquestionably the most prominent and acceptable element of her uncertain cuisine. The other fresh food, of course, was eggs. She kept some twenty or thirty hens to whose care her life was dedicated. Much of her day was devoted to preparing what she called 'the hens' meat' and, each day she collected the eggs and sold them, mainly to the wives of the miners from the nearby pit. Her hens and their eggs were her staple presents to her family. When Bella and I left after a holiday with her, we usually carried each a basket of eggs and a hen whose neck had been wrung and the feathers plucked the day before we left. In the years she had a turkey cock, it was usually sent to my mother for Christmas. In those days, there was no difficulty in packing a large turkey. Her practice, to which no one took exception, was to wring its neck, tie a label round its neck addressed to us, and post it. Its smell preceded its actual reception at Falkirk.

Agnes' life was without laughter or even company and all the years I knew her, she was crippled with rheumatics. The reason she never became housekeeper at Kirkbride was because she had married a man she had never loved and, by the time I knew her, detested. To her he had become an anathema. She never called or referred to him other than by his surname. When she spoke of him, it was always 'McCrindle will do so and so …' or 'McCrindle! Your tea's ready.' How she came to marry him was always a mystery to the family. She told me once, when I was in my teens, that she never wanted to marry him, but he was a widower with a large family who – I may say took nothing to do with him – who came to know her when she worked at Kirkbride and, as she put it, he 'had it all round Crosshill that he and I were getting married and when he had done that, there was nothing that I could do about it, except marry him.' Her employers, she had added, had strongly advised her against the match and, certainly, she spent the rest of her life regretting it. Sir James and Lady Houldsworth had condemned the match but they gave her a silver tea service with solid silver teaspoons as a wedding present, a gift which was never used until I eventually inherited it. Thereafter, every month or so, they would visit her, take tea, in which she did not join – that would not have been her 'place' – and they would sit for an hour talking to her. In winter, if there was a shoot at Kirkbride, Sir James always saw to it that a brace of pheasants were sent to Agnes. This was the kindlier side of life in 'good service'.

Her existence I could only describe as grim, solitary, unrelieved by companionship, even by a radio. There was a daily paper which came with the milkman and the only time I ever saw her relax was when occasionally of an evening – in the light of summer – she would sit down on a hard wood settle, read the paper and, from its contents, lament the state of the nation and the disappearance of the gentry, and deplore the amount of money it was said Gracie Fields was earning. Agnes was indeed a female version of one of Cunningham Graham's characters of about 1914, an 'old Celt' who could as he himself said: 'discern a gentleman a mile away ... Gentry and gentlemen, by which he understood those of old family, for money could not make nor want of it mar, in his opinion, were the chief objects of his creed.'

Her life in Dalquharran Mains with McCrindle came to an end about 1950 when they were no longer physically able to continue to live there. They split up – McCrindle was given a home by one of his children, who had always ignored his second wife, and Agnes came back to the family home her father had built in Union Street, Stenhousemuir. There, in about 1953, she took a massive stroke which incapacitated her from speech or movements but she was still able to make us understand how ashamed she was that she had been reduced to such a state and, I think, was relieved that the life that had given her so little joy was soon to be over. I can date this, because the last bit of diversion she knew was my taking her in my first car, a little pre-war Austin 7, from the house in Stenhousemuir to Linlithgow Palace, to see the illuminations on the night of the Coronation of Queen Elizabeth. She was a little stunned by the lights and the crowds and I recall that, during it all and all the way home, she sat silent,

17

as if it was all too much for her and the world had got beyond her and she was tired of it.

If much of Agnes' life had been a negative, disillusioning and unlovely experience, largely spent in one miserable place, Chrissie, her sister, aspired to and achieved the opposite. To use her own phrase: her 'lines had been much cast in pleasant places'. In her appearance, as in the life she led, she differed from her sisters. Bett and Agnes were physically small, but solidly built. Bella was small and slight. Chrissie may not have been tall, but she gave the impression she was – tall, slim, animated and civilised. She, too, left the family home early and I never heard her speak of where and how she first entered service, but that is what she undoubtedly did. By the time I came to know my aunts, however, she was the one who appeared only occasionally at the family home and then for short holidays or between jobs. She always came from faraway places with faraway names and, until the late 1930s, most of her life was spent abroad. Just how she became the woman she was, is very difficult to appreciate. The education she would have received at Stenhousemuir School as a child would have been elementary. Her accent must have been the unpolished and the same Scots tongue that my father spoke throughout his life. But escape she did, by her own efforts. She made herself a reputation as a governess to children and, latterly, a ladies' companion. It was still an age where wealthy and lonely women liked to have a companion and were prepared to house and pay them. In her earlier life, parents with children who were travelling and who wanted a governess who could teach their children manners and the fundamental three Rs were numerous. Chrissie was able to fill these roles. She lived for long periods abroad, in America, especially in New York, India, Ceylon, Australia, Tasmania and Paris – in the house of the Aga Khan, the erotic decoration of whose toilets she never failed to comment on as inappropriate for a maiden lady like herself. Certainly, she remained a spinster and one can only speculate on whether she had affairs with men. She certainly had male friends and distinguished ones at that. I have from her a coconut with the shell hollowed out to make a drinking vessel. The lip is encased in a rim of silver and silver also forms the base and stand. It is the donor, however, who is remarkable. There is a coat of arms and a motto, presumably his, on the silver stand and on the base, the words 'To Chrissie Smith from her friend, Admiral J. Moresby RN.' He was the founder of Port Moresby, the capital of New Guinea. He also gave her a copy of his book, *Two Admirals*, written about his father and himself, inscribed 'To Chrissie Smith from her friend, the author', dated September 1913.

In the late 1920s, she became governess to a wealthy American family with two children, George and Kathleen. When she was in Scotland the names of these two children, their doings and their behaviour, which was apparently angelic, were never off her lips and, at the age of about six, I came to develop a passionate resentment, and later a hatred of, the reported behaviour of these two children. The great crash of the Wall Street stock exchange in 1929 eventually put an end to the ability of this family to live in Paris and on the Riviera and to have a nanny for their children. What happened to these children, I never knew and neither did their nanny: the break was complete. Thereafter, her services as a companion to elderly ladies continued, mostly in the south of England. She was an inveterate letter writer and, throughout her life, kept an active correspondence with her family in Scotland and with friends in all parts of the world from which, as a child, my stamp collection derived considerable benefit.[1]

She continued to lead her somewhat nomadic existence until about 1953, when she returned to the family home for a brief spell to live with her sister, Agnes – an ill-assorted couple – until the latter died. Thereafter, her health gradually failed. Her mind went and she eventually died in March 1962; the last survivor of that large family which set out in life from 22 Union Street, Stenhousemuir. Even at the end, she displayed independence of spirit and practicality. After her death, I arranged for the funeral to take place at the family grave in Stenhousemuir Cemetery. The grave was partly dug when I obtained a copy of her will, which required that her remains be cremated and disposed of by the cheapest means possible. Cremations are never happy occasions. This one, attended by three people, – my second cousin, my oldest friend and myself – of a woman who had seen and known so much of the world and people, was among the most melancholy I have known.

Isabella – 'Bella' – was the youngest of the Smith sisters I knew, and the first to die. When her parents died and the other sisters left home, only Bella and the two brothers, John and my father, were left. Bella was their housekeeper. She, like Chrissie, never married and her life must have been a monotonous drudgery. What she relied on for money I do not know. She had certainly no income and there was then no social security. She never considered she could afford a wireless. Probably her parents had left her a little and she would save from the wages her brothers brought in, when they lived with her. I know that she had saved money, and the best kind of money, because at my birthday or at Christmas, her highly acceptable gift was a gold sovereign. It gave me a little collection of them which, in the foolishness of youth, I exchanged for £4 each when I found myself short of cash as an undergraduate.

In the mid-1930s, she developed diabetes and, thereafter, every day I was with her I saw her injecting insulin into her leg, an operation which saw liberal use of iodine before and after the needle was used. I still associate the smell of iodine with these days. Her annual diversions were the holidays she had at her sister, Agnes' home, the Sunday school outing to which she invariably took me, attendance at meetings of the local Liberal party, and an annual Christmas visit to the Royal Princess's Theatre pantomime in Glasgow, taking me with her.

On Saturdays and school holidays, I spent much time at her home and I have no doubt she gave me much of my own way. As a child, I always wanted a dog. Since, however, we lived, as my mother put it 'up a stair', she considered we were disqualified from having a dog. The only pets allowed in our home were budgerigars and, at one time, goldfish, each species being replaced when their brief lives came to an end. Bella, however, allowed me more ambitious and experimental pets. Someone made me a cage, into which I proposed to put pigeons and breed pigeons. A pair was acquired from a small zoo in Glasgow. They proved fertile and I soon had three pigeons, which my aunt fed during the week and I saw at weekends and holidays. Unfortunately, I was ignorant, as was Bella, of the ways of pigeons and this experiment came to an end when the cock bird killed its chick. That ended the keeping of pigeons. The pigeons were followed by Java sparrows whose principal merit was that they were cheap to buy. They proved so lively, however, that I never found a way of opening the cage door without one of them escaping and, when Java sparrows escaped, they never returned. That breed ended my experiments with pets until 1959 when, having married a patient wife, I at last acquired my first dog, a black Labrador bitch.

At the start of the War a new play place came to Bella's garden, in the form of an Anderson Shelter. It kept out the rain and it was hoped that it would keep out bombs and their consequences. There when it rained we could sit, talk, and even, when an older boy found us, be introduced into the mysteries of a pack of playing cards.

Bella died very suddenly in about 1942 and I had my first experience of seeing a dead body, a freshly dug grave and a coffin, of which I held a cord as we slowly lowered her into the earth. The pigeons and goldfish excepted, it was my first experience of death.

## THE IRVINES

The family from which my mother came was dominated by her own mother, who was indeed a formidable woman. She was born in 1855 and died in 1948 at the age of ninety-three with her faculties clear to the end, and able to care for herself in the room and kitchen house in which she had spent her whole life from the time she married, and in which she had reared her family, until six months before she died, when she went to live alternate months with my mother and her youngest daughter in Glasgow. All my childhood, from its earliest memories, were dominated by that grandmother, who early on impressed that she was made of stern stuff and, from what I know now, was made of even sterner stuff than I had realised. She was born in Slamannan and, in her early days, was in domestic service to one of the local gentry. She married Samuel James Irvine, who was two years her senior, in 1879. They had four children: Mary, my mother Anna, one son James and the youngest daughter, Jean. Mary went to London before 1914 and returned to Scotland only occasionally to see her mother and her sisters. Beyond giving his wife four children, and then deserting them and her, I know nothing of Samuel James Irvine. The date of his desertion must now be a matter of inference. Neither my grandmother nor my mother ever mentioned his name to me. I was told, when in my teens, by the older cousin I referred to, that our grandmother had been deserted by her husband and left to bring up the children with no support from him. He was said to have gone to sea on merchant ships. Nothing was heard from him for years, until he appeared at the door of what had been their home and where his wife still lived. She went to the door in answer to a knock, opened it, saw who it was and slammed it in his face. She brooked no excuses, no pleading and, therefore, she allowed him no words. She was, undoubtedly, a strong woman and had her values of what she had a right to expect from a husband and had not received. How she fed, clothed, housed, brought up that family as a single parent in the late Victorian age with none of the social security benefits of today, and in doing so, kept the respect and regard of her neighbours as she did, I know not, but I marvel at it. The old-age pension was payable from 1909, but would not give her any benefit until she was seventy. Certainly, her daughters and her son, when they began work, would bring in wages and, when I remember her in her old age, the two younger daughters were unquestionably good to her, especially in kind and especially my mother, whose married home was a five-minute walk from my grandmother's little room and kitchen house with an outside stair, a landing and an outside toilet beneath the stair. My mother went to see her every day after she came home from work. If we had anything special to eat, like chicken, then very much a treat, I was sent round with a portion for my grandmother. She still managed to have a little cash by her. I recall when I was about seventeen and becoming an enthusiast for classical music, she was able to give me five shillings when I asked for it, the price of two plaster busts, of Beethoven and Mozart, which I had seen in a second-hand shop in Camelon and which I greatly coveted. I still have them and still recall the readiness with which she parted with those five shillings. She brought up her children alone and I think she could claim she did it successfully. Her second daughter, my mother, was one of the earliest businesswomen in Falkirk. It was because my mother had her business and attended to it, that I saw so much of my grandmother, because she, with my Aunt Bella in Stenhousemuir, was always there to look after me.

Her youngest daughter, Jean, married David Ferguson a son of a Perthshire farmer, a gem of a man, who eventually had his own modest dairy business in the Gorbals of Glasgow. As a boy I used to deliver milk there and got to know that legendary area very well, where, I must confess, I never felt afraid or threatened and had many kindnesses from its people. David Ferguson and Aunt Jean had two children, a girl and a boy, the only cousins with whom I had any contact and familiarity. Both older than me, they were regular visitors to their grandmother's and our home, but I realise now I was always a little jealous of the generosity and affection my mother always showed them. Willy – the son – we took on holidays with us to Morecambe and the Isle of Man. Jess, who looked very like my mother, took I fear what looked like very unfair advantage of my mother's affection for her. When my mother's mind failed she gave to Jess – and Jess took – any jewellery she had and any that belonged to my father.

I saw much of these cousins. I spent two weeks of each summer holiday with Aunt Jean in Glasgow and there were there only three beds in the house. I shared a cupboard bed with Willy. Aunt Jean

– like my mother – had a piano. She however had taught herself to play the tonic sol-fa scale on it: many a wet afternoon during my Glasgow holidays I spent listening to her playing the songs of the First World War. It was there I learned the words and the tunes of these evocative and tragic songs. I can still sing them. On dry days, in the afternoons, I would walk a mile or so to Queens Park – on my own – to sail a model yacht on its boating pond. I would doubt if any-responsible parent or aunt could allow a ten year old to do that now, especially carrying a model yacht.

My grandmother's only son, Jim, a conscripted and reluctant soldier, was one of the many to be killed at Passchendaele in the First World War. He must have had at least one leave from France before he was killed when he brought back two brass *Pickelhauben* from German helmets, which sat at either end of her mantelpiece and were polished every day. Framed and hung on the wall, in the centre of her mantelpiece, was a printed *in memoriam* notice with a list of the battles of the Great War, with a facsimile of the signature of George V. There must have been as many of these notices as there were deaths in those battles. There were photographs of some at the memorials. In the centre, was a small type-written slip of paper giving the name and rank of the soldier from that family, who had been killed.

My most familiar recollection of my grandmother is of her sitting, knitting or reading, in a chair before her grate with a low fire burning. She knitted every pair of stockings I had as a boy. For her reading she was fascinated by the politicians of the great age she had known – the Gladstones, Roseberys and Disraelis – and I often brought her political biographies from the local public library. Until my early teens I was with her every Saturday night. My mother usually came late from work to collect me. My father would go off for the day and I would spend the morning and afternoon at my aunt's in Stenhousemuir and come back in the evening to my grandmother and sit there reading, learning multiplication tables, doing homework and, when she eventually was given a battery wireless by my mother, listening to that. I can still see her when George V was dying, kneeling beside the wireless that she might not miss any of the many health bulletins on the monarch. Her house was always illuminated by gas, and I still vividly remember sitting in the chair reading with the hiss of the gas mantle as the only background sound. In her eighties, the veins in my grandmother's hands stood out, and as a child I recall tracing them as I can now trace them on my own hand. She was the oldest member at the end of her days in the congregation of St Andrew's Kirk in Falkirk and to the end she subscribed to the *Falkirk Herald* and the *People's Friend* for the serialised stories of Annie S. Swan, as well as to the weekly *Christian Herald*. Each week, she dutifully sent copies of the *Falkirk Herald* – one her own, the other my parents' copy – to her daughters in London and Glasgow.

## MY PARENTS

I was my mother's only child. She married in 1924, late in life for those days and was forty-two when she had me. For me and her household, she worked till she could work no more and her mind went into senile dementia. In everything in which I was to show an interest, she not only encouraged me, but also strove to make its pursuit possible.

My grandmother's idea of a career for a young woman was what was called 'good service' i.e. domestic service. Indeed, pre-1914, this was the only opening for most girls from working class families and was a way of life that ceased to exist after 1918. My mother, however, had other ideas. She began by apprenticing herself to a Mrs Henry who had a small milliner's business in Grahams Road, Falkirk, and remained there until 1919, when she set up her own millinery business near the town centre. She was a milliner; she not only sold hats, but she made hats and trimmed those she bought from the millinery warehouses in Glasgow to suit the individual requirements of her customers. Every Wednesday on the shop half-day she went to Glasgow for this purpose, and when I was on holiday from school, between the ages of seven and twelve,

I used to be taken with her. Millinery warehouses offered few attractions to a child and, in order that I might pass the time and be diverted, I was regularly left alone in Argyll Arcade for up to an hour or more, expressly to look at the window of a particular shop known as the Clyde Model Dockyard. Its windows fascinated me. I gazed at them, coveting their contents: model aeroplanes, model ships, all the fitments for each of them. I may add that we only made modest purchases there at birthdays or at Christmas. I should also add that neither my mother nor I considered there was then any risk in leaving a boy alone, to stand at a shop window or wander up and down the Argyll Arcade, waiting for the arrival of a parent.

In the 1930s, when the shop had three other employees, she still did much of the sewing herself. It was open from 9 a.m. until 5.30 p.m., which were the hours the employees worked. My mother's own hours were much longer. She was usually home from 6.30 to 7.00 at night, but at what she called 'the busy season', the spring, especially before the celebration of communion in the local churches – for which, in those days, a new hat would at least appear to have been as essential as a desire for salvation – her hours became much extended. At such times, she would not be home, having walked the fifteen minutes from the shop to the house, until 8 or 9 p.m. and, even then, she brought work home with her to be done that night. As a child, when I could not sleep, I often went downstairs to the living room, where I knew I would find my mother and there, at 11, 12, 1 o'clock in the morning, she would be industriously trimming hats at a table covered with the jobs she had done and had still to do that night. It was often my function to deliver these to the customer the next day, travelling around by tram or bus to Larbert, Camelon and Grangemouth and, from past experience, knowing the houses where I was likely to receive tuppence or a threepenny bit for my labours. It was, of course, an age where women wore hats every day and on every occasion. It was only after the Second World War that the fashion declined, though my mother's business continued until 1965, four years after her own death, when I had made over the business to the three staff who had been with her through all these years.

The only time I remember her having time to herself was on Sunday afternoons, when she would be cleaning cupboards, doing general housework and occasionally some millinery and, all the while, singing to herself Moody and Sankey hymns or hymns from the Church Hymnary. Moody and Sankey were American revivalists who visited Britain in the late nineteenth century but whose hymns long outlasted their stay here. They believed in simple sentiments and, like General Booth of the Salvation Army, in good tunes. Some of their sentiments would earn little sympathy today. One I still remember had a verse whose meaning could have been in the mind of Karl Marx when he described religion as the 'opium of the masses.' It ran:

> When you look on others with their lands and gold,
> Think how Christ has promised you a wealth untold.
> Count your blessings, count them one by one,
> And it will surprise you what the Lord has done.

I still remember the words of most of these hymns she used to sing, I heard them so regularly and so often. She was a woman who had hope, quiet determination and optimism. I would add courage to these qualities – courage, that she would be able to carry through whatever hopes she had for her only child; a courage that when business in the shop was slack, made her call personally on customers who were, as she put it, 'bad debts', to obtain payment of what they owed her. The shop eventually became the main provider for the household and in many ways her dedication to it made possible the life we lived and for many years.

My father, following the family tradition, worked in Carron as a fitter until about 1945, when he finally became so crippled with osteoarthritis of the hips, that he could only walk, with difficulty, with the aid of sticks, in constant pain and living on painkillers. Surgery failed to help and, as a result, the house which had had

27

the support of two wages was reduced to existing on one. The two wages, admittedly, did not amount to affluence but, in everyday matters, they were careful of the pennies. The bank account, which was opened for me when I was born bore, on the bank book, the maxim – no longer true – 'Take care of the pence, the pounds will take care of themselves', and they both carried that maxim into their own affairs. Both my parents feared 'debt' and, to the best of my knowledge, never incurred any other than the mortgage. They brought their child up on the proposition that he should never buy anything he could not afford to pay for. My mother believed in buying the best quality she could afford in clothing, furniture and the like, and the furniture they bought when they married – a lounge suite, bedroom furniture, sideboard – was the furniture they were still using when they died and it then came to me. I still have some of it, as I still have the two items that came from the Smith family, a grandfather clock, made in Falkirk in about 1744 and my great grandmother's corner cupboard, both still in use, both splendid items, both much admired.

Their social life together was minimal. They would, very occasionally, visit friends of my mother, the MacDonald family, for a Sunday tea and the MacDonalds would sometimes come to us. My parents never went together to a cinema. My mother, to my knowledge, never went to a cinema. The annual holiday excepted, they never had a night out for a meal or a drink, except once, which was such a special occasion that I can still recall it in detail. It was to a touring company's performance in Glasgow of the musical *The Desert Song*. A childminder was got for the night for me and the shop had to be left early in order that my mother might catch the special bus. It was talked about, looked forward to, as in its day one might have looked forward to a flight on Concorde.

Their only joint holiday was their annual holiday, the first two weeks in July. We could never all get away on the first Saturday of that fortnight, however, because the shop required my mother's attention. Accordingly, their annual two weeks' holiday lasted only twelve days. We could only travel on the Monday, though I recall the odd occasion when my father went on the Saturday and my mother and I followed on the Monday. We never had a car until 1952 and, depending on public transport, if you wanted to go to the Isle of Man, or Southport, or Morecambe, which were the favourite resorts, you had to travel on the Monday. The boarding houses in these resorts – we were never in hotels – cost about ten shillings per person a day, for bed, breakfast, lunch and an evening meal. In selecting accommodation, it was an annual question whether we went to a house which served high tea, or to one which served late dinner. My parents preferred what they were used to, namely, high tea and they preferred it also for the additional reason that an evening dinner would be too much for their son and a high tea enabled us all to go out in the evening to the theatre because, if a late dinner was considered to be too much for me, the music hall certainly was not. For my parents and their like, theatre was not drama: it was where you were entertained, and that was the music hall.

It was then nationally in decline but, in these resorts we went to, it still flourished, supported by a generation which had enjoyed it in its and their prime. I have memories of dancers, acrobats, conjurers, damsels with dulcimers and, above all, comedians, comediennes and singers. The last of these holidays was in 1939, when we went to Douglas, Isle of Man, taking with us Aunt Bella. I cannot remember if it was then I saw and heard the great Florrie Ford. I certainly saw her, and more importantly, heard her once, and I can still recall that robust looking woman, with a voice that neither had nor needed amplification, singing 'Down at the Old Bull and Bush' or 'Kelly from the Isle of Man': songs that were peculiarly hers. There was no limit to what could be presented as entertainment in these holiday resorts' music halls. I think it was in 1939 an artist appeared whose performance I never quite understood. His name was Jack Doyle and he appeared on stage, in boxing shorts and with a punch ball, and proceeded to dance around this punch ball, punching it, apparently in the secure knowledge that it would not punch him back. I was told that he was a great boxer, or was going to be a great boxer though, from all I have learned, he never really fought in a big fight.

There is an essay on him by the late Patrick Campbell, called *The Gorgeous Indestructible Gael,* which described him thus:

> Jack Doyle, the well-known tenor, all-in-wrestler and former light heavy-weight boxing hope – a man who had once filled the White City even if he was carried out of it feet first thirty seconds later, having been felled by the first blow delivered by his opponent Eddie Phillips.

However, having danced round the punch ball he then disappeared and would reappear in full evening dress to sing sentimental Irish songs. There may have been straight theatre available but, if it was, it was not my parents' idea of entertainment. I doubt if either of them in their entire lives ever saw a three-act play. The following year, the year of the Battle of Britain, we still had our July holiday, but this time nearer home, at Callander in Perthshire – a destination which by its proximity to home and its then reputation for douce quietude, astonished my fathers' friends. There certainly were no music halls or dance. It was my first opportunity to become familiar with the Highlands – the start of a fascination that remains unimpaired.

These precious holidays were interrupted, I think, about three times by my taking some childhood ailment and being unable to go. On these occasions my father went off alone on a holiday which had been booked at Douglas or Morecambe. He would not have been lonely without wife and child since members of other families he had known in Stenhousemuir usually went to the same places, at the same time, and he 'teamed up', as he would put it, with them. There was, I am satisfied, nothing suspicious about this. The innuendos that would be inevitable today were unheard of as they would have been unjustified. This, however, left his wife without a holiday and when the patient had recovered it was to Rothesay on the Firth of Clyde, and then as now an hour and forty minutes from Glasgow, that my mother took me and usually, her own mother, for a week or a fortnights' holiday in a modest but comfortable boarding house in Ardbeg – then one of hundreds of such on the island. These were the only holidays in the real sense of the word my grandmother ever knew.

I have come to know the island well as I have had a house here since 1971 and lived here since 1983: I now know that there was no scarcity of splendid beaches as well as Ettrick Bay. When I went there as a child, however, with no car, we relied on local buses and I never recall going round the island or indeed going anywhere but into Rothesay, playing on the rocky shore of Ardbeg, or going to Ettrick Bay. Most of the island was under the direct ownership of what was then reputed to be one of the wealthiest families in the United Kingdom. It was obvious that they wanted to keep the island beautiful. An ambition which, when I came to holiday here in the 1970s, it was clear they had succeeded in doing. It is an island well-wooded and well-farmed which makes for a landscape which could have been part of the Wessex, Thomas Hardy described in his novels.

Such a holiday place gave my mother some of the rest she needed. For my grandmother, it was a novel experience. For myself, it was not like the Isle of Man and I can still remember being alone and bored by the monotony of passing the days especially when it rained, and then as now, the West of Scotland deserved the reputation it has of heavy rainfall. There were, however, three memorable exceptions to the boredom: one was Rothesay Castle, where I went frequently, enchanted by the allegedly haunted stair, the dungeon and the ramparts. At the castle they vended a guide book which contained a penny ballad – indeed a genuine 'penny dreadful' – about the ghost on 'the bloody stair'.

The second was the beach at Ettrick Bay. Third, and perhaps the most vivid in my memory, was the music hall entertainment given in the then elegant Winter Gardens. This was a small attractive theatre, characteristic of the Clyde coast holiday towns in the 1930s and earlier, which thrived on the holidaymakers, for whom it was the only live entertainment. There was, of course, the cinema in Rothesay but it was the Winter Gardens that offered the live music hall theatre. My memory is that one could go there twice a week and see a different show each time. The regular performers were familiar faces to many of their audience. In winter, they were part of the Glasgow Pantomime and Music Hall. In summer, they entertained the holiday-makers who, like the performers, had their favourite Clyde Coast resorts. As an example of this in the '30s, the Winter Gardens in Rothesay had two opera singers in their cast, a husband with the splendid name of Tudor Davis and his wife. They had the summer singing in Rothesay and in winter sang on the mainland with the Carla Rosa opera company. The ability of the men in these shows to appear night after night in immaculate white tie and tails and the humour of the comedians, male and female, the smiles and dances of the chorus girls created the magic of a special holiday which could help redeem even a rain-drenched west of Scotland day.

The star of the show in the '30s was the Scottish comedian Charlie Kemble whom I saw only in Rothesay. Jack House in his *Music Hall Memories* (1986) described him as, 'the great musical hall veteran', but does not elaborate on this. That he was a veteran was obvious even to a boy. Also obvious were his winning ways with his audience. He had an intriguing and popular variation on the traditional act of the Scots comic: patter and song. What he did was to make the subject of the verses of his song individual to members of the audience: to the orchestra's accompaniment, he moved around the stage looking for members of the audience whose appearance, whose dress, whose age he would then make the subject of the verse he sang. There was never anything rude or vulgar about this. It was an experience of good nature on the stage and from the audience. His verses had the appearance of spontaneity but must have involved a repertoire to match the many demands he made on it.

The last holiday I spent at Rothesay with my mother and grand-mother would have been in 1941. By then the bay was full of warships of all sizes, and submarines. The town was full of servicemen. During the Second World War, Rothesay was changed from a holiday resort to become part of the base for the war at sea; the Firth of Clyde.

I said their joint annual holiday was my parent's only joint luxury. It would be more correct to say it was their only joint activity. I except from this the one-night visit to my Aunt Agnes at the May or September weekend holidays – a tradition which was short-lived. It ended, I think, about 1935, by which time my mother had had enough of the sheer physical discomfort the visit involved. For my mother, her shop was all-demanding. From the start, she always employed a daily help in the house to help look after me, do the housework and make a midday meal. In about 1931, that role was taken by a Mrs Helen Lowe (Nellie) who stayed with us until she died in about 1956. She became one of the family and, if there was any entertaining done, it was confined to high tea on a very occasional Sunday, to which Nellie was invariably invited and to which Nellie invariably came, especially after she became a widow in about 1938. Indeed, her presence was one of the features of a Sunday tea and, I underline, it was a tea, there was no alcohol and Nellie was usually invited by the women present to 'read their cups', which became a well-known tradition in the house. There were some women, it was thought, could tell the future from the shape the tea leaves eventually left in the teacup. Whether Nellie was a good prophetess, I know not. I do know that she had a fertile imagination as to what was going to happen to the various people whose tea leaves had settled in a certain order in the tea cups she was studying. That apart, she was someone in whom my mother placed complete and justified trust. Without her, my mother could not have run the business she did. The negative side, however, to my mother's dedication to business, was that she and my father, while living together, largely pursued independent lives. Their relationship was not a particularly happy one. My father was never a demonstrative, emotional or ambitious man and would never have done what my mother did, namely start up a business on his own. There were quarrels between them, not rarely, and I have no doubt now that, if it had

33

not been for my presence, my mother would probably have separated from him, though in those days she may have been deterred by the knowledge that that would have been a dreadful thing to do in the eyes of her family and the community. There was never anything between them in these disputes but words, but these could be bitter and I have memories of being taken as a child from my bed, when she and I would go down the street to her mother's home until tempers had cooled. Time and time again, she reproached my father for not being willing to be something other than a fitter in Carron Company. Time and again, he made it clear he was quite content the way he was. He was not easily moved to make any changes and, the older he became, the more stubborn he became in every aspect of his life. In my seventies, my wife told me, that in this respect at least, I am my father's reincarnation. In the 1950s, even to have the front window frames painted was a source of friction and when my mother was no longer able to make decisions, he grudged even putting coal on the fire, and, if coal was put on the fire when visitors were present and, if any remained unburned when they left, he removed it to the hearth to be able to burn it another day. In the 1930s, his life was his work, for five days of the week, reading a paper at night and, at the weekends, going off with his own friends, as he had done in his bachelor days. I never recall him taking me out on Saturdays. He would take me to Stenhousemuir and leave me there at his sister's. He would go to the local football match: I was never taken, not that, personally, I had any great interest in going. Then he went off to see his friends, or – and that was his habit for several years – to go to Edinburgh, where his best friend's sister ran a successful public house in Leith Walk. He did not go to drink to excess. I never saw him the worse of drink but he wanted to meet company and have what he called 'a change.'

After such visits, he would invariably bring my mother a half-pound box of Cadbury's Milk Tray chocolates. The differences between them, however, never reached the ears of the public as a marriage in danger. My oldest and most perceptive friend, who lived in Larbert and came much about our house in our student days from about 1944 when I first met him at Glasgow University, was able to say, referring to my parents, when he toasted me at my sixty-fifth birthday, that I came from 'thoroughly decent folk'.

The fact, however, that my father took little part in my childhood and my mother was at her business, meant that I was – as I have already described – looked after by the housekeeper during the day on weekdays, but, more importantly by my grandmother and my maiden aunt on Saturdays and holidays. I visited my grandmother every day after school and, when I went to university, I visited her every day until, at the age of ninety-two, she came to live with us. For this situation, I allocate no blame. My father married late in life, his ways were set and he liked set ways, and the arrival of a son, I think, was a novelty to which he found it difficult to adjust. My mother gradually became the principal breadwinner and she knew and accepted the responsibility, and knew also that it was a responsibility she could only discharge by running her business to the best of her ability. Both my parents and, particularly my mother, wanted to do their best by me. On reflection now, I often wonder if their somewhat unsettled life in my childhood, created in me the sense of insecurity and uncertainty that has been part of my inner self for my whole life, and is the despair of my ever-patient and ever-understanding wife. It must, I think, have been my father's genes that made me leave the Bar in 1963 and seek the comparative security of the Sheriff Court. My mother would never have done that – she would have stayed in the Parliament House, especially when that adventure was proving rewarding.

One thing my parents and especially my mother did not lack was an interest and an enthusiasm for my doing everything they thought a child, in these days, should do. To my father, my total lack of any interest in, or capacity for, any sports must, however, have come as a disappointment. He, himself, had been a golfer much of his life and, in his youth, a footballer of some distinction. He did his best to have his enthusiasm reproduced in his only son but without success. I was enrolled as a boy member of the Tryst Golf Club at Stenhousemuir, where he arranged for me to have a series of golf lessons from the professional but, I fear, I derived no pleasure from the game of golf. At school, I detested football, the only game played there and, throughout my life, my interest in ball and team games has been non-existent. This is unusual and is a serious defect in a Lowland Scot.

Besides golf, however, my mother had other ideas. At home, we had the upright piano in the front room – not a particularly good piano, but one of those found in nearly every house at that period that aspired to better itself. There could have been no other excuse for my parents buying that piano when they married, because neither of them played a note, other than it might benefit any child they might have. Because of the presence, however, of that piano in the house, my mother's view was that I must have piano lessons and, for two winters, I attended a charming elderly man in Falkirk, who did his best to encourage my interest in piano playing. I was and am now passionately interested in music, but I am not – except for attempts at singing – an executant and any capacity to read music which may have resulted from my two years' tuition, has long since gone. I could only have learned to play the piano had I done what those of my contemporaries who succeeded in this did, namely practised every night between 5 and 6 p.m. At that hour, neither parent was in the house to make sure that I did. The housekeeper did not know what was expected of me in the way of playing notes on a piano. What I did then, in the front room between 5 and 6 p.m. was left to me and, I fear, I failed to take advantage of the opportunity given me.

# 3

# THE CULT OF SPEECH

The 1930s was still the age of the elocutionist, part of a Scottish tradition from the eighteenth century, when the elite of the land took lessons in how to speak English as against their native Scots. In Falkirk, in the 1920s and '30s there was a lively popular interest in the spoken word, not just the English spoken word, but also Scots. A teacher called Duncan Clark was the real begetter of this interest, as he was its inspiration, tutor and producer. Officially, he held the position of a teacher of English at Falkirk High School but, by the 1930s, his teaching of English was minimal, except for poetry, Scots and English, and drama, which were the materials of his regular class, known as 'speech training'.

For what I would think must be at least forty years, Duncan Clark ran elocution classes on Saturday mornings: Beginners 9.30–10.30; Intermediate 10.30–11.30; and older children 11.30–12.30. Ex Duncan Clark pupils were measured in the Falkirk of those days in their hundreds. One of his pupils from the 1920s was the daughter, Nan MacDonald, of my mother's closest friends, the MacDonald family. Nan was a splendid elocutionist. She became a school teacher and, in about 1932, followed her former master's footsteps and set up a winter Saturday morning class. I was one of her first pupils. It was said, by doting aunts and by some kind observers, that I had some talent for learning and speaking verse. The first book that I recall being bought for me in this context was Robert Louis Stevenson's *Child's Garden of Verse*, but the range was considerable. Each Saturday, we would be given a typewritten sheet with on it the poem or poems, we had to learn for the following Saturday. That, I apprehended, was not only an introduction to poetry – it was also an introduction to what I consider is basic to any command of language, namely learning good verse. In these days, there was much of John Masefield; there was a clutch of Scottish versifiers, like W. D. Cocker, Charles Murray, who passed in these days as poets trying to keep alive the Scots verse tradition. There were some of the easier poems of Robert Burns. There was Choric speaking, in which one might be given an individual part. It is only in later life that I have come to appreciate that it is not just reading good verse that helps to give one a vocabulary. Much more important is to combine the reading of it with the learning of it, as well as learning to speak what one has learned, and speak it frequently. Each year's tuition from Nan MacDonald had, at its end, a recital, a display of the pupils' achievements over the year and, for this, soloists and choirs performed on a Saturday afternoon to interested, sympathetic and enthusiastic mothers, grandmothers and aunts in the large Oddfellows Hall, which was above the hall in which we assembled each Saturday morning. My mother could never attend these performances, – Saturday was the busy day in the shop, – neither did my father. He had his own Saturday habits.

The Bellsdyke Hospital concerts which I mentioned earlier were not the only public performances I had. Nan MacDonald and Duncan Clark taught elocution, but they also taught it to be used in public performance. I attended these classes from the age of about five to twelve, and when I went to secondary school, Falkirk High, came under the influence of Duncan Clark. He was my teacher in this field until my late teens and I frequently remember and constantly give thanks for what Nan MacDonald and Duncan Clark did for and with me in this context. If I had any talent for speaking verse, which I'm told I had, I had it because of their teaching, their examples and their giving me the opportunity and the encouragement to use it. If I had and have a love of verse, spoken verse, which I think I have, I had it from the same two. Duncan Clark gave an education at Falkirk High School an advantage over any other school of which I had knowledge at that time. He gave all the pupils the opportunity to learn and speak poetry, to participate in drama and that drama, namely Shakespeare, is the best in the world. Undoubtedly there were many who were not interested in knowing poetry and drama, especially poetry, but the chance was there. I am convinced that when young, one should read, and above all learn as much verse as possible. To read poetry gives pleasure. To read poetry aloud is to make a child realise not just the capacity of words, to formulate and describe experience – 'to give to airy nothing a local habitation and a name' – but also to appreciate how alliteration, how rhyme, how rhythm can bring magic to the spoken word. To learn poetry moreover – and poetry because of its rhymes and rhythms is more readily learned than prose – is to acquire an ever-widening vocabulary. I was once, in Canada in about 1991, given an immense and all too kind compliment after I had proposed the Immortal Memory of Robert Burns to an audience of some 500 men at the Calgary Burns Club. I was approached by an American who said he had two sons and wanted to know how they could be taught, as he put it, 'to speak prose like you spoke tonight'. I thanked him, demurred to the compliment and I told him I thought, as we were all different, there was no one answer and that I could only tell him what had been my own experience; namely, to read the best verse and prose and to try to learn as much as possible of that verse which appealed to me most, and speak it at every opportunity and to whomever would listen. I have since learned that this method has long been a method used in Scotland, and was used by John Murdoch – Burns' teacher – to teach his pupil the accurate use of literary English with the spectacular results of which the world is familiar.

Then, by my early teens at Falkirk High School, we were not reciting individual poems, we were offering scenes from Shakespeare and it was here, under Duncan Clark, that I first came to worship the language, the poetry, the delight of Shakespeare. The parts I played included Sir Toby Belch in *Twelfth Night*, Bully Bottom in *A Midsummer Night's Dream*, part of *King Lear*, as well as speeches from *Hamlet*, *Macbeth*, *Julius Caesar* and *Henry V*. I became wholly fascinated by Shakespeare to an extent which justified the headmaster's comment in one of my reports: 'He spends much time on Shakespeare.' Whether his final comment, 'but Shakespeare will repay him', is correct is not for me to say but, certainly, Shakespeare became a part of me.

Childhood, for my generation, ended not just when we reached the age of twelve, but with the declaration of war between the United Kingdom and its allies and Germany on 3 September 1939. Not that that climate produced immediate dramatic changes in our lives. We were told about rationing and soon learned what it meant. We discovered that sweets were no longer available on the production of a penny or two. There was much talk among the adults, with comparisons between 1914 and 1939. There was talk of their generation having borne the brunt of 1914–1918 and now that it was all to happen again to their children, a prospect they faced with anxiety and fear. There was the immediate problem of creating an effective blackout in every room in every house, with shutters, heavy curtains and painting some windows, especially skylights, black. Some houses in the 1960s, where the occupants were then elderly, still had their painted blackout skylights. School attendance and classes were briefly disrupted and re-arranged. One thing that the blackout did give our generation of town children was their first experience of town streets lit by full moonlight, giving a clarity that was romantic, unbelievable and even magical. Here was what was meant by the phrase 'The moon hath raised her lamp above'. All of us became compulsive listeners to the frequent news bulletins on the radio, but while the Phoney War lasted there was a grim expectation that it could not last and there was an impatience that it did last until the following spring.[2] No one knew what would then happen, but certainly my recollection is that no one really believed that Germany could be retained by the famous Maginot line, although no one suspected how terrible was to be the realisation of that expectancy.

In 1940, as the Phoney War ended and disaster seemed to be everywhere, it was to a depressed and frightened people that the speeches of Winston Churchill came like the sound of a trumpet.

To begin with the older generation remembered him most for the disaster at Gallipoli in the Kaiser War, but that criticism soon disappeared. Here was a leader who knew where he was going, where he had to go and where he had to lead, and who was able to persuade his countrymen and women to go with him. When it was announced that he was about to broadcast a speech, everyone from the youngest in a household to the oldest congregated around the wireless set to hear him, and never left it without an uplift of the heart and a surge of confidence. Here was the whole nation's first experience, because of radio, of the power of words. Small wonder even an historian as left-wing as A. J. P. Taylor could say of Churchill, in *The Oxford History of England*, that he was 'the saviour of his country'. These speeches were unforgettable to a thirteen year old and some of the phraseology has stayed in many a lifetime's memory.

# 4

# THE YEARS BETWEEN

To a suggestion by the Rector of the Falkirk High School, the late A. C. Mackenzie, I owe what has been the life I have led: it was at his suggestion that I followed the academic and professional course that I have done.

For a week in about 1943, Michael Redgrave and Gwen Ffrangcon-Davies played Shakespeare's *Macbeth* in Glasgow. The Rector knew my obsession with Shakespeare and invited another boy and myself to be his guests at the Saturday matinee. After the performance our host took us for high tea to Ferrari's Restaurant, then one of Glasgow's best restaurants. It was in the course of that high tea that he raised the question of what we hoped to do. At that time I had no idea. My mother's only contribution to any speculation was to express the hope that I would get a job where, as she put it, 'You will not need to take your jacket off'. At one point she thought the job of a draughtsman might be suitable. My father had no suggestions. I had never considered law as a career. I did not even know what being a lawyer involved. The Rector's comment to me was: 'You are good at History and you are fond of public speaking. I think you should consider trying to do a History degree and then a Law degree and go into the legal profession.' That suggestion having been made and having appealed to me, and as no one ever suggested that I should consider other alternatives, from that day on I hoped to be able to follow the Rector's advice.

I left Falkirk High School in June 1944, grateful to the members of staff there who had shown me encouragement but without much regret that these days were ending. The friends I had made there, whose friendship survived the inevitable diaspora of our year, were two in number, who are now both dead. Most of my year who went to university went to Edinburgh and I was the only one who attempted a degree in History at Glasgow. The initial stage of disorientation and loneliness there was mitigated by the friends I made travelling. My impression was at that time that nearly all students in Glasgow University, who did not have their homes in the city, travelled daily from these homes to and from the university. The early arrivals had coffee in the Men's Union – then a male preserve – where the student travellers congregated from Ayr, Hamilton, Stirling, even Callandar; indeed from all communities surrounding Glasgow from which daily travel was practical by train or bus. I knew of no students then who possessed a car.

Once you arrived in Glasgow by train or bus, travel to Gilmourhill by tramcar or underground was a matter of pennies. You saved a penny as I recall if you travelled to the university at Hillhead by the underground from Cowcaddens rather than Buchanan Street Station. Those of us from Falkirk, Stirling and district formed a group which tried, and usually succeeded, in occupying a carriage to ourselves in which other travellers tended to leave us alone. In those days the trains we caught were non-corridor trains and once a carriage had been occupied it was ours for the journey. These train journeys, morning and evening, resounded with the gossip of the campus or more frequently with arguments of great intensity on politics and religion. None of these discussions, as I recollect, ever reached a conclusion or persuaded any one of the contributors from the views they had and initially expounded with much conviction.

We all had a grant from the local authority for a first degree but while it enabled us – just – to travel by rail it would not stretch to paying for living accommodation in Glasgow and such an expense was not within the means of my parents, especially after my father could not bring a wage into the house. In 1945, the inevitable Medical Board rejected me for National Service and I was fortunate in being able to complete the MA degree without interruption.

43

When I graduated from Glasgow University with honours in History in June 1948 I had the problem that faces many arts graduates, namely, what was to happen now? I had no doubt what I wanted to happen. I wanted to study for a Law Degree and then to go to the Bar. I immediately applied for a student place in the Faculty of Law at Glasgow and was accepted. The question now was how the second degree was to be financed or as my mother put it 'afforded?' There were no local authority grants for second degrees and my parents, while they willingly provided a home, were in no position to offer the necessary financial help. The solution I found was a position as librarian to Baillie's Institution in Glasgow with a small salary of £300 a year. But the hours were such that I could attend classes at the Faculty of Law, which were generally in the early morning or the late afternoon.

Baillie's Institution was a library founded in the mid nineteenth century by a wealthy Glasgow solicitor, to offer a place of study for students and housed a modest but adequate supply of standard texts, and a selection of more recent publications. It had, in particular, a good history collection especially in Scottish history. As a result of the war it had had two unorganised removals in ten years and its stock, when I started, was in subsequent chaos. The books were tied in bundles with rough twine and delivered in any order that suited the carriers. Shelves had to be fitted and then the books had to be sorted out into a proper classification. This was not a task that was done or could have been done, quickly.

That library had its loyal regulars – so regular that many of them became my friends. It was a place that was small and intimate enough to enable the librarian to offer a share of his coffee or tea to the regular readers. One of the regulars was the late Tom Winning who became Cardinal Archbishop of Glasgow. After I left Baillies in 1952, I did not see him – though I heard much about him – until 1993 when I attended an honorary graduation at Glasgow University and saw him, an official guest, in his full canonicals, speaking to a small group. I asked his chaplain to confirm his identity to me which he did and I approached him.

44

As soon as he saw me, he recognised me and remembered my name. He looked across at me and said 'It's Irvine Smith'. A recall like that to me is remarkable in any man, but wonderful in a man whose life had involved seeing multitudes. He remembered me, he remembered the teas and the coffees with which I had plied him when he was studying, and he remembered the friendship we had enjoyed.

I completed the Law degree in June 1951; one of the two Law Degrees at that graduation passed with 'With Distinction'. The other was Phillip Caplan, later Lord Caplan and a High Court judge. That phrase 'With Distinction' made all the difference to what I hoped to do. I had been a student at Glasgow University for seven years. I envied what I saw of the academic life and was reluctant, and it must be admitted a little afraid, to abandon it. I found the prospect of the practice of law, the competition it involved, and its uncertainty intimidating, and while I was resolved to try to be called to the Bar it was as much, if not more, the prospect of an academic career in law, against the prospect of making a living in a field where a living was hard to come by, that attracted me. I took the first steps to enter the Faculty of Advocates knowing that for someone with no family or professional contacts in law, it was a leap in the dark.

Baillies Institution is no longer. It was wound up some time in the 1970s. Its passing was much lamented and its help acknowledged in several prefaces to books, by authors who had worked there and who had found the whole atmosphere and amenities of the place to be congenial.

As a student and at Baillies, cash flow presented major and interminable problems: the price of a rail fare from Falkirk to Glasgow being one major expenditure. However, if the pounds were few, in those days they did go an amazingly long way. You could have a two-course lunch for 1s. 9d. You could have a three-course lunch in the restaurants of several of the large stores for 2s. 6d, about 12p in today's currency. 2s. 6d. gave you entry to the Saturday night concerts of the Scottish Orchestra in St Andrews

Hall where I had my first experience of hearing classical music live. The same hall was the scene of recitals by some of the great singers who, when the War ended, were again visiting Britain.

You could have a gallery seat in any of the many theatres in Glasgow for two shillings i.e. ten pence in today's currency. In my student days, every Wednesday afternoon when no classes met, I went to a theatre matinee. I saw most of the plays with all the star-named casts that toured the provinces in these days before their London openings. I saw and heard operas from the companies that came on tour to Glasgow, and I still treasure as my most memorable theatrical experiences plays I saw sitting in the Gods for two shillings. One of these, remembered after sixty odd years, was the late Ralph Richardson playing Peer in Ibsen's *Peer Gynt*, peeling the onion looking for the heart it did not have. Another was seeing the Lunts, then the most admired actors of the American stage.

Funds certainly did not stretch to eating, even for special occasions in any of the then more famous Glasgow restaurants like Ferrari's or Guy's, and what was true of restaurants was also true of alcohol: there was never question of that at Falkirk High School or in the first years of student life. The abstinence this meant did not apply to the many servicemen who were then returning or coming to university to complete degree courses that the war had interrupted or prevented their starting. They certainly did not teach the younger generation to drink. Instead they did much to teach us *how* to drink. Their drink was beer and at the end of one term those in the History Junior Honours class took me on my first pub crawl along Woodlands Road. I did not care for beer and was persuaded by one of them that the liqueur Kümmel was a safe drink – it was also an expensive drink and it was my mature fellow students who saw that I was not deprived of refreshment on that occasion. They spent more money than I did or had. They were very generous and very patient. At the university there were stories about extravagant orgies by those who were then on the board of the then men's Student Union, but such luxuries did not come

46

within the ken of the average student, especially if he was a traveller who had to catch a train or a bus to outlying towns.

I did not continue to drink Kümmel. Beer as a drink seemed to have one effect on me, that was to put on weight and it was only when I went to Baillies that I began very gradually, very economically, very slowly, but remorselessly, to have an interest in wine and food. The stimulation for this came mainly from literary rather than nutritious sources. During the war and the immediate postwar years, there was little opportunity for anyone to pursue gastronomy as one of the fine arts and certainly no knowledge of nor interest in it in the house where I was brought up. Nevertheless, the idea of what it meant was kept alive by such books as *We shall eat and drink well again*, and the other numerous publications of André Simon, a French champagne salesman originally, who made the conversion of Britain to good living *à la France* his life's ambition, and, be it acknowledged, his life's achievement. His classic creation was the *Concise Encyclopedia of Gastronomy*, with separate sections for sauces, vegetables, cereals, fruit, fish, meat, birds and eggs, cheese, and wine. These were first published, amazingly, section by section each year during the war and up to 1949. Then in 1952 came a one-volume edition at forty-two shillings, which became a bible for budding cooks and a bedside book for enthusiastic and/or ambitious eaters and drinkers. Simon also wrote and contributed to many books, especially on wine.

His own writings apart, he edited and published many anthologies of prose and verse on wine and food. About 1952, I found a quotation in praise of claret, written in Scotland in the fifteenth century and thinking, rightly, that it would be one with which he would not have been familiar, I sent him a copy. I have seen the quotation quoted in only one modern anthology and I give the beginning of it out of interest, it reads:

Claret wyn is helesum til all complexioun, nocht ower poignant or ower sweit bot delytable of hew and gust, chosin be the odour, colour, and savour, grund and nature. Sik wynis

47

confortis the stomak and helpis to the natural heit and to the
guid digestioun, and kepis the stomak fra al corruptioun....[3]

He wrote a kind letter acknowledging the quotation although I
have never been able to discover if he used it. André Simon was
indeed the founder of a school of authors on cooking and the
culture of wine, whose activities changed the British cuisine and
the British way of drinking. It is said that today more wine is
drunk in the United Kingdom than beer. If that is correct it is a
revolution that was started by André Simon long before foreign
holidays became popular.

My own cautious adventures into these fields were largely
inspired and encouraged by a distinguished Glasgow surgeon,
Archibald Goodall, who represented the Royal College of Physicians
and Surgeons on the Governing Board of Baillies Institution. He
had many medical qualifications and also had many interests
outwith his profession, two of the principal ones being the history
of medicine, particularly in Scotland, and wine. He and his wife,
Elsa, entertained me often at their home and there I owe my introduction to the successful marriage of food and wine. At that time
I was interested in a seventeenth-century divine called Zachary
Boyd, and Archie Goodall was interested in a sixteenth-century
Scottish surgeon called Peter Lowe, who founded the Royal
College of Physicians and Surgeons of Glasgow. Each of our interests led to France. Zachary Boyd and the Ayrshire family he came
from had French connections, whilst Peter Lowe was physician
not only to James VI of Scotland but was also to Henry IV of
France and a suspected privateer. The pair of us, with his wife,
went to Paris, he to the *Bibliothèque Nationale*, I to the library of
French Protestantism in search of our subjects. Neither of us discovered anything new there but we did discover something of French
food, wine and eating. In the Goodall household the pre-dinner
drink was a very dry sherry. For the meal there would be a named
claret, and if fish were to be served, a white burgundy. The aspiring
gastronomes of that period were all familiar with Thurber's

48

cartoon caption: 'It's a naïve domestic Burgundy, without any breeding, but I think you will be amused by its presumption', and Archie had a talent for coining like commendations. The talk would often involve comparisons between what we were drinking, and what we had drunk in the past, and hoped to drink in the future. Archie died prematurely in 1961, his widow died forty-seven years later, courageous, competent and independent to the end.

In those days there was nothing like the choice of wines that there is today. Australia and New World wines were unknown. France and Germany and, just starting, Spain, were the producers who exported to the UK. A wine shop at Charing Cross sold what they called a 'Spanish Sauterne' (these were the days before the Trade Description Act), which sold at 6s. 9d. a bottle, i.e. about 30p. It was sweet, it was powerful; when you drank it you were aware of the fact and did not hesitate to drink more.

I remember one day the shop had a large sign in the window, 'Burgundy 5 shillings a bottle'. I cannot remember the taste but all my contemporaries in Glasgow Law School contrived to buy some. It will be appreciated that at that price it did not last long. In my then early twenties I came to be asked to houses where a glass of wine was part of the routine and where the civilisation of France, its food, its wine, were worshipped and practised.

However, enthusiasm for food and wine in one's early twenties was an expensive enthusiasm, even then, and one in which our group could only indulge on special occasions. A group of five of us, largely at my instigation, decided that we would form a Wine and Food Society of our own which would meet in my parents' home, and for which I would do the cooking and to which, in turn, each could bring a guest to the dinners. The cost of this was the cost of what the company ate and drank, divided by five. The dinners were for special occasions: New Year was one, but the others all related to what we were all trying to do academically or professionally. We had two accountancy students, Willie Gold and Ian Taylor, a language student, Robert Sturrock, an actuarial student, Douglas McKinnon, and myself, and when one of

49

us passed an important exam or qualified, that was deemed a special occasion within the constitution of the society and a dinner was held.

We took ourselves very seriously. I determined what the menu would be. We then sought quotations about each member and guest for the menus which we had typed and, on two or three occasions, we persuaded an art student of Glasgow Art School, now an established Scottish painter, Frank Donnan, to draw and paint original designs for each of the menus. We all looked for bargains in wine and it would be bought and kept for the next dinner. Robert Sturrock came back from France on one occasion at New Year and brought with him a bottle of 1914 cognac which was really too good for the palates of the Society by the time we reached it at the dinner in question. Our guest that night who had taken full advantage of, to use a phrase of my father's, 'all that was going', described this vintage cognac as 'jungle juice'. He, I may say, was not asked back.

I used to set aside the whole of the day to prepare the meal which was always on a Saturday or a holiday, fortified by cookery books and guided not a little by my mother's home help, Mrs Nellie Low, who stayed to the end of the dinner and whom we always toasted and presented with a bouquet – both new experiences for her. I bought and prepared the food and set the table. We started with sherry or Dubonnet, no spirits. The preparation and presentation of the food could present problems. The age when a refrigerator was regarded by all as an essential part of domestic equipment was just starting, and my parents had not yet joined it. In short, they had no fridge. I aimed at five courses and we tried to have a wine with each course. We met at 7.30 p.m. and, depending on what was happening in the kitchen, I would announce that dinner was served when we all trooped through to the recorded strains of the Grand March from Wagner's *Tannhauser*. It became indeed our signature tune: latterly one only had to play the opening bars of it for the whole company to abandon or consume their aperitifs and make for the dinner table. We would break up about 2 a.m. or when the wine was finished, whichever was first, and then three of our party, who lived in Larbert, would walk the three and a half miles to their homes, a process which had the double effect of getting them home without the expense of a taxi and enabling them to sober up. One had to walk to an aunt's about one and a half miles away. I went to bed leaving all the clearing up until the next morning. My parents tolerated all this. They went to bed when the company assembled and did not appear again that night.

These dinners lasted for about three and a half years. The first break was Ian Taylor's tragic death in a road accident, then Robert Sturrock became an interpreter in the Foreign Office and departed for England. Willie Gold became the accountant at Dundee Docks, married and went to live there, which left Douglas McKinnon and myself. Douglas was by then a highly respected actuary. He became general manager of the Scottish Mutual Assurance Society. He still lived in Larbert and while two might be company and were close friends, it was not what the Society had intended. We remained close friends until his death, but evenings like those organised by the Wine and Food Society were over.

# 5

# FORTUNATE ENCOUNTERS

All lives, especially long ones, gather their characters. Most of mine – family apart – belong to my adult life, but there are a few I associate with my youth and early twenties, and of whom my memory is clear and my gratitude unquestioned.

The first two, Nan MacDonald and Duncan Clark, I have already mentioned. They both taught elocution. They both taught me to love poetry and did their best to teach me how to speak it. To them I owe any capacity I have for public speaking. It was another, James F. N. Fyfe, who introduced me to the world of music.

## JAMES F. N. FYFE

It was through my enthusiasm for reciting verse that I had my introduction to serious music which, for me means the classics. In the 1940s and '50s concerts by amateur singers and choirs retained their popularity in Falkirk and district. The town then boasted a choir originally called the Falkirk Select Choir, but in the 1940s it modernised and improved its name and status by renaming itself 'The Falkirk Choral Society'. It further renamed itself in 1954 as 'The Falkirk Caledonia Choir', after an Edinburgh Festival performance. It was the only choir in the town, apart from the church choirs which would combine annually to produce Handel's *Messiah*. The conductor of the Choral Society when I came to know it in the early 1940s was James F. N. Fyfe, born and reared in the village of Airth, near Falkirk, where his father was the manager of the local Co-operative store. A pharmacist by profession, by instinct, enthusiasm and talents, Jim Fyfe was an all-round musician. He was an accomplished pianist, and he had a lyric tenor voice, rather like that of Webster Booth who was popular at that time. He would accompany himself singing and had the reputation of being a sympathetic accompanist for others. He took pupils for singing lessons but his first enthusiasm was for the choir which he conducted.

This was the period when the Glasgow Orpheus Choir was a national institution in Scotland. Its one conductor, during its whole existence, was Sir Hugh Roberton, who was knighted in 1931 for what he had made of that choir.

Jim Fyfe was a protégé and admirer of Sir Hugh Roberton and his ambition was to model himself, his choir, its singing and its repertoire on Sir Hugh and the Orpheus, for which end Sir Hugh gave him every encouragement. The Orpheus concerts were given entirely by the choir and the soloists came from its own members. The Falkirk Choral Society eventually adopted the same presentation. However, at least in Falkirk, it was still a familiar practice to have as part of the programme what was then called an 'elocutionist', a speaker of verse or 'readings', beloved of the Victorians. I came to know Jim Fyfe when he had me, as an interlude at a choir concert, recite a poem by Cecil Roberts called 'A man arose'. It was a long poem in praise of Winston Churchill, which exactly suited the mood of the time and with which I, at the age of about fourteen, had been so impressed that I had learned the whole poem off by heart. I performed this at a number of the choir's concerts and in so doing became an admirer of their conductor who had me recite with the choir until about 1955, when I took part in a concert given by the choir in the Usher Hall in Edinburgh. That was my last recital with them. I had a hint from a senior member of the Faculty of Advocates that this was not something a member of the Faculty should be doing. That restriction appears to no longer apply, but at the time it probably also recognised that the audience acceptance of the spoken word at a choral concert was passing.

From Jim Fyfe and his wife – in whose company I spent much time and several holidays – I had my first real introduction, not only to choral singing but also to the classics of music. I had heard some of them on the radio but had no idea how to start to appreciate them. As a result, listening to them has become one of the major pleasures of my life. My wife and I listen to classical music every day. We have it at our meal in the evening or listen to an opera if we sit for the whole evening. I have been through the whole gamut of the recording media, 78 records, LPs mono, LPs stereo, cassettes, and now CDs and DVDs. It is very much a part of my life which I owe to Jim Fyfe. He suggested I start by listening to Beethoven's *Pastoral Symphony*. To do so I needed a recording to play on our ancient gramophone. We had the wind-up gramophone which reproduced sounds in a way which would now be unacceptable. Nevertheless, any pocket money I earned or received went to buying one record at a time of Beethoven's *Pastoral Symphony*, recorded by Paul Paray. I still have that recording on 78s. It was played repeatedly and while this apprenticeship was being served I began to listen regularly to orchestras on the radio. There are a few works, like the *Hebrides Overture* or the *Peer Gynt* suite I could enjoy at a single hearing. The great advantage of the records though was that repetition created familiarity. Jim Fyfe's next recommendation was Mendelssohn's *Symphony No. 4, 'The Italian'*. Here again, over many weeks a recording by Sir Henry Wood and the Queen's Hall orchestra was acquired and became part of me.

Jim and I regularly performed musical monologues together; myself speaking and he accompanying me on the piano. They were popular at that time in the musical hall and popular at the various smokers, i.e. male gatherings where food, drink and tobacco were the feature of the evening.

One of the major pleasures of my life has been music: live and recorded. I owe that to the late Jim Fyfe. One of the most vivid and cherished memories of my late teens and early twenties is of Jim Fyfe at my parents' piano, his wife and I on either side of him and the three of us, to his piano accompaniment, singing our hearts out in Schubert's setting of 'Who is Sylvia?'

His premature death in 1970, at the age of sixty, grieved the lives of many in many quarters. What he did for me in my youth and early manhood I could never repay, and it is now my regret that I did not do more to try. I am but one of the many beneficiaries of his counsel, advice and goodwill. His adoring wife apart, music was the most important thing in his life. It would be my contention that it is no small thing to have been one who inspired in many its making, spread its performance and encouraged its appreciation through the whole community in which he lived. He conducted the choir for thirty years. He was for me, as for many others, a teacher not only of the art of music but of the art of living.

## REVEREND D. J. FERGUSON, 1880–1967

I was reared in the Church of Scotland but it was its now smaller rival, the Scottish Free Church that, in my twenties, produced a Minister who made the greatest impression on me. That was an unlikely occurrence. I was and am an enthusiast for the carnal things of life: wine, food, music and company. The Minister I refer to here belonged to a Church which, in the twentieth century at least, was regarded as the last bastion of narrow Calvinistic theology, and of a way of life characterised by stringent Sabbath observance and strict morality, with marriages but no 'partnerships' and total sexual abstention until marriage, the prohibition of dancing and all such frivolities – in short, all things that were popular and enjoyable for the majority. The words of Sir Toby Belch to Malvolio in *Twelfth Night* – 'Dost think since thou art virtuous there shall be no more cakes and ale?' – expressed the general Lowland attitude to the Wee Frees. Theirs was not a faith that appealed to the generation that had experienced two World Wars, and in which the old conventional moralities were increasingly rejected. By the 1940s and since, the power of the old Free Kirk and its theology were mostly confined to the remoter parts of the Scottish Highlands and the Western Highlands and Islands, in particular.

I only ever knew one of its ministry, with whom I did not discuss either my own or his church's views on morality. However, I say with confidence that in that Minister, the Reverend D. J. Ferguson, then of the Parish of Easdale near Oban, I encountered, on a chance holiday in Easdale, a man steadfast in his faith and possessed of qualities which made him to me, and to the many friends of my generation to whom I introduced him, a saint, as well as a man of courage and of profound common sense. When it came to the sea, which from his earliest he had known – he was born on St Kilda – he professed a profound respect, courage and realism. I am no sailor, but when it came to small boats the Reverend D. J. Ferguson commanded such respect and confidence from me that I would have gone with him anywhere he chose to sail. He was a born seaman. With him you did not mess about in boats – you sailed with a purpose.

Easdale, when I met him, was a small village some thirty miles south of Oban; an area dominated by the sea and its islands with fierce tide races between them, some of which, like the Corryvreckan, have entered legend. I had never heard of it until the early summer of 1948 when a very close friend was demobbed from the Army and I had just completed an arts degree. For each of us a chapter had ended and another was about to begin, and this holiday was to mark that time, which it certainly did. We both wanted a holiday. Neither of us had a car. The budget was modest. One of my mother's shop assistants knew a family that had just taken over Easdale Hotel and suggested we holiday there. It was sound advice. The place, the atmosphere, the scenery, its character, charmed us.

I had had only by then one other experience of the West Highlands when a school friend and I holidayed several times in a cottage at Crinan, occupied by a widow and her disabled son. In the years 1942–1944, she had us to stay in the summer and gave us bed and board for ten shillings a week each. Everything being rationed, we carried as much food by way of tinned foods as we could. Crinan was beautiful. I will never forget the holidays there, but Easdale, its hotel and its food were different from Mrs MacPhee's and the two of us who went to Easdale felt we were

56

now at the stage where we should begin to act and be treated as adults.

The only church in the area was the Free Church, a wholly unlovely and uninteresting building situated, nay isolated, on a hillside about two miles from the village. On the first Sunday we walked there really because we had nothing else to do. There was no church organ or even a piano. There were no hymns with familiar tunes. The sparse congregation did its best to sing the metrical psalms which alone were permitted in the Free Kirk. There should have been a Precentor to lead the singing but no such figure, and indeed no real singer at all, belonged to that particular congregation. The manse pew, situated at the back of the kirk, contained the Minister's wife and his daughter, Dolly. The latter had a spine deformation but made up in spirit, fun, humour, laughter and normality what her physique had denied her. We, the two visitors, were conscious that the few other worshippers there were examining us with avid curiosity: our clothes, behaviour, looks, our unfamiliarity with and attempts at singing the barely tuneful psalm tunes, the degree of expected reverence we would show of the time and the place. The curiosity of their visitors was likewise intense, for here were a number of features we did not recognise as part of a conventional church service. The prayers were long and extempore. The readings were long, and the Minister did not read them like a well-graced actor. The sermon, which was also long, was also wholly extempore. I can still remember his theme: Communion was to be celebrated that day and the burden of the sermon was 'Dare you stay away from that Communion?' The second part was 'Dare you come forward for that Communion?' because to take Communion there meant your rising in the face of the congregation and going forward to the front of the kirk where the 'tables' were 'fenced' i.e. set apart. It was a theme that left one in some perplexity over what to do. In the end we both took Communion and, at the end of the service, were welcomed by Mr Ferguson, his wife and daughter and asked to the Manse that night after our meal at the hotel.

We went that night to a warm and uninhibited welcome. The Minister talked of his origins and it was for both of us the first time we had heard at first-hand what it was like to have been born and brought up on St Kilda, an island which because of its isolation was evacuated in 1930. To the end, the population of St Kilda was loyal to the Free Kirk. They were intensely religious: an emotion probably explained by the physical isolation of their island and its community. Education there is said to have been sporadic, but it had been sufficient to qualify our host for the Ministry and given him a vocabulary we had heard exercised that morning. The St Kildans' occupations were crofting, fishing and the taking of seabirds – puffins and fulmars – which thronged the island and its seas. These birds were the principal diet on the island, and our host attributed the absence of rheumatism among the folk on that rain-drenched island to the oil from the flesh of these birds. The Minister was a good narrator. He had a quiet sense of humour often betrayed by a twinkle in his eye.

So started a friendship and practice which lasted for five years. Whenever I had a holiday, or went on holiday with friends, it was to Easdale. In Easdale I and any of these friends of my generation who were with me were welcomed and included in the Minister's non-ecclesiastical activities. His enthusiasm for fishing was unlimited. The seas were mackerel-crowded. We would listen to his plans, watch him assess the wind, tides, sea, and help him launch his boat, which was his own making. It was very heavy and launching required a concerted effort. Then we fished but Mr Ferguson was not content only with fish as a fruit of the sea; he certainly believed that God had indeed given man dominion over the beasts of the field, the birds of the air and the fish in the sea. The birds of the air which attracted him were the cormorants – now a protected bird – which he assured us were a part of the diet of the St Kildans. So, in addition to fishing for fish, of which we caught many, we had a twelve-bore gun with which we pursued, with the active encouragement of the Minister, any sea ducks or cormorants that came within range. Each night we returned with our catch or kill to the Manse. Each night Mrs Ferguson fried the fresh mackerel and would call 'Come along now children' when the fish was ready. The Minister would say a grace and we fed on the freshest fish that we were ever likely to taste. This is more than can be said for the cormorants. Once, a group of us were asked by the Manse family to taste a cooked cormorant. Its reputation was a bird of very 'salt flesh'; a salt which, according to D. J. Ferguson, was cured on St Kilda by burying the dead bird in a peat bog for three or four days, which he claimed made the bird more edible. That night when we had the cormorant-tasting, we had the experience of eating what seemed to be solid salt. If the fulmars, sea ducks and puffins tasted anything like cormorants, the St Kildans, whatever other characteristics they had, undoubtedly possessed strong stomachs and hyperactive digestive juices.

That first night, when we visited the Manse in May 1948, and had tea and talk, ended with the Minister rising and kneeling before his chair. Nothing was said; he simply rose, turned, faced his chair and knelt. His family did likewise and we guests followed suit and there he prayed. We were sent on our way with the memory of the long evening prayer, heard by us all on our knees, and the blessing which followed. We were to learn this was the routine in that house every evening.

One thing on which Mr Ferguson had talked much was the harvest of fulmar and puffins, on which St Kildans depended for food and for what exports they had. In his love of fishing and for the flesh of cormorants, our arrival must have seemed a godsend to him. For here were now two young men who had with them a twelve-bore gun for shooting rabbits – a local farmer allowed us to do this; two young men who could help him launch and sail his boat, fish for and carry mackerel and shoot cormorants.

On the shore in front of the Manse lay the Minister's boat; a long, stoutly built rowing boat of his own handiwork. We were to learn much about that boat and its idiosyncrasies on that first and subsequent holidays; holidays which were in fact 'made' by the Minister and his boat. In it he carried an outboard motor and oars, the losing of the latter he regarded as one of the hazards of sailing and, as a result, usually carried several pairs of oars. He believed the boat needed ballast and this lay ready to hand in the mountains of slate which were everywhere on Easdale Island, once famous for its slate quarries. It will be appreciated that the result could be a somewhat heavy vessel to launch and, at the end of the fishing and hunting expedition, to drag up on to the beach.

The last time I holidayed in Easdale, after a lapse of some years, was in 1957. In the hotel was an English family with their son and his friend, both students at Keele University and both avid to be out in the Minister's boat when told about it. They were the only youths I ever knew who had reservations about the Minister's fishing and shooting. The older one had never seen a gun, much less a gun fired, but both never missed an expedition or a voyage. They said they had never had a holiday like this and, like the rest of us, I doubt if they will ever forget that determined old man and his ways with a boat.

His talk, when not about God, – and to us he rarely spoke about religion – was about the sea, boats, the birds of the sea and the fish in the sea. These subjects were in his blood, in that of his forebears, and in the skill of building boats. He had left St Kilda in 1900 and was apprenticed ship's carpenter at Yarrow's Shipyard in Glasgow. His apprenticeship completed, he worked there until March 1914 when he became a late entrant in the Ministry of the Free Church. He became Free Church Minister at Minard – where, in time, his own son became Minister – then Ayr, Scalpay, Fort Augustus, where he was on friendly terms with the Catholic Abbot, and, in semi-retirement, at Easdale. Each of these places adjoined the sea and throughout his whole Ministry he owned a boat. During most of it he owned a converted fishing boat called 'The Dolly', the name of his disabled daughter, and when from Ayr he went to his new charge in Scalpay most of the flitting went on the boat – and the flitting included sheep, hens and dogs, as well as most of the family possessions. On the way they put in one night in a Bay on Skye where they were overlooked by the Free Church

Manse. In the morning the little boy, who was the son of that Manse, saw the boat with all its livestock and ran to his parents to say that Noah had arrived in the Bay. This converted fishing boat, its size, the places it had been and could go to, the seas it could take, the joys it gave its owner, were the inspiration for a suggestion from him, made to some of us younger generation, that we should buy a boat like it, which he would find, and then teach us to sail. He was very persuasive and we very nearly accepted, though I think he might have tired of instructing us on the elements of seamanship because, unlike him, we were not born to the sea and feared it more than we could ever have loved it.

Just how serious and enthusiastic he was for this project, can be seen from the top half page of a letter he sent me in 1953. I found it recently when clearing out some old papers. It obviously refers to the proposed boat and begins with the word 'Requirements' and continues:

> You would have her whenever you wished to use her. Say if six persons were agreeable to form more or less a company and this boat costs say £12, engine £80, deck and alterations £24, cabin fittings £12, say a total of £150, all the alterations to be carried out by ourselves. I intend going to Glasgow for 2–3 days on the first week of November and if possible will have a look at the boats which Arnot and Young may have in their Dalmuir yard.

This shows the Minister's optimism that he might make a seaman of some of the younger generation, as well as the value of money in 1953. Of this, however, I have no doubt, if we had joined him in his project, for him to have had a boat to renovate, would have been indeed a labour of love.

As he got older his wife began to fear for his safety when out fishing alone. In particular, she feared for him in Cuan Sound where the tide could run fiercely. She begged him not to go out alone, but for him fishing was life, and he continued to go out.

61

On one occasion the weather he encountered was such that when his outboard failed he then lost every one of his many oars, and ended by losing his boat. He was himself washed up on the rocks at Cuan Sound. He went home to his wife who expressed, along with relief and thanks, the hope that this would be a lesson to him and that he would no more go to sea to fish. I do not know what promises were or were not given, but I do know that next morning, the storm being over, it was found that his boat and his oars were all washed up on the shore in front of his Manse. After that God-given return of his boat and its oars, the lament 'We'll go to sea no more' he regarded as no longer applying to him.

After that holiday in 1957 I was not again in Easdale until I went in 1961 with my wife and our first child, Richard, who was then a year old. The Manse had now been sold, his wife had died, and the Minister and Dolly lived in the nearby village of Balvicar. He died in 1967. Dolly I understand lived on alone there and died in the mid-1970s. That she should live on in the cottage alone after her father's death was characteristic of her courage, optimism and resilience. She was a great, cheerful character, as indeed was every one of that family I had the privilege of knowing.

## MRS GLADYS POLLOK OF RONACHAN, CLACHAN, ARGYLL

Ronachan House, in Kintyre, was the home of Mrs Pollok. It was built in the nineteenth Century by the head of one branch of the McKinnon family, who owned the British India Shipping Line – in its day one of the biggest of British shipping lines. When the *Pax Brittanica* was at its height in the late nineteenth century, British India had ninety ships at sea on eastern routes. Mrs Pollok once told me that she remembered how her uncle kept a steam yacht in the bay, with the steam always up, so that he could sail immediately to where he might be needed – a nineteenth-century equivalent of a modern private jet. Mrs Pollok, who at her death bequeathed the house to the Church of Scotland, was one of two

McKinnon children, a boy and herself. The boy was killed in the First World War and Mrs Pollok inherited and continued to run the estate. She had two sons: one emigrated to Canada; and the other, Tom, ran the farm, and he is the Tom referred to in the Barney Noon letter quoted later.

Mrs Pollock, who became a very good friend to my wife and me, was a generous, versatile and formidable lady. She held strong views on most subjects and was one of the very few women, in my experience, who knew and could argue the complex subject of Scottish Church history, and enjoy doing it. Her enthusiasm even stretched to reading the works of John Knox. When she heard of a neighbour keeping poultry in batteries for the production of eggs she referred to the book of Genesis where the Lord is said to have decreed, 'Let man have dominion over the fish of the sea and the fowl of the air and over cattle and over all the earth and over every creeping thing'. That dominion, she claimed. did *not* extend to keeping hens in batteries. As she put it, 'that goes beyond what we are entitled to do'.

I first met Mrs Pollok in 1954 when she arranged a series of lectures for her tenants and neighbours. She chose the lecturers and gave them the subject on which they were to lecture, which must have caused one, at least, some difficulty. The Professor of Astronomy at Glasgow University, for his subject – I would have thought a formidable subject for a Professor of Astronomy, but perhaps she considered the fact that he had a brother who was a Minister of the Church of Scotland would predispose him to a sympathetic interpretation – she gave him 'The Star of Bethlehem'. I do not know what approach he took when he lectured on this subject at Clachan, but lecture on it he did.

She invited Professor J. D. Mackie, the Professor of Scots History at Glasgow and a significant influence in my life, to lecture on the 'Tobermory Galleon', the Spanish galleon, allegedly the treasure ship of the fleet, sunk in Tobermory harbour. It had been part of the broken Armada making its way round the north of Scotland and down the West Coast. However, she did not only give Professor

63

Mackie his subject: the Galleon was the property of the Duke of Argyll and she arranged with the then Duke, that he invite Professor Mackie and his wife to lunch at Inveraray Castle to discuss the subject of the lecture on their way from Glasgow to Ronachan. At that time, with the help of Royal Naval divers, the Duke was trying to find the wreck, but the attempts were not successful. For the last of the series she wanted a lecture on the history and character of Scots Law. Professor Mackie suggested me. It seemed a crowded lecture but it was a small hall and perhaps thirty-five people were there. Mrs Pollok gave a dinner which started before the lecture, and after the lecture we returned to Ronachan to complete the dinner with port being circulated. I was offered a fee by her which, in view of all the kindnesses she had shown me, I refused. She told me to take my car and have it filled with petrol at the estate petrol pump and gave me eggs and butter – 'produce of the Estate' as she put it. Even more valuable, she gave a warm invitation, to use her own words: 'As David said to Jonathan, "Be sure you come back here again."' I did so many times – at first on my own – then with my wife and children. We had the freedom of the whole of Ronachan Estate, including a delectable and almost inaccessible hill loch where there were fish. Certainly although Ronachan became a Home for Alcoholics, its later prohibition of alcohol in my experience had not been one of Mrs Pollok's enthusiasms. She was one of the most generous of hostesses, and if Ronachan was left to the Church of Scotland with all it contained in her day, Barney Noon, referred to later, and his fellow inmates would have had at their disposal a library which would have given them all and more of the poetry they would ever have wanted to read and learn.

# 6

# EDINBURGH AND GLASGOW

The Faculty of Advocates, to whose membership I aspired, was in those days a small and exclusive fraternity, almost entirely male; there were only two practising women members, Margaret Kidd and Isobel Sinclair. It was a fraternity in which Sir Walter Scott would have found much of what he had known and relished of the same faculty 150 years earlier. Some members had had themselves called to the Bar – as Robert Louis Stevenson had done – for no other reason than that it was regarded as the profession of a gentleman in which if you had, or had inherited, money you had status with no necessity for putting your qualifications to mercenary and practical use. If you were at the Bar to pursue a career in law, real or academic, you found a company of about 100 active brethren amongst whom all the work of the Supreme Courts, both civil and criminal, was distributed by instructing solicitors, according to the experience, reputation, ability and personal or family influence of the advocate in question.

Admission in those days – the rules are now changed – imposed academic and financial limitations. An arts degree or passing an examination set by the Faculty on general scholarship, was the first requirement – evidence that you had what used to be called 'polite learning' – and this had then to be fortified with evidence of legal knowledge; a law degree which contained passes in listed subjects. I had the written qualifications which entitled me to try to become an intrant to the Faculty, a status whereby you were prohibited from earning money for a year, and during which you became a pupil or a 'devil' to a practising junior member of the Bar, i.e. not yet a QC (Queen's Counsel). This first year's 'devilling' meant assisting your master in what was then one of the main functions of a junior: drafting opinions, summonses, defences, petitions and the like, by which the business of the courts were governed. In the Court of Session it was usually the 'silks', i.e. the senior QCs, who conducted civil jury trials or a proof, accompanied by a junior who had drafted the pleadings – a practice which I heard the late Harald Leslie claim that, in his view, was to the advantage of the client. Since I had no personal connections or influence, the Clerk of Faculty found me a devil master, the late John Wilson, who I doubt really had time for a devil, though he had had an earlier one in Isobel Sinclair. For me this, in one way, was as well. I had been awarded the Faulds Fellowship by Glasgow University, which gave its holder the then respectable sum of £350 a year for three years. The expense of joining the Faculty in these days – including contributions to the widows fund and faculty dues – were in the region of £700; a small sum now but then substantial, especially if your only other income was £350 per year. These entrance fees, which used all I had, plus the year's obligatory non-earning condition, were major deterrents to anyone seeking to become an advocate. It was these things that, in my opinion, made the Bar the exclusive society it then was. Fortunately, the non-earning condition did not apply to an academic award like the Faulds Fellowship. Attached to the fellowship was the condition of independent research. My obligation was to pursue research into Scottish Legal History, which for the first time in its history was attracting attention and requiring recruits.

The Faculty was certainly interested in anyone who aspired to join them. And let their reputation for exclusiveness be what it was, so far as I was concerned, once I had started on the course which let me be called to the Bar the following year, in July 1953, I was accepted and given friendship and encouragement, not only from contemporaries but from established members of the Faculty. I think here in particular of Professor David Walker as he became (who was then a practising member of faculty), Hector McKecknie, QC, Campbell Paton, Manuel Kissen and Ian MacDonald.

I was called to the Bar, about the same time as James Patterson, who had devilled with me and who became a Border Sheriff. He was the son of a distinguished oculist. Jim undoubtedly belonged to the Edinburgh establishment. On the day he was called – when I may add he also received his first brief – his parents gave an evening party for him, to which he did me the compliment of inviting me. It was my first experience of being introduced to, and accepted into, the Edinburgh social and legal scene. That company demonstrated to me the calibre and character that Edinburgh Academy impressed upon its youth. I had never before been to anything like that party. This sort of thing did not happen in the Falkirk I knew. The champagne, and everything else one wanted, flowed freely. The young of the company were friendly and ebullient and treated me as if I had been one of the school's rugby fifteen, to which it seemed in their day, all of them had belonged.

It was a rule of the Faculty that once called you addressed all other members of Faculty, whatever their seniority, by their first names. Shortly after I was called, I met Professor Dewar Gibb, who had been my Professor of Scots Law at Glasgow and of whom I was a respectful pupil. When I called him Professor, he stopped me with an admonition that henceforth, as both of us were members of Faculty, we were to be on first-name terms. With him, as with other seniors, first names did not come easily to me but they all enforced this rule.

For the Faulds Fellowship, I undertook a transcription of the manuscript in the National Library of the *Practicks (1610–1634)* of Sir Thomas Nicolson of Carnock.

In sixteenth- and seventeenth-century Scotland, there were many such collections of *Practicks,* these being notes or jottings of cases in which the author as a pleader had been involved, or cases in which he was interested. Some of these Practicks, like Hope's *Major Practicks,* offered a digest or encyclopaedia of the then law. Others contained only case notes or jottings. Some of the digest Practicks were printed and were the earliest legal textbooks. Most of the 'only cases' Practicks remained unprinted, and if they all partook of the same characteristics as did Nicolson's *Practicks,* this is not surprising.

In the first volume of the Stair Society in 1936, the late Hector

McKechnie, QC, listed nine unpublished 'only case' Practicks which included Nicolson's and a similar collection by the Lord Advocate Hope. He described both the Nicolson and Hope as 'worth printing'. Nicolson's work was one in which the Stair Society was interested and when Hector talked of printing he had the Society in mind as publishers. He and Campbell Paton, who became literary director of the Society, spoke to me about publishing Nicolson, and made it clear that the Stair Society did not want just a transcription – they wanted an editing where necessary of individual cases, a biography of their author, and an introduction on the civil procedural techniques of the seventeenth century.

Nicolson's manuscript was a bulky volume containing some 600 cases, mostly briefly noted, but some giving arguments and submissions. Transcribing them was not an easy, rapid or stimulating experience. It took me some months to become able to read, admittedly slowly, the seventeenth-century handwriting in which they were recorded. In the court session of 1952–53, with the consent of my devil-master, I spent at least two hours each afternoon, four days a week, in the National Library in Edinburgh – the only place you were allowed access to the manuscript – transcribing the volume. It was an unfinished work. An anonymous preparatory note to the manuscript describes the cases it contains 'as being the foundation of a larger work designed but not perfyted'.

The next two years were, for me, lean years at the Bar and I worked frequently in the National Library to complete the transcription and collect material for the introduction. I had thoughts that a biography of Nicolson, the need for which Hector emphasised, would not prove difficult. Nicolson was a busy counsel in the Civil and Criminal Courts, described as 'the only man fit to be set up' against the Lord Advocate. In 1637, he purchased a Barony of Nova Scotia from Charles I, which gave him his title. He advised Charles I when the troubles of the Covenant commenced. Of his personal life otherwise, I could find nothing. What I hoped for was information on his personal and family life, and hoped to obtain this from his lineal descendent, Sir Harold Nicolson, the diplomat and author. When I wrote him, however, all he could tell me was that all the family papers had been destroyed when Carnock House was burned in the early twentieth century. My hopes that there might be family anecdotes or traditions about the founder of this family – what lines he had taken in the turbulent politics of the day, what were his interests outside his practice …? It would have been interesting to know if his 'cases Practicks' were recorded in the same way as the Lord Advocate had compiled his; 'without any study or application, being dictated to his sons in the mornings while he was dressing'. Some of Nicolson's jottings read as if they had been given a like treatment. Family tradition however could not help me.

The Faulds Fellowship ended in 1955. By about then and certainly the following year (I am writing from memory), I was beginning to have some practice as an advocate. An example of this was being instructed by no less than Lawrence Dowdall to defend one of the accused in the first Glasgow Bank Raid trial. If the practice continued and I was to make anything of the Bar, I became increasingly aware that I could not devote the time that I knew was required to continue, much less complete, the work of editing Nicolson's *Practicks*. By 1955, the transcription of the manuscript had been finalised, and I spent what time I could in the next year or so in editing it. I concluded by about 1956–57, however, that the only practical and realistic course open to me was to resign from the Nicolson project. Moreover, my conclusion was that, without the editing the Stair Society had required on the manuscript, the cases in the manuscript on their own would be of little interest and less use, except possibly to genealogists, and a waste of money for its publishers.

In short, I came to the conclusion that I could not accept Hector's judgement that Nicolson's *Practicks* as they stood were worth printing. I advised Hector and Campbell Paton of my decision. Both were realists. They expressed disappointment but accepted that my fears were justified and that, while trying to earn and keep a practice, I could not continue to edit the manuscript. They left me, however, with my transcription and the not insignificant material I had collected, and with the hope that if my circumstances did change and I had leisure, I could return to the *Practicks* and complete the work I had started when I was in my twenties. I write this at the age of eighty-four and have to confess that, since these meetings with Hector and Campbell, I have never had the necessary time and now, at the age I am, I fear it is unlikely I ever will.

In those days, most of those who were called to the Bar were from Edinburgh and had Edinburgh connections. It was the Edinburgh solicitor who instructed counsel, but solicitors from the rest of Scotland, who sent their Court of Session work to their Edinburgh agents, could nominate the counsel to whom the brief was to go. That, if you were non-Edinburgh, was perhaps the only way, to begin with at any rate, you would receive any instructions. One or two solicitors, with whom I had studied in Glasgow, sent me the odd divorce or opinion, but they were starting themselves and did not control the distribution of such Bar patronage as their office had. The outsider would get no business from the Edinburgh solicitor who did not know him, unless it was directed to him by the country solicitor. The Edinburgh side of the profession was said to have the proverbial and restrictive habit of the east coast fishermen, who allegedly 'gie our ain fish guts to our ain sea-maws' (give our own fish guts to our own seagulls). Legal aid in civil matters had been available for years, but whether the fees came from litigants, the public purse, trade unions or insurance companies, it still lay with the Edinburgh solicitor to distribute the patronage as he wished, unless his correspondent – i.e. the local solicitor who dealt directly with the client – designated the counsel who was to be instructed. Such being the situation, I have to report that during my first year at the Bar from July 1953 until July 1954, I earned the princely sum of ninety guineas – but for the Fellowship and certain other sources of income to which I will presently refer, and some good luck, the pursuit of academia seemed to be the only, and inevitable, course to follow.

In order to improve on my immediate economic status in my first year at the Bar, I was willing to earn money where and when I could, bearing in mind that as a member of Faculty, your range of opportunities was initially, at least, restricted. Nevertheless, as I now see it, I was fortunate. I had in these early years several strokes of good luck. This was the period of the winter evening classes, as television had not yet absorbed the adult's evenings. Courses were offered on all manner of subjects: public speaking, citizenship, languages, history, and crafts. Each summer lists were published by each university of the subjects on which they offered winter lectures and courses for a very modest fee. I started with lectures on Old Glasgow, organised by the Glasgow Corporation and given in one or other of the city's libraries. They went on for two to three years. You earned four guineas an hour and were expected to lecture for an hour and conduct a discussion session for another hour. For the evening you earned eight guineas, a significant sum in those day, had learned something of lecturing and made friends. I can recall one lady, a retired manageress from a large city store and an ardent Labour supporter, who attended these classes for two years, and who later got in touch with me to advise her grandson about what a career in law involved.

One series of lectures I gave over three winters were on Scottish History, sponsored by Glasgow University's extramural department. The lectures were given in Falkirk where I lived. Originally, they were to cover the whole of Scottish history in one session. Progress however was not rapid. The exploration of byways was popular with the class and led to much class participation. There were reminiscences of experiences and family connections, such that, often the teacher became one of the taught. By the end of the first session I had hardly reached 1603. It was agreed by the class and by the university that the course should be continued the following year and then it went on into a third year; 1955–1958, in all.

The personnel of that class remained substantially the same for the whole series. The lecture was on a Wednesday night and by the third year I had begun to have some practice in Parliament House and had difficulty in sparing the necessary time in preparing and delivering, and certainly for polishing, these lectures. This taught me how to use whatever competence I had in speaking extempore,

71

and I learned how to complete a lecture upon a note of finality for that night's subject, but with sufficient hint as to what was to come next week – the technique of the soap opera. Here again, friends were made. I was married in March 1958 and the Scottish History class held a party for the last of that session's lectures, and presented my wife-to-be and myself with wine glasses and a coffee percolator, the former still in active use. When we had settled in our home after the wedding, we had the class to a party. If that class learned something from me of Scottish history, I certainly learned from them whatever ability I had for speaking to a group on a fixed subject. It did me infinite good when it came to addressing juries, on what by then were unquestionably fixed subjects.

A more important contribution to economic survival came from the friendship I had with Sir Randall Phillip. In those days when a devil was called to the Bar it was the tradition that he lunched at the same table as his master. Then the Faculty was small enough to be accommodated in a lunch room in Parliament House to which only members were admitted. Accordingly, I joined what was called the 'Round Table' and found myself sitting with the Dean of Faculty, Sir John Cameron; the ex-Lord Advocate who became Lord Wheatley; James Walker shortly to become Lord Walker; T. P. MacDonald, the Vice-Dean; Frank Duffy and my devil-master who, until I joined it were the only two juniors at the table, and Sir Randall Phillip, a distinguished and respected senior who was Procurator of the Church of Scotland, and had been knighted for his services there at the time of the Queen's coronation. That table had a long history of sending its members to the Supreme Court Bench.

Sir Randall was a plump, good-natured little man who had the nickname of 'Sir Roundel' and he showed me a particular welcome and friendship. We took to one another despite the disparities of status and age. Sir Randall's practice was a lawyer's practice. I do not think he had had any contact with reparation or criminal work but in contract disputes, and on questions arising in trusts and executries, he was much sought after. By the time I knew him he had suffered a tragedy which darkened his later life. A few years previously his only son, Gordon Phillip, had died from injuries sustained in a school rugby game. His father had prepared a little bound volume simply called *Gordon Phillip*, which was his memorial to his son and of the way he had died. The first time I was in his house in Great King Street – when I may add the door was answered to me by a maid wearing the traditional black and white costume of a girl servant in the days when there were such beings, – he gave me a copy of that book. In the early 1950s he was in failing health and his clerk, who was also mine, once said to me that he 'could not get work out of Sir Randal'; meaning he was so long in producing opinions. He took the work involved in his procuratorship of the Church very seriously indeed, and there was so much of it that, in about 1955, the Church decided to give him an assistant – Assistant to the Procurator, not Assistant Procurator. Three or four of we juniors applied for the appointment and he appointed me. This was a big boost. It not only provided me with a very modest stipend but it gave me a status in the Edinburgh legal scene that, at my stage, nothing else could have done. My friend Alistair MacDonald's comment – and he was an Edinburgh man – was that I would never quite appreciate just what that appointment could do for me in Edinburgh legal circles. Sir Randal did need an assistant. He was inundated with requests for opinions on the various problems that seemed endemic in church administration. He encouraged such work. If he was asked for an opinion, he would give a brief answer and then say to the enquirer that if he was not satisfied then he should prepare and send Sir Randal a Memorial for the Opinion of Counsel, on which he, Sir Randal, would give a full written opinion. The ministers who sought his advice were not slow to send him memorials. Sir Randal died about two years later and was succeeded by T. P. MacDonald QC. In addition to the other work the assistantship involved, his successor had me prepare an index of Sir Randal's opinions. It was a task which taught me much about the problems that worried ministers, and much about the patience and thoroughness of Sir Randal Phillip's opinions. I hope the index and opinions are still available to whoever is Procurator now because they contain the advice of a learned, thorough and practical advisor in the proper workings of the Church of Scotland.

The early 1950s was the period when the law department at Glasgow University set about reforming its curriculum, its staff and its teaching methods. Prior to this, most of the teaching was done by part-time practising solicitors in Glasgow. The full-time chair was that of Scots Law, which was a Regius chair, and there were part-time chairs of Mercantile Law, Accountancy and Conveyancing. In 1954, David Walker, QC, was appointed full-time professor of Jurisprudence, and other full-time chairs followed in Roman Law, Mercantile Law and Accountancy. I had known David as a student in the class of moral philosophy when I was studying for an arts degree. The class sat in alphabetical order and Smith was followed by Walker. We became friends and at that time he encouraged me in my aim for a law degree and to aim for the Bar. He himself became Regius Professor a year or two later, and was undoubtedly the prime reformer in the Faculty. In the mid-1950s, he inaugurated a class in the Scottish Legal System; a historic and comprehensive introduction to the whole subject. This was novel and desirable. The classes of the 1940s and early '50s taught only their lecturer's subject: there was no introduction to the vocabulary, history, personnel, or techniques of Scots Law generally. For this new class, with characteristic thoroughness, David Walker had written and published a textbook that is still important. On this subject I was appointed part-time lecturer and lectured two to three nights a week, which meant a day in Edinburgh, a train to Glasgow in the late afternoon, and a lecture from 5–6 p.m. The class, I think, was a success; it certainly still continues.

Another of the reforms was the introduction of a class in the History of Scots Law, which was entirely new. The Scots had hardly ever shown much interest in the history of their law but, in 1935, the Stair Society was founded, dedicated *inter alia* to publishing the original sources of that law, which would enable, in turn, a serious scholarship to emerge. The first lecturer in the History of

Scots Law in Glasgow was Campbell Paton, a Glasgow solicitor who preferred the academic life to practice. He was the son of a prominent Glasgow solicitor who had practised in the brave days – his father had, I understand, been among other things, solicitor to the Caledonian Railway – Campbell, however, had no enthusiasm to follow his parental lead. He was comfortably off and a scholar and became a member of Faculty. He enlisted my help to index his addition of Baron Hume's Lectures on Scots Law which occupied six volumes. About 1958, he left Glasgow to take up a senior lectureship at Edinburgh where he had gone to live. His Glasgow lectureship was thus vacant and I had some of the qualifications necessary for it and the energy and enthusiasm to try to obtain more. It was a new subject; its theme and scope were still being explored. The materials for its study were also gradually being published. There was, I believe, no other applicant and I became part-time lecturer in the History of Scots Law with two lectures a week on Mondays and Thursdays at 5 p.m. I held that lectureship from 1957 until 1963 when I was appointed Sheriff at Glasgow and could no longer hold such a remunerated post. The university then invited me to become an honorary lecturer in the subject; I agreed and continued to run the department for twenty years as before, with a lecture two days a week at 5 p.m., without remuneration. I frequently caught a taxi from court to get me to the lecture hall in time.

The dual roles of sheriff and lecturer never interfered with one another. In some ways, in fact, they complemented one another and often the day's business of the court would provide material for the lecture – as, for example, in discussing criminal law with the class, comparing what the law had been and what it now was. If there was an emergency like a late sitting or illness, the assistant my predecessor had appointed would stand in. After him, Tom Friel, who had distinguished himself in an early year of the class, became assistant and made himself available, on call to lecture if there was a late emergency.

Those years in Glasgow were the happiest, busiest and most

satisfying years of my working life. The court was busy, the jurisdiction wide, the work infinitely varied. My colleagues numbered several giants as lawyers and as individuals. In lecturing I had the rewards that came from meeting, lecturing and getting to know a class of interested young people. The class was never large, varying from twelve to thirty-five. Its numbers increased with the years to which my lectures may have contributed, but which were more likely to have been the result of the dinner parties my wife gave for each year until 1974, when my first heart attack disrupted the routine. To the regret both of my wife and myself, the tradition was never resumed, but I have, in these my later years, repeatedly been approached by solicitors and advocates who took my class and who counted my wife's dinner party as their introduction to what they all called 'something really special' – and there were, and are many, who have kept in touch with us.

I left Glasgow in 1983 to go to the Sheriffdom of Greenock, Rothesay and Dunoon. I gave two or three lectures at the start of the new session, but the logistics of travelling from Bute and Greenock to Glasgow demonstrated that a permanent commitment was impossible, and the Faculty of Law was aware of this.

The balance between court and classroom, which I had for twenty years, suited me greatly. I have many a time regretted that I was ever tempted to give it up for the country living and the shrieval jurisdiction that accompanied it. By 1983 we had been owners of the house, known as 'Garrochty', on the Isle of Bute, for some twelve years. We had acquired it as a holiday house and with a view to retirement, and occupied it during holidays, or let friends have it when we were not there. There became a stage, however, when we wanted to live full-time in that house and that place, which we could only have done if I could have a transfer of jurisdiction from Glasgow to Greenock, Rothesay and Dunoon. That came in 1983 and we then gave up the tenancy of the Old Manse at Larbert, a gem of a house but becoming too small for us and our mutual addiction to the gathering of gear.

# 7

# FIRST BEGINNINGS

The start of a practice on which one could live, in my case, came mainly from two quarters. The first was the system, then prevailing, of recently called advocates appearing for the accused without fee in the High Court. The other was a Burns dinner I spoke at, attended, in particular, by three Glasgow solicitors.

In Scotland an accused person need never have lacked legal advice. Until 1964, solicitors and counsel acted in what came to be known as 'Poor Roll' cases. This had a long history and was normal representation until 1964, when criminal legal aid was introduced, and I never knew that assistance, if sought, to be lacking. My experience, in the 1950s, was that money was almost always to be found for bail, but few accused had access to funds to pay solicitor and counsel. The procedure here, for appearing for such accused in the High Court in the 1950s, was that the Clerk of Justiciary, Donald Stevenson, would approach a recently admitted and probably briefless advocate in the Parliament House saying he was looking for a defence counsel for a particular trial in the next Glasgow High Court sitting, and asking if he would act.

The Scots here had a long tradition of attempting to ensure that an accused, with or without means, was legally represented. There is an Act of the Scottish Parliament of 1587 (1587 C38) entitled 'All accused persons to be legally represented by advocates and prolocutors', and a later Act (C91) of the same year, empowering the court to compel advocates and procurators to appear for those 'accused of treason or for quatsumever crime'. Practice demonstrated that the court was prepared to use this power, and to use it regardless of the station of an accused. In 1597, even an aristocrat like the Countess of Earl had counsel appointed for her by the court. The system under the name of the Poor Roll, which prevailed in the 1950s, entitled an accused in the lower court to be represented by a solicitor in cases that were to be tried there, and if the case was to be taken in the High Court the solicitor instructed counsel to appear there, acting without fee. It was a tradition of the Scottish Bar that, in murder cases, a QC and a junior would gratuitously defend such a case. Junior counsel was available on this basis for all other High Court trials.

The only financial element then for a junior counsel conducting a Poor Roll case in the High Court was a payment of four guineas per day to cover travel expenses. I do not recall if this four guineas applied only to travel to Glasgow, or if a High Court in Inverness or Aberdeen merited an increase. The sum was modest and did not encourage extravagance in the beneficiary, but its source was intriguing and suggested long and high historic respectability. To receive it you made an application to an official known as The Queen's and Lord Treasurer's Remembrancer, which I take to mean the official who reminded, or *remembranced*, the monarchs and their Lord Treasurer, an office I did not then know existed, that the Monarch was expected to pay the subject of the exercise his share of the Royal Bounty to enable him to conduct a trial in Glasgow. I confess I did not even know there was still a Scottish Lord Treasurer who needed a Remembrancer. At the Court of James VI, with the unfailing capacity of the lieges of all classes and all ages to look to a Crown, chronically short of cash for favours, the Remembrancer in those days was unlikely ever to be without duties. It might, however, have been thought that modern accountancy and banking might have rendered not only the Remembrancer, but also the Lord Treasurer, a thing of the past. Then, however, it was not so. My recollection is that you addressed your application for the Royal Bounty to the Remembrancer through the Clerk of Justiciary, who of course was able to vouch for the validity of the application. The cheque for the four guineas, or its multiples depending on the length of the trial, duly came, though I never recall ever having seen either a Lord Treasurer or his Remembrancer. The nomenclature, however, of the exercise was a harmless and congenial link with the history of Royal finance. Certainly, the word Remembrancer conveys the impression of a gentle aristocratic figure, in contrast with his modern equivalent the Dun or the Debt Collector.

The Poor Roll system was a far cry from the elaborate preparations that were often claimed to be necessary after the introduction of criminal legal aid, but the system had worked and served generations of accused. In the ten years I appeared in Criminal Courts for the defence I rarely heard a client complain that his solicitor or his counsel had not done their best for him. So far as the pleader was concerned, the system gave him his first baptism of fire, his first opportunity to hear his voice before, usually, a Glasgow jury.

The young solicitor and advocate of today have courses in civil and criminal pleading available to them in all their aspects. He does not have to learn these matters for himself by experience and by watching others who already have experience, as our generation and the generations before had to do. Experience was the critical element. It alone could teach the individual where his talents lay and where his weaknesses existed. If he improved the former and rid himself of the latter, it was in the hard school of contested cases. Whatever contribution the adversarial system, which we have, makes to the elucidation of the truth, it is a system by which the pleader very quickly learns his trade and, in my day, unless you had friends and relatives who were solicitors and prepared to instruct you, your only opportunity to show what forensic mettle you might have was appearing for the defence in the High Court, instructed by a Poor Roll solicitor.

In practice then, in the 1950s, you were usually given your first chance by the Clerk of Justiciary, Donald Stevenson. He planned the sitting of the circuit that was to take place, knew the number of cases, the instructing solicitors, how many counsel were required to act and who would do so gratuitously. He found out which counsel were free and which were not, and put those who were free, and willing to act, in touch with the solicitor for the accused who was appearing on the same basis as the advocate. This was how I received my first and unpaid defence brief. It was to be the first of many. I always appeared for the defence and gradually came to be instructed by solicitors who had been put in funds for the defence.

When you were acting gratuitously neither you nor your instructing solicitor had much time and no financial resources for preparation. There was rarely elaborate taking of precognitions or numerous consultations. Certainly you and your solicitor saw life and the pair of you had always to be ready to rely on your own resources, both mental, and in a long trial, physical, to sustain efforts to maintain the accused's plea of 'not guilty'. There were no 'refresher' briefs here. Sometimes all the defence had was a list of witnesses that the accused hoped would speak in his favour. This was of little use, of course, unless the witnesses in question were sufficiently enthusiastic to be bothered to attend a solicitor's office and give statements. What you normally heard, on the Parliament House or solicitor-counsel grapevine, was a recent, and generally depressing, account of the client's criminal record: how he had treated his solicitors and counsel who had acted for him in the past; and how strong was the present charge against him. Usually, there was a statement from the accused himself and where he was not content to leave all the investigation to his solicitor, he would often supplement his precognition with letters to solicitor and counsel. Occasionally, if the accused had failed to show any interest in the efforts being made on his behalf, which was not unusual, there was little or no time for a full precognition from him. I can recall one accused handing me what he called his 'statement', which he had written personally and in which he set forth his version of the event. It ended with the line, 'Do you think this will do? If you don't, tell me where it goes wrong and I'll sort it'.

Even in cases where witnesses had been precognosced there was always the chance of the unexpected revelation of your client's resourcefulness or cynicism. I recall one example of the last, in a case I defended in the late 1950s. A man, who had been able to pay for his defence, was charged with theft of a TV set by house-breaking. In those days television sets, in size, resembled small coffins. They stood about four feet high, and some eighteen to twenty inches square. They were not readily portable, unlike that popular object of theft of the 1960s in Glasgow, the 'wee tranny' i.e. transistor. If you stole a TV set the operation required that you move what was a substantial piece of furniture. The bulk of the then current television models, however, presented no obstacle to their owners being deprived of them by the thief in my experience. He would usually have his own television but was well aware where there was a ready market for others he might have for disposal. My client here was accused of breaking into a flat in a tenement and removing a large TV set. One witness to this exercise brought something new to the case. He testified that he had seen my client standing, on the afternoon in question, at the entrance to the close or entry, in which the house broken into was situated, and clutching a large television set. This was not in the statement the accused had given, or in that of any of his witnesses, and since I had to have his comment on this somewhat damning evidence I went over to the dock, as was sometimes necessary, and done in the presence of the judge and jury. My client was no stranger to sitting in the dock and was not one of those who was overawed by the might and majesty of Scottish justice. I went over to him and whispered to him 'Where were you? Were you standing in the close or were you somewhere else?' To which I received the highly circumspect reply 'It all depends. Where do *you* want me to be standing?' I forbore to answer his question.

In situations where preparation was basic but slight the cross-examination of the Crown witnesses frequently became an exercise in instinct as to where and how far you would go, and what you would get when you got there. The books on witness examination advise that you do not ask a question unless you know what the answer is going to be. This is all very well if you had a fully prepared set of precognitions of all the witnesses but since the possession of such precognitions bespeaks much time and money, you were rarely in that position and your cross-examination was a process which necessitated following the old advice of 'gang warily'.

Criminal practice for the defence in these days demanded a readiness to take over the defence at a week or a day's notice. I have had papers delivered to my home at 11 p.m. for an appearance the next day, with a consultation in the cells before the trial, if he was in custody, where you learned what your client looked and sounded like. The visit to the cells before the trial was always important, especially if you had a jury. I remember one case where I saw the client in the cells for the first time. In profile, he looked like Ivor Novello: face-on he had a face like a ferret. I did not think it would be to his advantage that the jury see him face-on and for that, among other more cogent reasons, I advised him not to give evidence on his own behalf where he would have to face the jury from the witness box. He took the advice and was acquitted. Had they seen him face-on they would have believed him capable of anything, which to judge by his record of previous convictions he undoubtedly was. It does not help with a jury if the client looks, as unfortunately some of us do, 'capable of doing anything'.

For the young advocate, however, being on one's feet addressing a jury was for me a wholly thrilling as well as a new experience. This is what one had dreamed about. That exercise to me is the most thrilling thing of all in criminal practice and gradually as I gained experience I came to the view that in the criminal jury trials, while the evidence may seem to be the most important element, it is the speech about the evidence that often determines the result. After that first trial the Clerk of Justiciary had me appear frequently and, on this basis, I had the experience of nearly the whole criminal calendar, an experience which was extended when I began to be instructed by solicitors such as Lawrence Dowdall, Bill Dunlop, Joe Beltrami and Len Murray who, in Glasgow at that time, were the masters of their craft and from all of whom I learned much.

Back then I think I learned something about addressing juries.

Before I ever entered a court I had been used to speaking to an audience. From my youngest days I had been one of those, as I have already mentioned, who recited poetry to any audience who would listen to him and if the elocution lessons, to which I was sent all through my childhood, taught me anything, I think it taught me how to make myself heard by an audience. Appearing before a criminal jury has many of the characteristics of theatre. You have to make the jury listen to you. You have to speak to them audibly, hold their interest. You must not bore them, which means you must not address them for too long.

I have known pleaders who would speak on and on and on to a jury for no other apparent reason than to impress them with their ability to speak at great length on very little. Length must, to a certain extent, be governed by the amount of evidence that has to be discussed, but I regarded the optimum time for addressing a jury for the defence in a criminal charge, unless an exceptional one, as thirty to forty minutes: an hour at the most – if you wanted them to hear, listen, understand, remember and be persuaded. No modern Scots jury will willingly sit through five-hour speeches as their great-grandfathers did. If a juror yawns you are speaking far too long. If jurors stop looking at you they are thinking of other things than you want them to think about. If one of them goes to sleep and you only notice it when he stirs in that sleep, you are well on the way out. Once sitting in a sheriff and jury trial where a pleader was boring the jury, one of the jury, a decent-looking wee Glasgow woman looked up at me on the bench, smiled faintly and shook her head. The rhetoric, oratory and gravitas of earlier generations have, I am told, no place in a modern jury trial. My humble opinion is that if this has no place it is because the modern pleader does not know what that gravitas is, or how it should be used because to use it, to seek to achieve it, requires a definite form of speech, different from that now popular, but then, call it what you like, I have seen and heard counsel indulge in extreme rhetoric and seen a jury eat from their hands.

In January 1954 the annual Burns supper, at the Plough Hotel, in Stenhousemuir, was organised by a local solicitor, Robert Turpie. He had a local practice and lived in Larbert. He had also a Glasgow office. His political sympathies lay with the nascent Scottish Nationalism of the day and he was on friendly terms with some of the Glasgow solicitors of a like mind – John McCormick, who founded the modern Scottish Covenant and William Graham, another solicitor who supported him. Robert's organisation of the Burns supper involved two visiting speakers – Ian Hamilton, now a QC, then a national figure for his part in the theft of the Stone of Destiny from Westminster Abbey, and me, whose father's family had been in Stenhousemuir for four generations. Ian Hamilton was called to the Bar a year after myself and, like all young advocates, we welcomed any attentions which might be paid to us by members of the profession who might instruct us in cases in court. Ian proposed the Immortal Memory. I proposed another toast which, to me, was new to a Burns dinner, namely the toast of Scottish Literature. This was a working man's Burns supper. There was nothing sophisticated about it, but there was sincerity, or there would have been no place for the toast assigned to me. At the top table Robert had invited three guests – all legal colleagues from Glasgow – Willie Graham, Peter McGettigan and George Wallace. For me the presence of these three men was to make that Burns supper the most significant and important Burns supper of the hundreds I have spoken at.

I was sitting next to Willie Graham who was a blunt, outspoken individual who did not hide his prejudices from strangers who sat next to him. I was, however, neither in the position nor the mood to argue with him. Ian proposed an admirable Immortal Memory. I proposed Scottish Literature and when I sat down my neighbour, Willie Graham, demanded how long it had taken me to prepare what I had had to say. He was very kind in his remarks of what I had done, as were his two colleagues and before he left that dinner he said he would send me some business in the Parliament House and might be able to use my services occasionally in Glasgow in the Sheriff Court. I should underline that Willie was a solicitor whose firm had much court business.

Peter McGettigan did not have the volume of business that Willie Graham had but he was also kind in his remarks and also sent me what business he could. Peter became a friend of my wife and myself for the rest of his life. He was a man of immense charm, immense courage, immense civility and a devout Roman Catholic. His wife, when I knew her, was in indifferent health. He had one daughter and one son. His son tragically died, and with his death something died in Peter, not the charm, not the politeness, but I doubt if he was ever the same man he had been.

Courage ran in that family. Peter's brother, who was his partner in the legal firm of McGettigan and Company, lost the power of speech as the result of a stroke but never lost his sense of humour or his courage. I met him once in Highburgh Road, Glasgow, after he had suffered this affliction. He carried a little pad around with him on which he wrote down any 'conversation' he was having with you. He shook hands with me, took out his pad and wrote, 'I am Tom McGettigan – I am the only dumb lawyer in Glasgow'.

The third of these guests from Glasgow at that Burns supper was George Wallace who had been a practising solicitor in Glasgow, and Peter McGettigan's partner at one time. Since the war, while remaining a solicitor in the Supreme Court, he had gone into business and created a highly successful company, Wallace Cameron and Company, which earned one of the Queen's awards for industry. They manufactured all manner of medical dressings, cleaning material, antiseptics, and polishes and were so successful that they were eventually taken over by Smith Kline and Company when George was given a seat on their board. Simultaneously with managing a successful business, he was Chairman of the East Kilbride Development Corporation and eventually a Peer of the Realm as Lord Wallace of Campsie. The night of the Burns supper George gave me every encouragement. He liked what I had said and the way I had said it and told me so. He asked if I would speak at dinners for him. This was praise indeed even if he did not mean it. In fact, however, he did mean it and thereafter helped my wife and myself in many ways because George was an extraordinarily kind and generous man. He was one of the friends of our married life and we saw much of him and of his wife until we left Glasgow in 1983. He was a man well-known in the city with much influence and he gave me his good will and encouragement: in Glasgow then these were valuable things to have in my situation. George was the first man I was privileged to know who really did things in what my generation called 'style'. He was the first man I was privileged to know who answered to the Eartha Kitt's description of 'an old-fashioned millionaire'. His tailoring was invariably immaculate and undoubtedly expensive. He had a large car and a chauffeur. When he was made a life peer he asked me to go over his maiden speech with him. He took me to lunch in the old North British Hotel and ordered smoked salmon for us both with half a bottle of champagne and added to the waiter, 'vintage', to which the waiter nodded in knowing acquiescence. George used to carry a small wad of new five-pound notes in his jacket handkerchief pocket, along with a gold swizzle stick. He would take one of the notes out and give it when he thought it was deserved. My son, aged about nine, still recalls being given one and his younger sister recalls her resentment that she was not there to get one with him. His Christmas presents were the talk of the family.

I had done some after-dinner speaking locally in the 1950s and early '60s at some small functions, but it was George who introduced me to the real Glasgow scene. Besides being Chairman of East Kilbride Development Corporation he was president of the Institute of Marketing, and became Deacon of the Craft of Gardeners, one of the ancient crafts in Glasgow whose members were and are the aristocracy of trade, commerce and the professions there. In 1966, George had me speak at The Gardener's Dinner, when he was their Deacon, and I believe that the dinners at which he asked me to speak in Glasgow and East Kilbride gave me the entrée to the Glasgow after-dinner scene which I greatly enjoyed, and which, if my experience of 2009, is any indication, was an entrée which has not yet been denied me.

A milieu such as the Faculty of Advocates and Parliament House might have been expected to impress an indelible and unvarying stamp upon all its members. Such, however, was not the result. There were many characters, not to say the odd eccentric among the members. I never experienced any unpleasantness from among them, but there is no doubt that there was a general interest in any new entrant by nearly all established members of Faculty, even by the seniors. They were interested in his history, his antecedents, his potential as a pleader, his politics, and about these they undoubtedly gossiped and kept in mind any of the information they had on the new entrant that might be of value to them.

I remember early on in my membership being approached by the late Sinclair Shaw, QC; a man with an approach and a voice that suggested a gently spoken medieval scholar. He had a French wife and was, in fact, an ardent supporter of the far left in politics. Shortly after I had been called, he approached me once or twice with the suggestion that I should make some motion at a Faculty Meeting, or be the junior who proposed a left-wing candidate for some vacant office in the Faculty. Why he should choose to approach me I never learned, for in Parliament House I never discussed politics. The only explanation I can give for his approach was, I think, his knowledge, which was common, of my comparatively plebeian origins. An end, however, was brought to these approaches when for some forgotten reason I expressed my admiration for General (then President) de Gaulle. Sinclair's reaction to this was almost cosmic. For him my admiration was political heresy. He assured me at some length of many wicked tyrannies of which he said de Gaulle was the author. He appeared to be genuinely horrified that anyone could harbour such a heresy as I did and remain socially acceptable. He was a Queen's Counsel when I knew him but rarely appeared in court, but when he did he conducted his client's case with such care and thoroughness that the patience of his instructing solicitors, even those who shared his political opinions, was tried and he had little business.

Another character who had an early comment on me was the late J. A. K. Lilley, known as Jake Lilley, who was Sheriff Principal of Fife when I went to Parliament House. He had known that institution from the 1920s and written an admirable but now unobtainable book on the Faculty of that period. By the time I knew him he was reputed to be getting deaf but I learned the truth of this rumour when, in a very early jury trial, I appeared in front of him and a jury in, I think, Dunfermline Sheriff Court. The accused was alleged to have been involved in supplies to the dockyard at Rosyth and some criminal intent was alleged. Sheriff Lilley not only wanted to hear all the evidence in the trial, it was *essential* he hear all the evidence, and because of his deafness there were many questions and answers he had to have repeated. If, however, he was slow on the hearing, he was not slow in his law because his charge to the jury, which was unappealable, destroyed the defence case and the accused was found guilty. The morning after the trial, round the Parliament House fire, I am told Sheriff Lilley's contribution to the group was about the trial in which I had just appeared. I heard from one of the group that his comment on the defence counsel, myself, was that, 'He will do all right once he learns how to speak up'. It is the only occasion, of which I am aware, where I have been accused of inaudibility.

Parliament House was a place for making acquaintances. All members of Faculty were your brethren. It was not, however, a place where you made many friends, but friends you did make, and any one of these friendships bred what Robert Louis Stevenson called 'subsidiary friendships', that you met at the Friday and Saturday dinner parties, then beloved of Parliament House. Not living in Edinburgh I was less involved in socialising than most but certain brethren I regarded as more than just brethren. I recall some in particular.

One man in Parliament House, who from my start there gave me his friendship, his help and his advice, was Manuel Kissen. When I first knew him he was a junior counsel with the reputation of being the busiest junior at the Bar. It was his practice that if instructed to draft, say, a summons on one day the summons was drafted that night and back in the hands of the instructing

88

solicitor the next morning. His energy was prodigious. He required very little sleep, was known to have drafted up to a dozen Court of Session summonses in one night, and never seemed to stop working. His idea of relaxation was to return to Glasgow every weekend, where he belonged when his mother was alive, taking with him six paperback detective stories, or what he called 'rubbish novels', and to spend the weekend reading these and occasionally dining with friends. When he was a senior I was frequently his junior in Reparation claims tried by a civil jury. When he went on the bench our contact did not stop. When I was in hospital recovering from a heart attack he sent me a parcel of paperbacks, and when I eventually issued the Ibrox judgment he wrote to me commenting on the day's press reports for the case. 'My gladness at reading the report was due not only to the fact that you had returned to duty but also to the fact that you had cleared yourself of the burden of the Rangers decision. It worried me that you had this hanging over your head while recovering but, thankfully that is now out of the way.

A word of advice – if I may be permitted to give it. *Please* cut down on your work, not only for your own sake but for the sake of your family . . . *Please* also cut down the outside engagements.'

He continued that his wife 'would be delighted to learn that you are back in harness like a faithful old work horse.' He rarely appeared in Criminal Courts but I was his junior in a case referred to later in this book – namely, Christina Flanders – where all the talents I have been attempting to describe were displayed.

Another was Ian MacDonald who later became a judge as Lord Mayfield. He had had a distinguished career during the war and after it had devilled to Manuel Kissen. When I went to the Bar he was a busy junior, but one who with his wife, early showed Diana and I many kindnesses. He was a good-natured, entertaining companion with a broad sense of humour for which he found many subjects among his brethren. When I was courting Diana the MacDonalds patronised her father's hotel in London and to the questions of her mother, who had no experience of Scotsmen, spoke well of my intentions towards their daughter to whom I was engaged.

At the Bar I was senior by a few years to Ranald Sutherland, later Lord Sutherland, who was another of our group. We had very different backgrounds, but in the mid-1950s became friends. He was a frequent visitor at our home and came to know Diana's family in London. He was a groomsman at our wedding in 1958 and Diana and I came to know well and prize the company and kindness we had from the Sutherlands, both father and son. Ranald and I shared two interests: Parliament House in all its facets, and music. I recall in particular a sheriff and jury trial in Perth of a number of prison officers from the then recently set up detention centre there. They were charged with ill-treating detainees. Ranald was the Advocate Depute who was prosecuting. I was for all the accused and sought to persuade the jury (as the presiding sheriff told them) 'that what was on trial here was the object and methods of the recently introduced sentence of three months' detention' – the object of which was to give what was called 'a sharp, short lesson' with strict discipline to young offenders. It was the discipline which had led to the complaint here of ill-treatment. The jury did not take long to reach their conclusion. They did not accept the evidence of the ex-detainees and in doing so acquitted all the accused – and with that verdict, the institution itself, as well as its objects and methods. In that trial, I still recall the pleasure it was to appear against a pleader who was not only eminently competent and fair, but courteous to all who were involved.

Listening to classical music, and in particular opera, was an enthusiasm Diana and I shared with friends like Ranald, who had the same love of it. That enthusiasm was fed on long playing records of complete operas. In the 1950s, I was just beginning to acquire these. Diana and I – to her dismay – rarely dined out in restaurants: any spare cash saved thereby was spent on LPs, and playing the recording of a complete opera, with a home-produced evening meal between two of the acts was, and remains, our greatest pleasure. Mr Sutherland senior did not always share this pleasure.

His brief comment on the soprano and mezzo in Verdi's *Requiem* was that they were, in his view, 'bawling women'. Ranald, however, did more than listen. He was a talented pianist.

When I left the Bar in 1963, the friendships and contacts there were kept up for a year or so, but even within Scotland, there can be tyranny of distance, and where contact is rare, it tends to become rarer until it no longer exists. In its last stages, as here, it declines to a Christmas card and eventually not even that.

The only two of this group who did not reach the Supreme Court were Alistair MacDonald and I. He and I went to the Sheriff Court Bench, he in 1961, myself in 1963. We both left Edinburgh and were 'seen there no more', nor at Faculty dinners nor on the dinner-party circuit. This was the experience of all I knew who left Parliament House. It was as if we were regarded as brethren who had deserted the ship. Contact with old friends gradually became less. Alistair MacDonald, as always, put his finger on the situation: 'If you leave Parliament House,' he declared, 'and ever want to get back there among them you have to be reborn.' Alistair and his wife Jill, however, were two of the friends with whom we had continued contact until his untimely death – despite the distance between Lerwick, Kirkwall and Glasgow and Bute.

# 8

# SHERIFF ALISTAIR MACDONALD

About a year after me, Alistair MacDonald came to the Bar. And from his arrival there he and I were boon companions. Any problems we encountered in our respective practices we discussed walking up and down Parliament Hall. He acted as my junior when we defended the two capital murders, Watson and Miller. In 1961, he left the Bar and became Sheriff of Shetland, the most remote of all Scottish sheriffdoms. It was a move no one could understand because he was a man given to talk, gossip, company, and the life of Edinburgh, his home city, and he adored the life of that city. When he collapsed and died so prematurely in 1998, for his friends there was eclipsed the unfailing gaiety that always attended him. His widow's belief, which she told me two years ago, was that he had found the stress of the Miller case and the subsequent execution of that accused so stressful that it determined him to leave practice at the Bar, and when he was offered the Sheriffdom of Shetland, he readily accepted it.

To those to whom he gave his friendship, he was the greatest, most original, inexhaustible and inventive wit of our time. His sudden and untimely death produced many testimonials, but none more appreciative and relevant than the article of Lord McCluskey, published in the *Glasgow Herald*, in which he celebrated Alistair's wit. Along with his wit he had a ready command of the language of the Authorised Version of the Bible.

Where Alistair was, there was laughter. He was a Yorick who did not need a table to keep his companions in a roar of laughter. Indeed, he was not an enthusiast for addressing after-dinner audiences, but was at his best when he discoursed on the characters, scandals and rumours of Parliament House, the weaknesses of judges, idiosyncrasies of characters there and the passing social and political scene. Any hypocrisy he detected in great and small was the subject of his unceasing irony, especially if they were members of the Faculty of Advocates. His was a wit that was respected, admired and sometimes feared by all who heard it. The late Manuel Kissen, one of the busiest counsel of his day, always had time to listen and talk to, and laugh with Alistair MacDonald.

His wit was not of the kind that can be readily recorded for repetition. It was spontaneous, essentially original and intimate, arising out of the particular conversation, company or event. I recall one incident where he and I were together at a reception in the home of the late Lord Justice Clerk Thompson. I came from Falkirk and that prompted some talk on the Lord Justice Clerk Craigie Mason Aitchison, who died in 1941, who was a Falkirk man and the son of a Falkirk manse. He had a reputation not only as a pleader but as being fond of alcohol. One of the many stories about Craigie in his cups was mentioned in that conversation with Lord Thompson, who shook his head over it. Alistair's immediate comment was, 'Of course, nowadays, we have a better class of judge than they did in these days', which appealed greatly to his Lordship.

I was with him once at a function where wine was flowing, and his comment to the waiter who came to replenish his glass was perfect. 'Just to the brim, please,' he said. In the same context, at a dinner where his glass stood empty for too long, his comment was: 'Gentlemen, the toast is Absent Friends, coupled with the name of the wine waiter'. He loved the reality, and the old Scottish description of 'Gentlemen daffin [drinking] at their wine'. Another of his phrases was: 'A problem shelved is a problem solved'. His tongue could on occasions be biting, if not cruel. One January, I had undertaken to propose the Immortal Memory at an old-age pensioners' Burns supper. I had also mistakenly agreed to do the same elsewhere and I persuaded Alistair to toast the Immortal Memory at the old-age pensioners' function. On the night I took him there to introduce him to the organiser and chairman, whose welcome to us both was far from warm. He appeared to be under the impression that two members of the Bar were to be treated as hostile to all he believed in. The tone of his attitude was exemplified in his comment to me, which was: 'We will use you next year?' To Alistair he was barely civil and certainly his hospitality was not what was expected at a Burns supper. Alistair was a man who was fond of wine. That night there was no wine and no whisky. Indeed, all Alistair was given to drink was what was given to all the others who attended that dinner; namely, a small bottle of beer. This, together with the Chairman's hostile reception, did not make for a congenial evening. Alistair told me afterwards that he had difficulty restraining himself from opening his Immortal Memory by wishing all the company of old pensioners the hope that they would enjoy this Burns Supper, because for some of them it would 'probably be the last Burns Supper they would ever be at'. Fortunately, he did restrain himself.

The annual Christmas cards from him and his wife, Jill – a delightful woman and respected consultant – were the reverse of conventional. He filled them with news and fun. As what I consider proof of this, I print two of his letters to me that accompanied Christmas cards, in 1967 and 1985. They each give the inimitable flavour of the man. The first letter is dated 'Feast of St Catherine 1967':

My dear Irvine,

I have just finished prayerfully redding up another year's stewardship of my Sheriffdom. Another year in which no Shetlander went to prison, no Shetlander child or youth went to any penal institution or was placed on probation. Indeed, brother, my efforts here are wonderfully blessed. It is difficult to over-emphasise the value of the resident sheriff's personal example. But enough of my poor concerns. I am very sorry that I was unable to do anything to entertain your friend Doreen because I had to leave quite unexpectedly by the very next morning for the Island of Unst. I was very sorry too that you did not find it possible to visit us in the autumn. We would be delighted to have you whenever you can manage to come – please believe that, my dear Irvine.

I do not know whether you have been following my TV appearances. They have added to my already fantastic status in the Sheriffdom. It is perhaps as well that I shall be the last sheriff of the Shetland Islands. It would be monstrously unfair to anyone to follow in my footsteps. Thank God I have been able to save my unhappy people from 'XY' [a potential candidate for the vacant Sheriffdom of Orkney]; this I owed to them. I am looking forward eagerly to becoming Sheriff of Orkney and Shetland and to sitting in the shadow of the magnificent Earls Palace. I want to hold a court again from time to time in the Great Hall of the palace. I shall have heralds and trumpets … It will be glorious!

I am under the doctor the whole time now and I have to keep taking those sedatives. I have been advised to resign and take up gardening or weaving but I have decided to carry on until I commit some misconduct, like our other brethren – you get a better pension that way I am told.

Isn't it nice that we shall soon be eligible to become one of the five Sheriff Principals? I have read the Grant committee report carefully and as far as I can see, the only real duty this official will have is drawing up the sheriff's holiday roster. This post, together with a knighthood, will do me very well. I should, of course, pay a depute to perform the derisory duties and I would live with my family in Brittany!

Jill sends her love to you and Diana and we join in wishing you and your children a happy and a Holy Christmas.

West Hall
Shetland Island


Tuesday, 1 January 1986
My dear Irvine,
It was a great joy to hear from you, but I was grieved to

hear how ill you had been. I hope that rest will restore you to health. You should be in no hurry to return to duty. I know something of cold journeys to court and something of cold courts too. The heating has failed several times this winter at Lerwick Sheriff Court. It is misery; but I am lucky that my court here is ten minutes' drive from home. The Kirkwall Court is very snug and I would as lief spend a winter's day in it as anywhere else. I have a wonderful view from the bench at Kirkwall. I look over a garden full of tall trees to the Earls Palace and to St Magnus Cathedral. I enjoy watching the rain showers sweeping past while the agents argue far below me. It would be perfect if only I could read a book; but even this constraint is valuable since I enjoy reading in the evening so much more. That is the spirit in which I deal with all the little burdens and restrictions which life places on me: joyfully offering them up and using them as a means of spiritual improvement.

Your news of your family is good and, indeed, you are fortunate in Diana who has taken such care of you in your illness. I seem to detect in Jill [his wife and a medical consultant] a slight impatience when I suggest that I might be ill. Illness is for hospitals: not for the home. Our children were never in danger of swallowing dangerous pills. There is not so much as an aspirin to be found. There are some homeo-pathic preparations for the treatment of foundered ponies but they are not kept in the house. Jill has very much the approach of the old style army doctors when it comes to diag-nosing illness in me: two causes and two causes only: drinking too much and malingering. I am very lucky that no major internal system has yet failed. I have been able to carry on to date and I find that such illnesses as I have receive more sympathy and consideration from the Sheriff Court staff than they would at home. I am lucky that I spend a night each week in a very comfortable little hotel in Kirkwall, where I am very well looked after and treated with a respect and deference which is becoming all too rare in these days. Kirkwall must surely be one of the last bastions of the old decency. There are some elderly men in Kirkwall who address me in the street as 'My Lord'. True, they are usually drunk and, more often than not, have appeared before me, but I cannot help discern in them something of an older and better time when things were better ordered.

I saw the end of 1985 with no regret. For once, good fortune, for a while deserted Familien MacDonald, Jill and Cata [his daughter] were quite seriously ill in the summer. For a time I was alone at West Hall – alone, that is, except for a pony, three cats and a large Labrador/collie. I almost envied Job his boils. I was pretty sure they would yield to penicillin. However, with the approach of winter things began to improve. Cata is restored to health and Jill, almost so. All of us were at home for Christmas and it was a very happy festival. Ian [his son] took the final part of his MRCP early this year and is presently preparing to sit the first part of the higher qualifications in anaesthetics. He is not sure yet whether he wants to be a Consultant Anaesthetist. His difficulty is to find a medical speciality which can be easily combined with mountaineering, skiing and windsurfing. I have suggested 'skins' – a speciality in which there are no emergencies, where there is no scope for negligence or accident, where death is unknown and where, if one had the good fortune to hit upon a remedy for chronic itch, fame and fortune would inevitably follow. Of course, there are disadvantages. It is, perhaps, a little unexciting and since no one ever gets cured, there are large clinics of somewhat resentful patients. But one cannot have everything. You must have discovered that.

The New Year's Honours List was particularly dreary this year … How is the selection made? Don't bother to answer that. I have a fair idea. I met great numbers of civil servants during my time with the Montgomery Committee and was much confirmed in my views of their deleterious influence upon our national life. I can imagine the kind of mind which assists in the preparation of the final list ...

You will have noticed that the Law Reform (Miscellaneous Provisions) (Scotland) Act 1985 received the Royal Assent a couple of months ago. The most important provision of the Act came into force on 30 December 1985, removing the disqualification of sheriffs from holding 'any office not by statute attached to the office of sheriff'. You may not know that it was because of my insistence that this provision was included in the Act. Nearly three years ago, the Lord Lieutenant of Shetland wanted to make me a Deputy Lieutenant of the County, and was informed by Younger [then Secretary of State] that although Sheriff MacDonald was in every way suitable to the appointment it was, alas, statutorily barred. Now three years later justice has been done and the Lord Lieutenant has applied _de novo_ for my appointment. I welcome the appointment as yet another opportunity for public service, and I must say that you meet a very nice class of person amongst the Deputy Lieutenants of Counties. I believe the uniform and the insignia are those of a full Colonel in the Regular Army, but I care little for such gewgaws or whigmaleeries. I shall remain quite unaffected, you may be sure.

My dear Irvine, Jill and I were most touched by your warm expressions of friendship and heartily reciprocate. We remember you and Diana with great pleasure and affection. We would love to come and visit you on your island and will do so when you are restored to health. I still dine out on your horrified reaction to my offer to come and visit you when you had been ill: 'Oh Alistair, I'm not as well as that yet!' Jill had every sympathy with the sentiment. I am removed from sick rooms – much as flowers were at night in times past. My presence is found to be something less than soothing.

I, at last, surrendered to my hatred of the Scottish New

Year and last night was in bed with a good book by 11.30
p.m. I toasted Jill with a sustaining cup of Horlicks at
midnight and woke this morning feeling well and smug as a
Pharisee. How empty Shetland looked. The sun shone on
snow and sea. My heart went out to those who by intemper-
ance and irregularity of life were losing the beauty of the
morning. Gales are forecast and will no doubt greet the
misguided revellers when they awaken from their disordered
sleep.

Jill joins me in sending love and best wishes to you and
Diana. Get well soon, but do not charge back to work.

Yours aye, Alistair

P.S. I welcome the onset of gales. I had a phone call
yesterday from solicitors asking if I would be available to sign
a warrant for the arrestment of a ship at *ad fund junid* [arrest-
ment to found jurisdiction] on Saturday. It seems that a Bank
in America is owed forty-five million dollars by a company
which owns *inter alia* an oil platform in the North Sea. The
platform on Saturday is to be off the coast of the North Isles
of Shetland. It seems that a Sheriff Officer from Aberdeen (we
have none on the island) is coming with a Writ from
Aberdeen by helicopter and armed with my warrant,
proposes to fly out to the platform and arrest it! I have landed
on rigs from helicopters which were welcomed and expected
and had not found the experience re-assuring, but to land on
a rig from a helicopter which was not welcome …! And how
do you dismantle a craft the size of Glasgow Sheriff Court
which has no motive power of its own? I suppose the Sheriff
Officer might screw off a leg, and now there are to be gales as
well! The Sheriff Officer will probably get killed. Just as long
as no one tries to blame me. The last warrant to arrest a ship
which I granted was in the Galoil case. The action was for a
trumpery four and a half million dollars. When the defenders
petitioned to have the arrestment removed, I could not take
the hearing and it was handed over to Muir Russell in

Aberdeen [the sheriff there]. I assured him airily that the hearing would probably not go on (in my experience, such cases die a natural death. They are settled in hours by financial giants who have not a minute to waste upon the Scottish legal system, with its time and line methods of procrastination). It did go on. The hearing lasted nine hours. Muir was appealed to the Inner House and was upheld. An appeal was taken to the House of Lords where the Honourable Harry Keith, [one of the Lords of Appeal] hammered Muir Russell, Lord Wheatley and the second division into the ground like a tent peg. I shall take this case myself. A crave for forty-five million dollars will be a record for my little court. I am almost ashamed to say that $4,500,000 has been the largest to date. I can hardly wait for Saturday and the gales and the rig and the Sheriff Officer and the helicopter! I do like a bit of fun with my law.

A.

P.P.S. Do you ever wish you had stayed in PH [Parliament House] and been made a Life Peer like everyone else?

P.P.P.S. The last distribution of the judicial loaves and fishes was truly the feeding of the 5,000. Everyone was made a judge, it seems. Of course, the workload has been tremendously increased by removing divorce to the Sheriff Court. Criminal legal aid is now almost the sole source of income for the Bar, and no one is allowed to plead 'guilty', which means that the Lords Ordinary and indeed all the Lords are needed on circuit all the time.

# 9

# BAPTISM OF FIRE: THE FIRST HIGH COURT TRIAL

I do not remember much about my first High Court trial as a very junior advocate. I was called to the Bar in July 1953 and this trial was the following October. It was my baptism of fire in that court and caused no ripple on the surface of forensic life. I do not recall much of the detail except that those details I do recollect were the sort with which I was to become very familiar indeed over the next forty odd years. I had ten years at the Bar defending in such incidents, and twenty years in the Sheriff Court in Glasgow, plus fifteen in Greenock and other sheriffdoms trying them. What I do recall very vividly of the Circuit High Court was their openings. The High Court on circuit in those days was regarded and treated as an event, and its judges treated like royalty. I remember a sitting in Aberdeen in the late 1950s, which was a civic as well as a judicial event. During the sitting, the city extended its generous hospitality to all – the accused excepted – who were in attendance in that court. At the start of the sitting, the judge inspected a guard of honour from the local regiment drawn up outside the court in Union Street. In my time, Glasgow never had this for a High Court, but the arrival of the judges there was always memorable. A civic limousine brought the two judges – there were always two judges on a Glasgow circuit – to the entrance to the Judiciary buildings. There, on the pavements they were awaited by their respective macers; police on duty stood at attention. The car drew up at the appointed time, and their Lordships emerged, and at a measured pace, preceded by their respective macers, moved up the steps and entered the building between two lines of staff, lawyers, police and public. I once saw an elderly Lord Carmont make that entry in Glasgow for what was to be his last Glasgow circuit. For the start all those involved – except the accused – were assembled for the then traditional opening of a circuit, not just in Glasgow but at the opening of a circuit all over Scotland at that time. For me, my first opening turned out to be an unexpected combination of sight and sound. First there appeared two state trumpeters. Then there came from a macer his long drawn-out call of 'Court'. The Bar and the public got to their feet. There was the presence of a clergyman and then the appearance of the two red-robed judges. When all were assembled the state trumpeters sounded their long trumpets. I had never before heard them live. It was an experience which explained their long association with state events and great occasions. I can still remember the echoes of these trumpet calls dying away over that silent audience. To me it was theatre; magnificent theatre, and a realisation of why the scriptural phrase, 'The trumpet shall sound, and the dead shall be raised', was so apt. It was a sound that arrested the mind and the heart and lent the pride, pomp and circumstance of age to the whole proceedings; old ceremony calculated to thrill and impress everyone there that what was happening was nothing sordid or trivial. Here was the old Scottish way of proclaiming the status and dignity of the process of justice. It does not and could not I suppose happen today, not because the sound of the trumpet would not thrill, but because such pomp and ceremony are now discounted, and because High Court Sittings, at least in Glasgow, are no longer events, but part of an unending routine.

The trial that followed that experience was in marked contrast, but for a Glasgow High Court in the early 1950s it was archetypal. The charge was one of assault to severe injury. The scene was a flat in a Glasgow tenement. The time, a Friday or Saturday night. And the cast members of a large group of family and friends, who had congregated in the parental home, there to participate in the consumption of what in Glasgow was then known as 'a good carry-out' – a carry-out here was a quantity of alcohol which had literally to be 'carried out' of public houses when they closed at

10 p.m., if the night's festivities were to be continued. The adjective 'good' applied to a carry-out, was and is a synonym for 'large', and an adjective which puts the carry-out into a special category for volume, variety and alcoholic content. The eventual result was what the prosecuting counsel, who was born in and educated in Edinburgh, called 'a fracas' – a word which was new to most of the witnesses, who had a much cruder word to describe what went on. The consumption of the 'good carry-out', while it undoubtedly increased the enjoyment of the evening was not an asset when it came to its participants attempting to recollect, to the two police constables, who were eventually called by the neighbours, which of the men had taken exception to the remarks of the elderly father, and what precisely were the allegedly provocative remarks that had provoked the assault on him, or why they were made. While all had been present and could not have avoided hearing all that was said and shouted and, as far as the men were concerned, must have seen the assault, uncertainty prevailed as to who had carried it out, though it must have taken some time, since its result was what appeared to be a geographically and undoubtedly discriminatingly conducted session of surgery on the victim's face. The victim was not in an ideal position to be a witness, but he was not only ready, he was almost enthusiastic, to assent to the defence's proposition that his memory of what had happened was not as good as it might have been, and at one point was prepared to accept another defence suggestion that he might have sustained his injuries by falling on a fender in front of the fire, which was what one of the younger generation present said might have happened.

As witnesses, the women in the party were not particularly helpful to the police officers in their enquiry because, as they advised the police at the start of what the advocate depute referred to as 'the fracas', they had all retired to the toilet on the stair, I fear in order not to be able to see anything that followed. The male witnesses supplied many conflicting details – so many, in fact, that it became clear that they had witnessed so many assaults over the years that their evidence could only, with difficulty, be associated with the night in question. Clearly this was not an unusual occurrence in their experience after the consumption of a 'good carry-out'.

I recall addressing the jury and not being very happy at the little I had to say on the accused's behalf. Lord Strachan, an impersonal, gentlemanly figure, charged the jury, who promptly found the accused guilty – which suggests they found some of the witnesses more reliable than I confess I had done.

That was the first jury trial I ever conducted. It was not an important case but at least it set me on the way. Thereafter, in the first year or so, I appeared frequently in the High Court, mostly on Poor Law cases with no fee. Gradually, however, there came cases where a modest fee was offered and gratefully accepted. The great thing about the Poor Law cases was their putting you in touch with the reality of life as lived in certain parts in those days. It also gave you a good lesson in the extent of your own resources.

The more I saw of the Glasgow High Court as a defender, the more I realised that this first High Court trial had in it most of the characteristics you found in all such assaults and 'fracas': the witness, for example, who could not, or would not, remember events which would have riveted the attention of everyone in their vicinity. Sometimes such a 'witness' would offer an explanation of this admittedly improbable amnesia. One I recall claimed that he had seen all that had happened but his memory could not recollect a single thing about the whole incident: 'My memory is not good.' Another, present at an assault, described the preliminary skirmish and when he was asked, 'What happened next?' replied 'I do not know.' Asked 'why' he did not know, his reply was 'I shut my eyes'. One common cause of the commencement of such domestic hostilities was a complaint as to the quantity or quality of the 'carry-out', made by one of the guests, who considered that whoever had organised the elements for the evening's enjoyment should have made a better job of it. The universal amnesia these 'carry-outs' were able to produce, and the universal aversion of all present to being, or being considered as, a witness to whatever happened, were endemic. This last characteristic was seen at its best where there was a fracas in a public house. It usually began there with the collapse of the gantry at the hands of an unsatisfied patron who had probably been refused more alcohol. The collapse of the gantry, however, usually precipitated the emptying of the public bar. At its beginning all the men, not actively engaged in what caused the gantry's collapse, would retire to the gents' toilet. It was in these cases, often a matter of some wonder, indeed amazement, that the gents' toilets in certain Glasgow public houses were capable of accommodating such a congestion of patrons that the toilet could certainly not have been of any use to any one of them for the purpose for which it was built, and where the congestion was such that anyone desperate for admission to use the toilets in question would plead in vain.

As described earlier, legal aid in criminal matters was introduced in 1964. Before then the impoverished accused, if he or she sought it, never lacked free representation in the lower or the higher courts from both branches of the legal profession. There are two delightful examples of Walter Scott, as a young advocate, making such appearances. On one occasion, at the Jedburgh Assizes, he appeared for a veteran poacher and sheep stealer and persuaded a jury to find him not guilty. 'You're a lucky scoundrel,' Scott whispered to his client when the verdict was pronounced. To which his client replied, 'I am just of your mind and I will send you a maukin [i.e. a hare] the morn's morning'. In another one, again at Jedburgh, his client was convicted of housebreaking and sentenced to death. When he went to see the man in the condemned cell the latter said:

I am very sorry, sir, but I have no fee to offer you, so let me beg your acceptance of two bits of advice, which may be useful perhaps when you come to have a house of your own. I am done with practice you see and here is my legacy. Never keep a large watchdog out of doors – we can always silence them cheaply. Indeed if it be a dog, 'tis easier than whistling but tie a little tight-yelping terrier within, and, secondly, put no trust in nice clever gym crack locks. The only thing that bothers us is a huge heavy old one, no matter how simple the construction, and the ruder and rustier the key, so much the better for the housekeeper.

Lockhart says he remembers Scott telling this story some thirty years after at a judge's dinner at Jedburgh and summing it up with the rhyme: 'Aye Aye, me Lord,' said Sir Walter addressing Lord Meadowbank the judge. 'Yelping terrier, rusty key, Was Walter Scott's best Jeddart fee'.

This was a service for which, it has always seemed to me, the profession has never been adequately recognised.

Like every lawyer who has acted for the defence in criminal trials I have had the question repeatedly put to me: 'How can you defend a person that you know is guilty?' The answer was given long ago by Doctor Johnston:

A lawyer has no business with the justice or injustice of the cause which he undertakes unless his client asks his opinion and then he is bound to give it honestly. The justice or injustice of the cause has to be decided by the judge or in serious crime by the jury.

In fact, the lawyer does not *know* if his client is guilty unless his client tells him so, and if his client does that the lawyer cannot appear for him pleading 'not guilty' and conducting a defence directed at persuading judge or jury that the evidence for the Crown is untrue. I have known accused to say: 'Tell me what I've got to say'. That the defence cannot do. The lawyer must advise on the strength of a case and, if asked, give his views on the chances of a successful defence but if the client admits that he committed the crime then the lawyer's clear duty is to inform him that he, the lawyer, cannot conduct his defence and that he, the client, should consult someone else. Since a plea of 'guilty' today can result in a reduced sentence there will be cases where an accused will properly be advised that it is in his interests to plead 'guilty'. If, however, no matter how strong the evidence, an accused insists that he is 'not guilty, and wishes to go to trial', then the lawyer must undertake the defence and do his best for him. The accused is presumed not guilty until the prosecution produce evidence sufficient and acceptable to convince a judge or jury of the client's guilt and it is the lawyer's duty to conduct the trial to ensure that the standard required of the Crown by law is reached whatever his, the lawyer's personal views may be.

I had my lesson in this situation at a very early stage. I was instructed on the old Poor Roll system to defend a youth charged with rape. I have forgotten the names and the precise ages of those involved, but not the situation and what happened. The youth had been released on the day in question from serving a sentence in Polmont Borstal. That night he broke into a house in the neighbourhood where the lady was staying and entered her bedroom. The charge was that there he assaulted and raped her. His story to me, and I saw him for the first time on the morning of the trial, was that the woman consented to intercourse with him. I was given the Crown precognitions to read by the Advocate Depute. I saw the woman in the courthouse. I did not speak to her. Having seen her, however, a well-dressed woman who appeared and bespoke superiority, confidence and competence in whatever was her way of life – she looked like a successful professional or business woman and seemed like the last person, I thought, would have consented to sexual intercourse with this ex-Borstal boy in the circumstances alleged here. Having read the Crown precognitions and seen her, I had a session with him in which I advised him that he had very little chance of an acquittal, and that his interests would perhaps best be served if he plead 'guilty', and the woman was not subjected to the ordeal of the witness box. My advice was rejected. He insisted that she had consented to inter-course with him and that he was not guilty and he would not plead 'guilty'. In that situation we went to trial. In the course of her evidence the lady found herself in some difficulty. I cannot recall the details but seem to recollect it turned on the question of times. In any event, the jury clearly accepted the accused's evidence of consent and acquitted him. It was clear also from the judge's charge that he, too, was unhappy about there being a conviction.

That case was my lesson on the wisdom of Dr Johnston's defi-nition of a lawyer's function. Had that youth taken my advice and pled he would have been given seven or eight years' detention. I never again refused to defend an accused who insisted on going to trial where I had considered he or she had no chance and had told them so. The question of his or her guilt or innocence was and is for the jury to decide.

In the early 1950s a recently called advocate accepted all forms of business with which his instructing solicitors were prepared to trust him. If you had precognitions and instructions to draft a summons in a type of action that was new to you, you went to the 'Style Books', or you obtained a style from a colleague who had experience of this type of action. If you could find neither, you discussed it with those of your brethren who had probably been called a few months before yourself, or any more experi-enced advocate with whom you were on friendly terms. On several occasions, the late Manuel Kissen was very helpful to me in this respect. What you undertook ranged from divorce, affiliation and aliment, breach of contract and some, of what could be heavy, reparation cases, some of which it would turn out were being conducted on a speculative basis of which you had not been informed. The members of the profession in Glasgow, however, who had promised me civil business kept their promise.

Undefended divorces were the start of the civil business that came my way and with legal aid available, this type of action was in a constant flow. Each divorce paid counsel four guineas for the summons and four for the undefended proof. Most of these divorces were undefended. Divorce was not then, as it is now, competent in the Sheriff Court, but only in the Court of Session and, accordingly, such was the volume of business that one or two judges sat on such actions two days every week, and on Saturday mornings. Back in those days, the pursuer in such actions, and their other witnesses, travelled to Edinburgh from all over Scotland and had their day in court. On Saturday mornings, there would be two judges each with a list of eight divorces. The grounds for divorce in these days were not the 'Irretrievable Breakdown of the Marriage', which became law in 1976, but was what was termed a 'Matrimonial Offence' – adultery, desertion, cruelty – and the often complex financial consequences of today's law were unknown. The issue was the simple one – namely, was the Matrimonial Offence proved. It was the heyday of the private investigator in adultery cases. Their evidence was usually of a visit to a hotel bedroom, or to a house where the defender was cohabiting with the new partner, the details of which rarely varied. Custody of children was, in my experience, rarely a live issue in the undefended divorce, but latterly the court would not grant divorce unless it was satisfied that the best arrangements, that could be made in the circumstances, had been made for the custody and upbringing of the children. There were rarely difficulties in proving the Matrimonial Offence. If there were, the difficulties emerged usually before two judges – Lord Guthrie and Lord Wheatley – both of whom undoubtedly had an instinct for scenting the difficulties. These difficulties, generally, arose in actions for divorce on the ground of desertion. Here, the desertion had to be proved – a separation for three years – but also, during those three years, the pursuer had to prove his or her willingness to adhere.[4] If the pursuer knew that the defender was living with another partner in the three-year period, for example, the essential proof that he or she was willing to adhere had still to be proved. It was a law that not only placed a premium on hypocrisy, but gave what were called difficult judges the opportunity to question the pursuer in detail and, frequently, to have an undefended divorce set down for several hearings, for the party to try to satisfy the judge of his or her willingness to adhere. In those days, Decree of Divorce was not a formality. The judge had to see the pursuer and accept his or her evidence and that of their witnesses before he would grant Decree. Today, the undefended divorce in the Sheriff Court is proved by affidavits, for whose reliability only the makers of them can vouch. Few would assert that the oath that accompanies the affidavit was or is a guarantee of honesty.

Reparation actions gave more remunerative business for the junior who was instructed for the pursuer. The law involved in the claim was based on common law of negligence, on alleged breaches of the Factories Act or other legislation, and it was the junior's duty to draft a summons which set forth the circumstances of the accident and the law which it was claimed entitled the pursuer, proving these facts, to a remedy in the form of damages. In the Court of Session in those days most of such actions were then tried by a civil jury, and the junior who drafted the summons was expected to stay with the case, having been joined by a senior, a QC, during its course. It was the senior who usually conducted the leading of evidence and cross-examination at the jury trial. There was no limit to the type of civil work the new advocate might be called on to undertake – not only in the Court of Session but also in the Sheriff Court.

I was fortunate to obtain the support of several experienced Glasgow Reparation solicitors, *inter alia* John Maillie and James Murray. Some of them I came to know through husband and wife cases or criminal business, and others through appearing against them. Fraser Cook, a very experienced and successful reparation lawyer, who invariably acted for the defenders, was one of the latter. I was involved in a case against one of his clients in Airdrie Sheriff Court. The details now escape me but I do recall a point where one of the defender's witnesses said something he should not have said. Whatever it was, it was a gift for a cross-examiner and I cross-examined, I think to some effect. The result did not please Fraser whose witness it was, but he obviously appreciated the way I had conducted myself as, thereafter, he frequently instructed me – usually with Manuel Kissen – in reparation cases. We, and our respective wives, became friends. He has been dead now these many years but we are still in touch with his widow.

Some counsel had a successful practice in Licensing Courts and I occasionally appeared there. In these courts, members of the licensed trade applied for licences for the sale of alcohol. The character and atmosphere of these large and invariably busy Licensing Courts could vary. They were thronged with those applying for a licence for the sale of alcohol for a public house, a hotel or a restaurant, or for the renewal of an existing licence, along with their advocates and solicitors. The court required that while the application was being made by the lawyer, the applicant stood facing the bench.

The 1950s and '60s were the decades when Reo Stakis was expanding his hotel and restaurant enterprise, and each application he or any other applicant made for a licence required that he appear personally before the court. I recall him as a physically small man but he had a zest for expanding his business. I remember the late Peter McGettigan musing on Licensing Courts, and saying that there was usually one member of its bench who dominated the proceedings: it could be the magistrate in the chair, the lawyer from the Town Clerk's Office or the Chief Constable. In Glasgow however, in Peter's opinion, when Reo Stakis was the applicant and appeared before the bench, the court was dominated by him alone.

If Licensing Courts were hectic, the hearings of planning application appeals before a commissioner, which at that time were in their heyday, were the reverse. My memory of them is of protracted, prolix, generally tranquil affairs, wholly divorced from any hint of urgency. They could last for weeks, even longer. In the course of these planning hearings, one sometimes found it difficult to resist a sense of unreality as planners, architects, environmentalists and surveyors gave their views on potential population densities and the effect on the environment, and on those likely to be affected by the proposed development taking place. All these were canvassed in a language – a jargon – that the planning experts seemed to have developed for their own use in such matters. Against this, however, the financial rewards were usually more certain than in some of the criminal cases in which one could become involved, and variety in one's practice was then a welcome thing. Now, I understand, much less so.

A very different tribunal than these planning appeals is the conduct of business before the General Assembly of the Church of Scotland sitting as a court. I had the then unusual experience for members of the junior Bar of once appearing there.

In 1625 King James VI presented (i.e. appointed) the Reverend Andrew Norrie as Minister to the Joint (i.e. adjoining) Parishes of Larbert and Dunipace, in Stirlingshire. By the twentieth century, both parishes had substantial church buildings and widely scattered congregations. Larbert Parish Church, known also as Larbert Old, had the majority of the joint membership, but the Larbert Minister had the additional duties of serving the Dunipace Church and congregation, and the Larbert Kirk Session came to the clear opinion that to properly service this joint charge placed too great a strain on the Larbert Minister. These were the days when, compared with now, joint charges were unusual. The Dunipace session and congregation were content with the old arrangement. For one thing, it ensured that they had a minister of experience for Larbert Old had a tradition of attracting able ministers, and they did not accept that there should be a change. They were the smaller element but their parish was the home of the Anderson family – a well-established and respected Glasgow legal family, a daughter of which was Miss Betty Harvey Anderson, who became a Member of Parliament. The Kirk Session of Dunipace looked for and obtained support from her and her family. In this situation the only course open to the Larbert session was to petition the General Assembly of the Church of Scotland, to 'disjoin' the two parishes, and the session wished me to appear for them when their petition was heard.

The first manse of the new joint charge was completed for the Reverend Andrew Norrie in 1635. In 1799 it became 'The Old Manse' of Larbert. That house meant much to my wife and me, and to our three children. It was our home as tenants for the first twenty-five years of our married life and after us, when the house was sold, our daughter and her husband purchased it.

This was the first manse then of the first Minister of the Joint Charge of Larbert and Dunipace, which it was now my function to try to persuade the General Assembly should be disjoined, and the preparation for my submissions had to be completed in a place where Andrew Norrie had lived and conducted his ministry. I confess I had some misgivings about how the spirit of Andrew Norrie might react to what I was doing, especially on the night before the hearing. The possibility of occult influence was not just fantasy. During the Civil War, the kirk and manse were the scenes of some violence. In 1650, they were at the centre of military operations between Cromwell's Ironsides and the Scottish army. Each of our children, when they were infants and slept in the small top bedroom, – the house was small but it had three storeys – spoke of violence and unexplained events: 'a man in strange clothes hitting a lady' (Richard); 'a man with a sword killing another man' (Claire); 'doors opening and closing' (Alison). Each of them was, and still is, convinced that the manse was and is haunted. Neither my wife nor myself ever had any personal experience of the occult, but on the day before the Assembly hearing, and on the day after, when the petition was granted, I wondered if the spirit of the Reverend Andrew Norrie was in a position to show his displeasure at the disjunction of that which King James VI had joined, then this would be an appropriate occasion for such a demonstration. Nothing so far as I am aware occurred.

My instructions and all the information, on which my submission to the General Assembly was based, came from the Session Clerk who devoted himself to the work. He was the retired Classics Master from Stirling High School who lived about 200 yards from the Old Manse. As the date of the General Assembly hearing approached, regularly – my wife said it was nightly – we heard his steps as he passed the roadside window of the house bringing the most up-to-date information.

The Assembly hearing was lengthy and thorough. I made my submissions. Representation, arranged by Miss Betty Harvey Anderson, replied on behalf of the Dunipace session, then the case was opened for general questions which came from all quarters of the hall. For the answers to some of them I had to refer to Mr Murray, the Session Clerk, who sat with me and he addressed the Assembly. After the question session came the discussion which again involved anyone who wanted to speak. It was long and sometimes acrimonious. The fear we had was that a suggestion from the Minister of Paisley Abbey, that the case should be continued to the next General Assembly, would be accepted. We could see no purpose in such a move. In the result the petition was granted and the Parishes of Larbert and Dunipace, joined by James VI in 1625, were disjoined in 1960.

As I have already alluded to, my interest in this case was not just a professional one. When James VI appointed Andrew Norrie in 1625 the then kirk stood on the same location as does its modern successor. The kirkyard was the kirkyard for Larbert Parish and has many old, distinctive and distinguished stones and memorials. In 1625 there was no proper manse for the new minister and one was built for Andrew Norrie. It was and is a delightful and beautiful piece of seventeenth-century Scottish domestic architecture. The suggestion is that its architect was Dutch and was responsible for a similar building in Aberdour. It now has the main road on one side, the church hall on another and part of the old graveyard on the other two sides. It was and is a rather romantic graveyard, and contains the grave of Robert Bruce, the Minister James VI exiled from Edinburgh. It also holds some of the dead from the Battle of Kilsyth (1645), buried in what had been its old, now roofless, Session House, and near it is the grave of James Bruce, 'Abyssinian Bruce': the eighteenth-century explorer who 'traversed the deserts of Nubia and discovered the fountains of

114

the Nile'. About 1956, the local authority, mindless of the architecture, age and significance of the building (there are few
seventeenth-century small houses now occupied in Scotland)
proposed to demolish it, and sent men to take off the roof. They
were seen by a local ironmaster, Mr Robert Hunter, who lived
nearby and who stopped any further destruction and purchased
the property. He and his daughter Doreen thereafter restored the
house with taste and love to its former beauty. In doing so, there
emerged carved on one windowsill '1635 A N'; the year the building
was completed and the initials of the minister who had it built. It
had continued to be the manse for generations until 1799 when it
became a slum. Lesley Hunter ensured its continued survival. My
wife and I were married in 1958 just after the restoration of the
house was complete. We were offered the first tenancy and considered we were privileged to occupy such a gem of a house.

# 10

# THE FIRST GLASGOW BANK RAID

On 19 July 1955 there occurred what came to be known as 'the first Glasgow bank raid' – at the time, referred to as 'the crime of the century' – in which a man was brutally assaulted and £44,025 stolen. Other bank raids in Glasgow followed, as if the success of this particular one had whetted the criminal appetite of some native Glaswegians. Its planning and execution would have been entirely at home in the Chicago of the 1920s, with the difference that here no one was shot, but they were, in detail and in character, new for the Glasgow of the 1950s. Compared to the then accustomed run of Glasgow High Court trials this was in a class of its own.

It was the work of a well-organised gang from London whose mastermind, prosecution and defence were agreed, was an Australian, George Gray, known as the Monocled Major: 'a very jolly, popular man' according to one witness. George Gray did not figure at the trial of the five accused that eventually went to trial in the High Court in Glasgow. He was then a prisoner in Wandsworth Prison in London.

The plan was to rob from a particular bank van making deliveries of banknotes to branches of the British Linen Bank in Glasgow. The preparatory moves were made in England and were taken well ahead of the planned robbery. In short, this crime not only involved planning, it involved very long-term planning. Fast and reliable cars were deemed essential, and to obtain these the gang resorted to one of the commonest, cheapest and most efficient methods of obtaining them. In May 1955, they stole a Rover motor car from a parking lot in London; a site which no doubt enabled them to select the vehicle most suitable for their purposes, whether in Scotland or England. Having acquired the vehicle, they fitted it with false number plates. One Rover, however, must have been deemed insufficient for their purpose since a month later a second Rover was stolen from a 'recess at Palace Gate, London', which was also fitted with false number plates. Even two cars were apparently inadequate for the duties expected of them for on 7 July, from a parking place near the Kensington Hotel, London, they stole a Riley Pathfinder which, like the other vehicles in their fleet, was given false number plates. At the end of this it was no doubt hoped each car had been given a new and unchallengeable identity.

Further long-term preparations for the raid involved familiarising themselves with the Rob Roy Roadhouse at Aberfoyle, selected as their headquarters and for its accessibility to and from Glasgow. The Monocled Major and one of his team, John Blundell, whom the witnesses apparently regarded as his right-hand man, first stopped at the roadhouse in June. They were back in July, when they were joined by other members of the gang, and their trans-port, the three stolen cars. There was never any question but that a robbery with serious violence was planned. The preparations demonstrated that, and included not only the theft of the cars and the acquisition of false number plates, but also the acquisition of a cosh, or blunt instrument, rope and equipment for tying up, blindfolding and muzzling any opposition. The selection of the Rob Roy Roadhouse gave them distance from, but ready access to, Glasgow. The Major, offering a couple of guests at the hostelry a lift to Glasgow, boasted that he could do the journey in twenty-two minutes and wanted to try to cut that to twenty. Rob Roy MacGregor, after whom the hostelry was named, had in his day, particularly in that part of the world, enjoyed a long and much chronicled criminal career as a freebooter, cattle thief and black-mailer. It is not known if the Monocled Major or any member of his team were familiar with that history. The planning here for the proposed crime was undoubtedly exhaustive, but I doubt if a reading of Sir Walter Scots *Rob Roy* had been prescribed reading for all participants, but if they did know of him, then this choice of a hostelry named after him must have seemed entirely appropriate, if not a historic and encouraging precedent. They settled in and explored the beautiful and historic surrounding countryside. It was the time of year that that countryside is usually at its best. They were civil and easy going guests and became popular with the hotel staff and other guests.

On the morning of 19 July the cavalcade set out from Aberfoyle for Glasgow at an hour that in the eyes of some of their fellow guests disqualified them as simple holidaymakers. One of the gang was seen up and dressed at about 6.00 a.m.; three or four were seen moving about at 7.00 a.m. Their cars were heard leaving. They not only knew the road to Glasgow, they knew the street in Glasgow – Paisley Road West – where they knew a bank van belonging to the British Linen Bank was due to deliver currency to a branch of the bank there. The timing of the Aberfoyle team was immaculate. They knew not only the branch of the bank that was to be supplied with notes, but also the details of how that delivery would be made, and the routine of the bank employees involved in it. They were in position to see the arrival of the bank van and the bank messenger and a guard start to deliver notes to the Branch. The other member of the bank team, a Mr Currie, was alone in the back of the van when it was attacked by men wearing overalls to disguise their ordinary clothing. 'The timing of the affair was as near perfect as could be' (the judge's words).

Once the driver and one guard were inside the bank, a paper was slapped in his hand by one of the waiting men – a signal for the attack: then came the sudden rush of two men into the back of the van to overpower the only guard, Currie, who remained; two into the front to whip the van away immediately. The cosh, the rope, the adhesive plaster were all there: the cosh to overpower the guard if necessary, and the rope and plaster to tie and gag him. They knew of the existence of an unoccupied house at Dunbrek Road, very close to the scene of the crime and the use they made of it was to take the van there quickly where, under partial cover of the back of the house, they discarded their overalls, and trans-

118

ferred the loot to some other less questionable form of conveyance; no doubt a Rover or a Riley Pathfinder. Currie, coshed from behind, had been rendered unconscious. While the van was being driven away the unconscious Currie's arms and legs were tied and his eyes and mouth covered with adhesive tape. He was severely injured as a result. The party then returned to the Rob Roy Roadhouse with a haul which even the late Rob Roy MacGregor would have regarded as enviable.

On their return to the hostelry the gang resumed their role of innocent holiday visitors. The Major arranged a party in the bar for later that evening. One guest, the wife of a banker, glancing into a bedroom occupied by the Major and Blundell, saw the bed strewn with 'a lot of bank notes', and a briefcase against the wall, which she interpreted as the occupants 'having had a good day at the races at Ayr'. It was indeed the day of Ayr Races.

The next morning the Major paid the bill for his whole party and all of them left before lunch. The Major drove one of the Rovers and abandoned it in Killin. Five suspects were eventually arrested – four in England, one in Ireland – and charged with the crime. They were brought to the High Court in Glasgow for trial on multiple charges of car thefts, assault to severe injury, and robbery, to which all pled 'not guilty'. The Crown list of witnesses ran to 203. This was not a Poor Law case. The funds – I know not from whom or where – were available for solicitors and counsel. The former were all doyens of the criminal Bar in Glasgow: Lawrence Dowdall, perhaps the most successful and realistic defence lawyer of his day; Bill Dunlop; and Freddie Levine. And by them the case had been thoroughly prepared. Of the defence counsel team, in the order of the clients in the dock, were: Frank Duffy, myself, Lionel Daiches, Euan Stewart and Ian MacDonald – two became High Court judges and two became sheriffs. Frank Duffy died a year or so later from a massive stroke taken while defending a murder charge.

I only remember clearly the faces of the first two of the accused. Frank Duffy, who defended number one, John Lappin, nicknamed him 'Captain Hook'; an appropriate name because in appearance he did look like the apotheosis of *Peter Pan*'s Captain Hook. I appeared for John Blundell, accused number two, regarded as the Major's right-hand man. Though he was pleading 'not guilty', it was proved – and no cross-examination had any effect upon the witnesses who testified to it – that when arrested in Fulham he said to the police: 'I expected you to pick me up sooner or later, but I want you to remember that I did not assault anyone.' This in itself was a damning statement, but he went further. He added: 'I was in it, but I didn't get as much out of it as you seem to think'; not comments, I fear, on which it was easy to base a successful or even plausible defence.

I sat next to Frank Duffy who cross-examined all the crown witnesses that incriminated his client. Frank was a congenial and delightful character; a combination of Ireland and Glasgow and good-nature. On his feet he could be brilliant. He was clever, had an irrepressible sense of humour and stood out, in the Parliament House of his day, as a character. Like me, he never lived in Edinburgh but travelled to Parliament House from Glasgow every day when he was appearing there. He was, however, not there every day. He had built on his Glasgow connection a substantial criminal and reparation practice. In the 1950s, in what were colloquially called 'drunk driving charges' – statutorily called 'driving while unfit to drive through drink or drugs' – Frank was a popular defence counsel, and he had some remarkable acquittals in these trials which were almost invariably before a sheriff sitting alone. He undoubtedly had a way with juries. He was always asking them 'to bring down condign punishment' on whoever committed the crime his client was charged with, provided they did not bring down the condign punishment on his innocent client. He was a member of the Round Table at the advocates' dining room and accepted by all the seniors and about-to-be judges, who were members of that table, for his humour and good nature. I remember the late Lord Blades saying to him at a Round Table dinner: 'Frank, you've only got to turn your big brown eyes on a Glasgow jury and they will give you anything you want.'

In the trial the first few witnesses incriminated Captain Hook. Frank cross-examined them all and after the last sat down turned to me and said, 'Well that's me finished until [witness] number fifteen', which according to the statements we had, was correct: Lappin was not mentioned there again till witness number fifteen and, accordingly, Frank paid little attention to what the next witnesses were saying. In particular, he paid no attention to a witness who testified that he had seen one of the stolen cars. The witness was asked if he saw anyone in court he recognised and he obliged by identifying 'Number one', i.e. Frank's client, as driving the vehicle, and what is more, testified that he was so interested that he took down the registration number of the vehicle in question.

This was to prove significant and intriguing evidence. At that time, I understand, the letters which preceded car numbers gave much information about the car. The first alphabetical letter on the number plate gave the year of the car's first registration in its licensing county. The other letters gave the county in which it was registered. In counties with many registrations the first letter would change each year. In counties with few registrations one letter would serve for a number of years.

When the witness identified Lappin, I gave Frank a nudge and told him his client had just been identified driving the car. Frank's first reaction was a profanity. He then conducted a quiet but animated conversation with Lawrence Dowdall, who sat behind him and had instructed him, on why this was not in the precognitions (statements). This exchange terminated when the Crown examination of the witness ended and Frank had to cross-examine. He did his best on the witness's personal identification, but there was very little he could do about the car number. Then as a last resort he asked the question, 'Why had he [the witness] noted the car in the first place? What was so particular about a man driving that car?' The answer the witness gave was devastating. It was, 'Well, the car had a Sutherlandshire registration number and I knew that Sutherlandshire [i.e. the car registration authority] had

121

not yet reached that letter of the alphabet that was on that car's number plate'. In short, his expertise on the then system of numbering cars was such that he could – as he did here – recognise a false number plate on sight.

A somewhat shaken Frank sat down. He turned to me and said 'Jesus Christ!' And glancing up at the witness turned to me with the remark: 'Does this not show you how much f— useless information some people carry around with them?' It may have been useless information but it helped to do for his client.

There was another episode when two of the gang, Captain Hook and Blundell, as I remember, joined company to drive south in their stolen car. On the way they stopped at Auchen Castle Hotel near Dumfries for refreshment. It was a good hotel and no doubt its reputation appealed to them, which may be the reason they chose to leave the main road to visit it. Be that as it may, they went into the bar. Only one barman was on duty from whom they ordered two lagers. One of them wanted a special kind of lager and the barman obligingly went out to get it. While he was doing so the two removed a safe and its contents from behind the bar and went on their way. Frank's comment to me, on the barman's indignant evidence on this episode, was, 'Irvine, our clients won't be asked back to the Auchen Castle Hotel: two lagers and a safe, please'.

At the end of the trial two were found 'not proven'. Three were found guilty despite the eloquence of the Bar and were sentenced, as I remember, to imprisonment of eight years for number one, and six years for numbers two and three – which for 'the crime of the century' could not be regarded as severe.

The Crown evidence against the three convicted, as I recall, was overwhelming. When your client makes replies like mine did, about 'not getting as much out of it as you seem to think', and when that testimony is wholly resistant to cross-examination, the chances of the defence having any success are obviously slim. Blundell was arrested in a flat in Fulham in London and I showed my youth and ignorance of London, as well as the difference between its retail and hotel establishments, by suggesting to the jury that if Blundell had been in the bank raid, the police would not have found him in the poor accommodation they did, but would probably have found him in a luxury suite – I should have said in Claridge's but instead of saying 'Claridge's' I said 'Selfridge's', but only the judge, as far as I could see, smiled at that blunder. There was, however, no smile from the Presiding Judge, Lord Patrick, when he came to charging the jury. That charge became a classic exposition of the law of concert; a concept of which the case itself was a perfect example.

This case, so far as the solicitors and counsel involved were concerned, concluded with something which I very much doubt could take place today. None of us had ever heard of it taking place before and I never knew of it being repeated since.

The head of Glasgow CID at that time was a quietly spoken, patient and immensely perceptive man, Robert Kerr. We got to know him as Bob Kerr. He is now dead. He had been head of the whole investigation and, when it was over, all the defence solicitors and counsel involved wanted to know how he had gone about it and what the details were that did not come out in the trial. It was decided unanimously that we ask Bob Kerr to meet us over a dinner. He accepted the invitation and I arranged a comfortable and private room in the old Literary Club in Bath Street, Glasgow, for a Saturday night.

The food was unambitious but good. The wine was ambitious, good and plentiful. Bob Kerr did not drink – the rest of us did. Come the end of the meal, Bob Kerr gave us his inside account. The lawyers listened, the interruptions were few, it was a sign of our fascination – we were entranced. Our guest held the floor for the rest of the evening. Neither I nor any of the others kept notes of what Bob Kerr said that night. I do know he gave us the inside story of how the crime, then one of the biggest money thefts in Scotland was investigated, how the witnesses were traced, the evidence obtained, the prosecution prepared and the part he played, and I do remember two of his comments. Speaking of George Gray, the Monocled Major, who was an Australian and who had a substantial criminal record, his comment was: 'If an Aussie is bad, he can be really bad'. Speaking of an investigator's luck he told us that at one point he and his team were looking for possible hiding places for wads of banknotes. He had interviewed Gray, the Monocled Major, in prison in London, who told him that he had dumped some on a hillside between Callander and Lochearnhead, a fairly wide geographical area. His own view was that some of the money was still in the Aberfoyle neighbourhood and, driving along a loch side near to Strathyre, he saw a clump of bushes and said to his driver, 'Let's investigate that'. They did, and found some items and, in particular, twelve jute bank money bags but, unfortunately, all empty. Someone had been there before them.

It was an unforgettable night; an example of mutual respect, confidence and trust, which in my experience was and is unique.

When Bob Kerr met with the Monocled Major he was in Brixton Prison where he charged him with the Glasgow crime. The man he met then appeared to have become something of a philosopher and was by no means indignant at the accusations made against him. He wanted to discuss what the evidence was against him. From that conversation it would come as no surprise to Bob Kerr that when Gray, in 1957, was eventually brought to Glasgow, he pled 'guilty' to the charges against him, and was sentenced by Lord Guthrie to six years of imprisonment, to be served after the completion of the seven-year sentence he was then serving for a crime in England. He appealed against the consecutive order in the Scottish sentence on the grounds that, while a sentence of imprisonment may be imposed in Scotland to run consecutively to a prison sentence being presently served, that did not apply where the sentence being served was imposed by an English court. The matter was decided by the Appeal Court on 27 October 1957 when it dismissed the appeal and confirmed Lord Guthrie's sentence.

Six years' imprisonment for the organiser of the crime – the same sentence as was imposed on two of the assistants – seems unduly lenient. I appreciate that little value is to be placed on hearsay evidence – especially some fifty years later, but I have recently been given information, which if correct, would explain the lenience of the sentence on Gray. It is that when he came to be sentenced the defence plea in mitigation, apparently not challenged by the crown, was that 'the Police no longer regarded Gray as the leader and he did not take an active part in the crime'. If this is correct, I for one would certainly be fascinated to learn who was nominated for the allegedly vacant role of leader in this robbery, and what his qualifications for the part were. If there is any substance in this story I am satisfied it would not be the opinion of the then head of the Glasgow CID, who investigated the case, and who spoke to Gray at the latter's request when he went to charge him. It certainly is not the opinion of the only surviving defence counsel who took part in that trial.

# 11

# CAPITAL MURDER TRIALS

In Scots common law the death penalty was the legal sentence for all murders. In the eighteenth and nineteenth centuries, it was also competent for many other crimes – though not for as many as was the practice in England – and was only gradually restricted. By the twentieth century it remained the sentence for murder and treason, but by then was the subject of a vigorous and protracted debate conducted in and outside Parliament, for and against its retention. It was suspended for a short time in the mid twentieth century but was reintroduced by the Homicide Act of 1957 for a limited class of murders only. These came, thereafter, to be known as 'Capital Murders'. The categories of capital murder, as provided in Section 5 (1) of the Act, were murder done in the course or furtherance of theft; murder by shooting or causing an explosion; murder commited while resisting arrest or during an escape; and murder of a police or prison officer on duty. These were regarded as the most reprehensible of killings and those which, it was considered, required that the ultimate deterrent should remain. It was, however, a political compromise which satisfied neither those who wished the sentence retained nor the abolitionists, and that act was repealed in 1965 by the Murder (Abolition of Death Penalty) Act; a statute whose wisdom continues to be the subject of public debate. The body of opinion which considered that the issue should be settled by a referendum of the electorate won no support from any of the political parties.

During the currency of the 1957 Act, I defended five capital murders: three as a junior, and two with seniors, namely Ewan Stewart and Manuel Kissen. As murders, I doubt if these five cases lend much weight to the arguments of either the retentionists or

126

the abolitionists. While, however, capital murder prevailed, before and under the 1957 Act, it was the crime regarded as being of the utmost gravity and to be prosecuted as a matter of the utmost social importance. A trial for murder was thus regarded as very serious business indeed.

In today's climate, where the numbers of all crimes have escalated and murder along with them, the modern trial for murder appears to take its place as part of the ordinary scheme of criminal justice. Before and during the 1957 Act, the murder trial was regarded as calling for special measures. The jury, once impanelled, was not allowed home until they had reached their verdict. They were housed overnight in a hotel and were incommunicado, except for telephone messages to their family supervised by the Clerk of Court. This could go on for weeks, as it did in the trial of Peter Thomas Anthony Manuel, with the Clerk of Court and the Court Macer having to organise outings at the weekends to pass the time for the jurors. The jury in the Manuel case came to know one another so well that they planned a reunion a year after their ordeal, and were only prevented from having one by the press publicity given to that particular proposal.

There was never any question in a trial for murder of waiting for the shorthand notes to be produced. The shorthand notes of each day's evidence were taken by a team of shorthand writers, and each night, judge, prosecutor and defence had the typewritten notes of that day's evidence, such that when counsel came to address the jury, or any debate arose on evidence, each was able to refer to the precise page of the notes for verification of the evidence that was being referred to.

There are few Scottish counsel left who have defended trials where if there was a conviction for murder, unless youth or insanity or some special circumstances precluded it, the death sentence would follow. Whether it was carried out was a decision that depended on considerations and officials, with which and with whom the defence had no contact. I suspect that I am the only member left of the Scottish Bar who has unsuccessfully defended

127

a nineteen year old for a capital murder who was eventually hung; the last man to be hung in Barlinnie prison. The knowledge of that potential in all capital cases unquestionably introduced an anxiety and a stress into their conduct which for me was not resistible. Dr Johnson's comment was: 'Depend upon it, Sir, when a man knows he is going to be hanged in a fortnight, it concentrates his mind wonderfully'. My experience suggests the same conclusion applies to the individual who defends anyone in such danger. Each of these five cases lives on in my memory, and their characteristics, and even the faces, have not been erased with the passing of decades. This, it is hoped, explains my trying to describe each of these capital cases in which I was involved.

## JAMES KEELINGS WATSON

The first was James Keelings Watson for a murder committed allegedly on 7 August 1959. The trial commenced on 11 November 1959.

My introduction to him was unexpected and unconventional. In those days the Court of Session did not sit on Mondays. I was at home in Larbert, where I then lived, when about midday Len Murray, a friend and a partner in Levy and McRae, phoned me with the question: 'Are you doing anything tomorrow?' To my answer of 'No' came the question, 'Would you like to defend a capital murder charge?' There is nothing like the confidence here on my part of 'green unknowing youth'. Len was doing me a great compliment. Here was an unprecedented opportunity and I accepted immediately, knowing full well that the rest of the week would be devoted exclusively and exhaustively to the doings, real or alleged, of the accused James Keelings Watson, and knowing also that whatever funds the accused's father would put up would nowhere match the effort, risk and responsibility involved. It was unquestionably a crisis situation.

The accused had, long before the trial date, been seen by the Poor Roll solicitor, who had instructed counsel, a QC and a junior.

Watson, however, had been told about Len Murray while in pretrial custody in Barlinnie Prison and had on the Monday morning, when the trial was due to start, dismissed both his then counsel, confident that his new solicitor would, at this last minute, be able to conduct his defence, and find counsel who would do likewise, or might have the trial postponed. Len was seen by the presiding judge, Lord Russell, and explained the situation to him. He then adjourned the trial until 10.00 a.m. on the Wednesday morning. There was no question of a long adjournment to the next Glasgow circuit and we did not ask for one. Such was not the practice at the time under the circumstances as they were here, where the accused had sacked his counsel on the morning of the trial: it did not lie with him, or those representing him, to hope for a long adjournment. Modern practice, at least in the Sheriff Court, has become different. There I have been often asked for an adjournment on the most spurious of grounds, and in the most obvious expectation it would be granted as a matter of course. Then, it was different.

I phoned the Vice-Dean of Faculty of Advocates to try to find a silk, including himself, willing to lead; not because I wanted one but to conform to the conventional approach. I wanted to clear with the Vice-Dean that if I did not find a senior, two juniors conducting the defence were, in fact, acceptable and competent. I then contacted Alistair MacDonald who confirmed he would act as my junior. There was no doubt that in the twentieth century, Scottish QCs always regarded it as their duty to appear in capital trials if no funds were available. However, my efforts to find a silk willing to take the case at such short notice were not successful. The Vice-Dean's opinion was that if the accused wanted to be defended by two juniors, and gave a signed mandate to that effect, he could see no incompetence.

All this haste, the expedition which then attended the instruction of solicitor and counsel, the pressure which each of them underwent trying to master the Crown precognitions – of which the Crown, as always fair, let us have possession so we could read them at our own pace –was certainly unusual, if not unprecedented. Len Murray has given a blow-by-blow account of it, in wholly evocative terms, in his autobiography *The Pleader*. We interviewed the accused on the Tuesday morning and the consultation he would have had with his first defence team was repeated with the second. It would be interesting to know what he thought of us all. By the Wednesday morning we were as prepared as we could ever have been, despite the urgency of that preparation.

The indictment against Watson alleged that on 7 August 1959, in the basement of a tenement in the Woodside area of Glasgow, he had assaulted a prostitute, Valerie Henshall, beaten her with his fists and a bottle, knocked her down, kicked her, tied a stocking and a handkerchief round her neck and robbed her of her handbag, a pair of shoes, a watch and £5 of money, and did strangle and did murder her, the murder being capital because it was done in the course or furtherance of theft.

The Crown evidence was undoubtedly formidable. It had the evidence of a taxi driver who had picked up the woman and the accused from a coffee stall in Glasgow city centre and driven them to about fifty yards from where the woman's body was later found. This taxi driver was of the view that when they got to their destination the woman wanted to return to town, but was pushed along the street by the accused; the street where her body was eventually found. The time of this incident was about the time the medical evidence concluded she must have died. In that taxi the woman had a £5 note which was not found on her body. When arrested the accused had a £5 note in his possession issued by the same Scottish Bank as the woman's had been. Shortly after the murder, the accused was identified washing blood from his clothing. To top it all, within an hour of the woman's estimated time of death, he had picked up another prostitute, had shown her a watch which could have belonged to the deceased, and, most sinister of all, had tried to persuade her to give him a false alibi which would cover the time of the victim's death. For a verdict of murder this evidence, if accepted by the jury, could be described as overwhelming.

130

The witnesses who testified to it were not to be shaken in their identification of the accused and in their evidence of what they saw him do on that fateful night. I can still recall vividly, the evidence identifying the shoes produced as those belonging to the murdered woman. When the body was found her watch and shoes were missing; a pair of shoes was later found in the possession of the accused's sister who claimed they were hers; a claim that was not convincing, not least since the particles of dust and dirt taken from them by forensic experts matched similar particles taken from the area where the body was found.

What was impressive and moving here was the evidence of the dead woman's son. I still see him as a boy of about twelve. He was in tears as he identified his mother's watch and handbag. He stood in that witness box holding the pair of shoes produced and identifying them as his mother's shoes, and adding to his general identification the fact that he knew they were his mother's because of a mark on one of the soles, which he and his mother had both noted and spoken of, and to which feature he pointed and said, 'These are my mother shoes'. After the boy's evidence there could have been very little doubt as to the ownership of the shoes found in the possession of the accused's sister, and even if there was any doubt, there was the watch and the £5. For a verdict of murder the evidence was there.

In Len Murray's book, his account of the trial is all too kind in his references to my own submissions to the jury. I had sat, such was the design of the North Court, at the Bar table during the trial with my back to the jury. When I rose and turned to address them Len's recollection is that I opened with the words: 'Ladies and Gentlemen for three days now I have sat with my back to you, I now turn to face you for the first time.' Len's memory is that at this point a female juror 'with immaculate timing' fainted. He is probably right, but my own recollection is that it was later, after my next words, that the juror fainted, and these words I do remember. They were not spontaneous. I had written them the night before. What I wrote of the rest of that speech were headings, but the opening and the ending were prepared the night before. I recall that opening, because I came to know it by heart: I was fond of repeating it later when there was talk of this particular trial. The opening, I thought, had to try to put the sordid drama we all had listened to into a setting which, hopefully, would arrest the attention of that jury, and I was not unmindful of the fact that it was to be delivered on a winter's afternoon in the North Court, where the atmosphere would be heavy with emotion and tension. As it turned out, I remember dusk was falling, the great window was dark, and the atmosphere was indeed heavy and tense. The Crown speech had been measured, undemonstrative, exhaustive and conspicuously fair. I hoped for an opening that would arrest. The opening of that jury speech was, as I recollect it: 'Ladies and Gentlemen for three days the curtains have been drawn on a dim half-lit world on the fringe of society, where all is unlovely, where all is sordid and where all is cruel'. My recollection is that it was at this point that the juror fainted.

The jury found Watson guilty of non-Capital Murder, which was the best verdict we could hope to have obtained, no more. We did not really ask for more. There was here, as always when a jury reaches a verdict that is unexpected, speculation of how and why they did it. The jury system may have much to commend it, but why it reaches the verdict it does, is, nowadays beyond enquiry.

Len Murray's view was that the jury had not been satisfied that the shoes had belonged to the murdered woman. His personal belief was that this was another case where a Scots jury was reluctant to return a capital verdict. I, personally, could see no reason for the jury not believing the Crown evidence, identifying the shoes as belonging to the deceased and rejecting Watson's sister's claim that they were hers. I cannot forget the pathetic but moving way that boy identified his mother's shoes. On the subject of the shoes, I did say to the jury that if they considered that Watson stole them, and murdered in the course or furtherance of that theft, they would surely be the dearest shoes ever bought by any man. I confess that in my opinion, on the defence pled before them, the jury had no need to indulge a prejudice against a capital verdict or to speculate on the ownership of the shoes. To have done the former would have been perverse and a breach of their oath to 'truth say and no truth conceal so far as they were to pass on that assize'. I believe that the jury returned a proper verdict on the evidence and on the law. If there was, in their verdict, a reluctance to return a capital verdict, that reluctance had justification in the defence that was laid before them.

The Homicide Act of 1957 made murder capital in a limited number of situations. One of these, and it was the one charged in this case, was murder done 'in the course or furtherance of theft': here the murder was alleged to have been done by Watson 'in the course or furtherance of theft of the handbag, the watch, the shoes and £5'. There was overwhelming evidence that he had murdered her but the defence submission was that the Crown had not proved beyond reasonable doubt that the alleged murder was done 'in the course of the theft', or 'in furtherance of the theft'. At the time, I recall no legal authority defining limits to the words, 'in the course or furtherance of theft', and, in particular, the latter word 'furtherance'. Our submission was that the Crown evidence was consistent with the articles being stolen after the woman had been strangled. Strangling requires two hands; she could be expected to resist, so the attacker's two hands would be occupied with the killing, not with the removing of her shoes and her watch. If these were taken after she was dead the defence submission was that her killing could not be said to be in the course or furtherance of the theft of the articles which were in her possession when she was strangled and already dead. It was improbable, it was submitted, that shoes could be taken from a woman standing or resisting.

It was an hour's speech which had much more than this in it, but this to my mind was its crucial point. The phrase in the statute is 'furtherance of theft': the defence contended that this could not apply to a situation where the victim of the theft was already dead. The phrase was, 'furtherance of theft,' not furtherance of removing

133

possessions of a person already dead. There was and could have been no other line of defence open to this accused, and Lord Russell, who tried the case, did not direct the jury that in law my submission was wrong. It would be my view that if the jury was reluctant to return a capital verdict they also had, in the defence submissions, a good reason for taking the course they did.

The strain, tension and anxiety that went with the conduct of such a trial and its result, I fear, received uncertain and short-lived appreciation from the accused. We went to see him after the verdict and his thanks were profuse at the time. His last remark to me was, 'You should be a f— minister'. Perhaps he was a judge of ministers but I very much doubt that. Certainly, if he was, their ministrations had not left James Keelings Watson with an active conscience. He was not, however, really satisfied with the verdict; seven months later he tried to appeal it on the ground that there had been insufficient evidence to convict him. The trial defence team was not involved. The appeal, not surprisingly, failed.

Any conscience he had had short recollection. Of his sentence of life imprisonment, the only competent sentence for non-capital murder, he served ten years and was then placed on a Training for Freedom Scheme, which means that it had been decided he should not serve the life sentence of the court. This scheme involved him working each day in the community. On one of those days he assaulted a seventy-year-old woman, punched and kicked her repeatedly, knocked her unconscious and stole a number of articles from her. The old lady was rendered unconscious; the prostitute had been made a corpse. He admitted this assault and robbery and was sentenced to a further twelve years.

I have no knowledge of what has happened to him thereafter, though when I heard of the attack on the seventy-year-old woman I wondered if our efforts in the earlier trial had, in the ordinary scale of things, been a worthwhile exertion. I understand that he died on 17 June 2005 of heart disease, in Wishaw General Hospital.

# JAMES MITCHELL

James Mitchell (28) was charged that, on 7 January 1960, at the house occupied by Robert Bernie Currie, he did assault Benjamin Hyman Furst and did discharge at him a loaded shotgun, shoot him in the body and did murder him, such being capital murder in terms of the Homicide Act 1957 Section 5 (1) (b). His trial started on 28 March 1960.

In France, the homicide in which Benjamin Hyman Furst – known as Benny Furst – died would probably have attracted the name of a *'crime passionnel'* because it was the devastating climax to the love affair the accused's wife was conducting with the victim. In Scotland, however, it took the conventional form of a charge of capital murder. There was no denying the involvement of passion: of a wife having an affair with the victim, her husband's consequent jealousy, distress and rage, and as its climax, the husband arming himself with a shotgun and going to the house where he knew Benny Furst would be, and there shooting him as he answered the accused's knock on the door. The precise charge he faced for this killing was in the terms I have quoted above; the use of the shotgun making the murder a capital one.

Mitchell was an engineer, aged twenty-six at the time. His wife was two years older. They had been married for some five years and the wife was expecting a child in June. Benny Furst and the wife worked for the same employer and in her evidence she explained to the jury the history of their association. They had made business trips together, became good friends and, about August 1959, became lovers. She was frequently from home. Certainly at first the husband did not suspect he was being cuckolded and accepted the explanations given of her absence as 'going out with the girls from work'. On 4 January, she claimed that Furst asked her to leave her husband and go with him; a proposition she agreed to, and claimed the decision as being the result of the then strained relationship between her and her husband. On

6 January, she told her husband she was leaving him for Furst, and when he asked about the expected baby she told him it was not his but Furst's. In evidence, she admitted that this was a lie. The husband's reaction to her confession of Furst's paternity was, on 7 January, a threat that he would shoot himself with a shotgun. He himself, in evidence, said he had tried to shoot himself with a German starting pistol which he had converted to take a .22 round. He claimed to have put a larger round in the chamber of the gun, put it to his head three times and pulled the trigger, but without result. Later, Mitchell's solicitor advised the police of his suicide attempt and the pistol was taken by the police for examination. That examination revealed that the firing pin rested on the rim of the cartridge which was in the firing chamber. The police evidence – and there was no challenge of this – was that it was designed solely for firing blanks, but a plug in the barrel had been removed and it was capable of firing a lethal missile. The .22 cartridge which was in the gun was too long and had jammed.

The wife's father described the shooting. He was in his house. Furst was there. There was a knock at the door. Furst went to the door and he, the father, heard a shot. 'Furst fell into my arms.' He saw Mitchell a few yards away with a gun in his hands. 'He pointed the gun right against me and said "Stand back, Dad." I grabbed Jimmy and the gun at the same time. He just stared at me. He was as white as a sheet.'

Mitchell himself in giving evidence spoke of his distress at what his wife had told him about Furst. He spoke of his attempts at suicide. On the shooting of Furst his evidence was that he did not know whether or not he shot Furst on 7 January. He did not remember clearly what had happened. The Crown disputed this evidence with vigour and led evidence which, it claimed, disproved his allegation that he did not remember what had happened. Police Constable Hugh Craig testified that he was on duty in the Information Room on the night of 7 January and about 11.08 p.m. received a call on an outside line. 'A man gave his name as James Mitchell of 90 Golf Drive. He said he was speaking from a tele-

136

Douglas, Isle of Man 1939 – the author with his Aunt Bella, for whose generation paddling in the sea was the hallmark of holiday.

The author as Sir Toby Belch in *Twelfth Night,* aged 16.

McCrindle, Aunt Agnes and two visitors. Neither Aunt Agnes nor McCrindle were used to being photographed but here McCrindle took to it more than his wife. The visitor took his hat off and hung it up for the photograph.

Grandma Irvine, aged 93 in 1946. A formidable woman who was a permanent figure of the author's childhood.

The author's mother and his Aunt
Jean at his graduation.

James F.N. Fyfe, who introduced
the author to the world of music and
thereby gave him one of the greatest
pleasures of life.

The Rev. D.J. Ferguson prepares for a fishing expedition. He is
seen with Dr Peter Doutson, one of the many friends the author
introduced to the Minister and to the Minister's boat.

June 1951, with the late Nick
Ross the day they graduated
in Law.

© MIRRORPIX.COM

W. R. Grieve QC and the author photographed
in the street while defending a High Court trial
in Glasgow in 1960.

This photograph shows the presiding Sheriff
and Parties' Advisors setting out to inspect the
subject of a litigation. The unexpected press
coverage produced a flood of photographs.

The author, Sheriff's Library
Glasgow. It is said the wig
depersonalises its wearer.

The Old Manse at Larbert, built 1635, restored 1958.

The ill-fated staircase 13 of the Ibrox Disaster.

One of the famous family coats, worn by the author and later adopted by his children for hill walking.

Addressing the Haggis, without which, to the Scot, no haggis tastes as it should.

A more informal version of a Burns Supper but none the less sincere.

Petroleum dinner in Glasgow 1986 – the author is receiving one of the many gifts he has been given over the years.

An example of the traditional photograph of the Top Table and guests, which preceded most of the Trade Dinners of Glasgow. These photographs traditionally showed a company who wanted to enjoy themselves and expected to do so.

The author with the first of many Lucias.

Speaking with a lectern of empty
bottles.

Dr John Dagg and the author at a
post-performance party of *Enoch
Arden* – all the recitals they have given
have been for charitable causes.

© SHEILA BURNETT

Dr John Dagg at the piano – the speaker is the author in the course of
a performance of Tennyson's *Enoch Arden* and its musical setting by
Richard Strauss.

A family photograph. The author and his wife with their elder daughter and nine grandchildren in July 2005.

phone box at Kelso Street and he wanted to pass a message.' He asked the man to carry on and the man said, 'I have just killed a man with a shotgun at 9 Halley Place.' When the Constable suggested the shooting might be accidental the reply was 'The killing was intentional'.

Mitchell was defended by Ewen Stuart, QC, later Lord Stuart, and myself. The defence did not dispute the killing. The issue was the mental state of Mitchell when he fired that gun. A special defence in those terms focused this issue; namely that 'at the time the alleged crime was committed Mitchell was insane and, therefore, not responsible for his actions'. In short, the defence accepted that he was sane before the time of the crime and sane after it, but at the actual killing he was not.

The law was clear on what an accused, advancing such a defence, must prove on a balance of probability. It is that no one is responsible for the commission of a crime, whose reason has been so overpowered on account of some mental defect, that he has been rendered incapable of controlling his conduct. An abnormal state short of that was not enough. The jury here had the unusual experience of seeing and hearing psychiatrists of the utmost experience, distinction and articulacy, on the one hand dismiss the suggestion of the accused's insanity at the time for the prosecution, and, on the other hand, for the defence, explain how and why a man can arm himself with a shotgun and appropriate ammunition, go to the house where he expects to find the victim on whom he intends to use that gun, load the gun, summon the householder to the door, aim the gun and when his intended victim appears, shoots him and be at that time insane. These psychiatrists in support of the defence talked of the sanity before the shooting and sanity after the shooting, but claimed insanity at the actual killing. Here, among others, was Dr Angus McNiven, Consultant Psychiatrist, who thought Mitchell was suffering from a deep emotional disturbance at the time of the shooting. He did not think Mitchell was insane at the time of the shooting, but there was not much difference between his state and that of a man

137

suffering from mental illness. Another experienced and distinguished psychiatrist, Dr Hunter Gillies, went much further in support of the defence. His evidence was that he did not think Mitchell intended to kill. He did not think he was capable of forming the intention. At that point in his evidence the trial judge intervened to say, 'Then it was only an ironic coincidence that the man who came through the door and was shot was the wife's alleged paramour'. To that question Dr Gillies answered, 'Yes, I think it is quite possible he would have shot anyone. I don't think he knew he had shot the man until his father-in-law told him'.

At the end of the evidence the prosecuting advocate, with that fairness and moderation which are traditional characteristics of the Scottish Crown Office, intimated on behalf of the Crown that he was reducing the charge. He told the court:

> Upon consideration of the evidence I have elected to restrict the libel to one of culpable homicide. While there are differences in the evidence of the accused's mental state, in some respects there appears to be one common denominator, namely that his responsibility at the time was diminished.

Culpable homicide includes intentional infliction of death in circumstances which the law deems blameable, though not such as to amount to murder.

The jury took twenty-five minutes to find by a majority verdict that Mitchell was guilty of culpable homicide, but found him not guilty on the grounds that he was insane at the time of the shooting. Scottish juries had a reputation of being reluctant to convict in capital crimes, and in modern times – as compared to earlier practice – only the jurors know what evidence they accept, what they do not and what facts they find proven on the evidence submitted. The jury here had before them, however, varied psychiatric opinions which gave them grounds for reaching the verdict they did.

Mitchell was ordered to be detained during Her Majesty's pleasure and was initially detained, I was advised, at The State

Hospital at Carstairs. I have been unable to ascertain the duration of Her Majesty's pleasure in this case.

## ANTHONY MILLER AND JAMES DENOVAN

The trial of James Keelings Watson resulted in a verdict on which the defence could feel some satisfaction, not just in the result but in the submissions which hopefully produced that result. On the alleged element which made his killing capital he was acquitted. On the killing, to which he had no real answer, he was convicted. No such emotion accompanied or followed the trial, conviction and sentence of Anthony Miller where the defence team was, as for Watson, Len Murray, Alistair MacDonald and myself. The evidence in the Watson case gave the defence material for a submission which the jury appeared to have accepted. In the Miller and Denovan case (starting 14 November 1960) the prosecution had no weaknesses. Its evidence could only be called overwhelming from every point of view and at every stage. It was one of the few jury cases, in my experience, where the defence was unable to find any evidence reasonably to support an argument to the jury in favour of at least a not proven verdict – the verdict indeed which I always tried to stress to a jury when I was addressing them with the words: 'If the evidence is such that you cannot say "he did do it," but also cannot say "he did not do it," then the Law of Scotland gives you the appropriate verdict in "not proven" for such a situation.' My experience was rarely to find them slow to take up the suggestion if the defence had something substantial it could call on in the evidence in favour of an accused. On the evidence here the verdict of 'guilty' was almost inevitable – a realisation that did not diminish the pressures and responsibility on the defence. It was not competent to plead 'guilty' to a murder charge. The Crown had to prove it and the defence to test the Crown evidence.

Anthony Miller, nineteen, and James Denovan, sixteen, had found a way, an easy way, and apparently a safe way, of obtaining money. Denovan, while in custody in connection with another case, seemingly wanting to clear his conscience or possibly obtain some advantage from confession, told the police that he and Miller had attacked many homosexuals in Queen's Park Recreation Ground. Their tactics were admitted: the younger one was the decoy. He made contact with the homosexual and while he occupied the victim's attention Miller came behind to assault and rob. None of their victims reported these assaults to the police, but then one of their victims died. Police investigation of that death resulted in a number of charges of assault and robbery in the summer of 1960, all relating to assaults on homosexuals in Queen's Park. The principle charge, however, was in relation to the man who died. That principal charge was one of murder by killing John Cremin. The date was 6 April 1960, the location again the Recreation Ground of Queen's Park. The charge was that they did assault John Cremin, strike him on the head with a piece of wood or similar instrument, knock him down, rob him of a bank book, a watch, a knife and £67 of money and did murder him. It was further alleged, as with Keelings Watson, that since the murder was done in the course or furtherance of theft the murder was capital murder. To the minor charges of assaulting men and robbing them, which they had admitted, both accused pled 'guilty' at the trial diet, and only the capital murder charge was the issue that went to trial, and the issue, in the result, was which of these two struck the blow with a baton of wood, causing a massive subdural haemorrhage from which Cremin died. Or more precisely for my client, whether the Crown had proved that he, Miller, alone struck the blow.

The evidence against them can only be described as devastating. The evidence of two pathologists established that it was a single blow on the head which fractured Cremin's skull and caused a haemorrhage of or into the brain. In their view, the blow was a severe one, 'a violent one', causing a large fracture and haemorrhage all over the brain. An attempt to suggest to the doctor who examined the victim that such a fracture could have been caused by Cremin falling, brought the reply, 'Unless he was struck by a motorcar and precipitated on to the ground you would not produce such an injury as this'. This opinion was confirmed by the evidence of Denovan that he had gone into the public lavatory as a decoy, met Cremin, and came out with him. Then Miller suddenly came up and struck Cremin on the head with a large block of wood some three feet long; a blow which knocked him senseless. After the assault there was evidence from their friends that they, and especially Miller, boasted of Cremin's fate and how he had come by it. The evidence of Miller boasting of the exploit was founded on establishing not merely an extra-judicial confession by Miller of actually striking the blow, but in addition proved his knowledge of the whole circumstances surrounding the actual commission of the crime, which would be possible only if he had had an important part in it. There was evidence that the two accused pointed out to their friends the spot where Cremin had 'flicked it', with Denovan suggesting a two-minute silence for him. They were identified as having possession of Cremin's bank book and brand new banknotes. The crux of the case was not a killing, but which of the two was proved to have used the baton of wood, since in terms of the Homicide Act 1957 only the one who had dealt the fatal blow could be hanged.

Miller did not give evidence, a fact which elicited from the Justice General, the president of the court which heard his appeal, the extraordinary, and it might be thought hardly judicial remark, 'He did not even have the courage to go into the witness box'. My reply to his Lordship was that 'I would not put it that way'. Advising this accused was an agonising matter, but he was advised by us all not to give evidence. We doubted that he would have been an impressive witness and we feared how he might react under cross-examination. There was, we considered, really nothing to be gained by leading him in evidence and there was, we thought, the risk that much could be lost. No such reticence characterised James Denovan. At sixteen he could not hang, whatever happened to his co-accused, but his evidence made certain that it would be the co-accused who incurred the capital penalty. He went into the witness box and swore that a three-foot long baton of wood was wielded by Tony Miller and not by him. He accepted that he was party to an assault, but claimed that he had no idea that Miller would strike quite such a hard blow. In short, he claimed he wanted no unnecessary violence while the victim was being robbed.

This then was a situation where all the Miller defence could do was to argue before the jury that Denovan's evidence was not to be relied on, that the Crown had not proved beyond reasonable doubt that Miller killed with the baton, and that in the whole circumstances of the case, had not led sufficient reliable evidence – submissions which had, necessarily, invited much criticism of the reliability of the younger accused's evidence.

It seemed to the Miller defence that the only possible line of defence, with any hope of success, was to invite from the jury a verdict of culpable homicide. I asked the presiding judge, Lord Wheatley, for a direction from him that the jury could consider a verdict of culpable homicide. Culpable homicide in Scots law covers among other things 'the unintentional deprivation of life in pursuance of an intention not to kill but to do some inferior bodily injury from which it was not probable that death would follow'. It followed 'that the degree of culpability of such excess must depend on the circumstances of each particular case and its punishment may in consequence vary from a day's imprisonment or a fine of a shilling to transportation for life' (Alison, one of our greatest criminal lawyers, writing in 1832). The defence submission that culpable homicide should be left to the jury did not have much to commend it. Alison refers to 'some inferior bodily injury' from which it was not probable that death would follow. The law, as it has been for hundreds of years, was and is that where you have corrupt disregard of the person and life of another, whatever your intention may be, that constitutes the malice, the depraved and violent purpose which the law requires to constitute murder. One judge, writing in 1815, put the law in a way that might have been with this case in mind:

That there was here a merciless blow struck on the temple of the deceased certainly with an aim for that purpose. Death might in all probability not have been involved, but indifference whether it should follow or not must have been experienced by the panel [i.e. the accused] otherwise the force exerted would have been less and the weapon used less violent. Now it is this indifference, this recklessness, as our books term it of another's life for which the law, when so indicated, presumes a degree of malignity against it in an individual or disregard to the safety of the innocent as imply the crime of murder.

Lord Wheatley rejected the defence request and directed the jury in these terms:

If you come to the conclusion that that blow was delivered as a result of Miller hitting Cremin over the head with this large piece of wood in order to overcome his resistance, in order that robbery might take place, then I direct you in law that there is no room for culpable homicide in this case. If it was homicide at all in that situation it was murder.

When the Jury's verdict of 'guilty' in the case of Miller was appealed, the Appeal Court expressly approved of the trial judge's direction.

Defending a capital murder when, on the evidence, it was impossible to find a viable defence was an experience none of us who were involved ever wanted to repeat. All involve some stress; a capital murder trial brings stress especially in circumstances such as prevailed here – a stress which becomes almost unbearable. We hear much today about stress. I know of no stress so concentrated as trying to save a man's life without any real weapons with which to do it.

After Lord Wheatley's charge it took that jury thirty-three minutes to reach verdicts, which does not suggest any of them had much difficulty in reaching a conclusion, and it is a comment on the strength and quality of the Crown evidence against these youths that the unanimous verdict on each of them was that Miller was guilty of capital murder, Denovan simply of murder. Juries in Scotland had a reputation of being unwilling to return verdict's in cases where the death penalty was imposed. Here they returned a verdict of guilty: they did so in thirty-three minutes and they did so unanimously.

That trial and its outcome left its mark on all three of us who were involved. Len Murray has described his traumatic reaction. I am told that during that trial I was white as a ghost and a worried and anxious man. Worried and anxious was also my own recollection of my state. It was his widow's view that the experience of this trial hastened the late Alistair MacDonald leaving the Bar and going as sheriff to the Island of Shetland.

In what was to be the second-last effort to save Miller's life, an appeal was marked in the Court of Criminal Appeal on the grounds of alleged misdirection by the trial judge. In particular, it was submitted he should have left culpable homicide to the jury. A further – and rather forlorn argument – was that the jury erred in accepting Denovan as a reliable witness against Miller. They had rejected Denovan's evidence that he was not involved art and part in the murder,[5] and found him guilty, but if they had found him an unreliable witness in this, they had erred in accepting him as a reliable witness against Miller. This argument, not unexpectedly, found no acceptance.

The appeal was heard on 7 December and Miller's legal advisors did not find the hearing given them by the Court of Appeal an easy one. Len Murray has written, in his biography, *The Pleader*, at some length on the matter and with some indignation. It was in its course that its president made the remark that Miller did not even have the courage to go into the witness box; a remark which if it had emanated from the bench in a jury trial might have imperilled the conviction. Their attitude to the other grounds was equally dismissive and they endorsed Lord Wheatley's decision emphatically to withhold culpable homicide from the jury. Their attitude was summed up in the closing remarks of Lord Clyde that this was an appeal 'completely devoid of substance'.

No other reasons were given at the time, but it would appear that by the end of that day reasons for the decision were available. Their decision is printed in: 'The text of the Opinion issued by Lord Justice General Clyde in the Court of Criminal Appeal on 7 December 1960 in the Appeal of Miller and Denovan v. HMA'.[6]

The decision was certainly not given in open court in the presence of those representing him. It would appear to have been written that afternoon or evening. There is reference to 'the contention put before us on behalf of Miller this morning'.[7] The judgment concludes: 'The grounds put forward are completely devoid of substance and indeed had this not been a murder charge we should not have felt it necessary to give detailed reasons'.[8]

The remaining final attempt to save Miller's life were the efforts made to persuade the Secretary of State of Scotland to recommend that the royal prerogative of mercy be invoked. A petition with some 30,000 signatures was presented, some 10,000 more than signed a similar petition on behalf of Oscar Slater, whose case is known as the worst ever miscarriage of justice in Scotland. It failed and, on 19 December, the Secretary of State advised Mr Murray that he was unable to find sufficient grounds to justify him advising Her Majesty to interfere with the due course of law. Accordingly, Tony Miller was hanged in Barlinnie Prison on 22 December 1960 – the last of many men to be hung in Glasgow.

It is unlikely that there will ever be full disclosure of how the Secretary of State and his advisors reached the decision not to recommend reprieve because Miller was just nineteen when he was hanged, and in Scotland, at least, there were few recent precedents for hanging in such circumstances. In 1960, there were four trials for capital murder in Scotland. One was Alexander Stirling sentenced to be hanged; he was reprieved. The second was James Mitchell who was acquitted on the grounds of insanity, then came Miller. Then, in August, one Robert Dickson shot a lighthouse keeper. He was found guilty and his execution fixed for 21 December. Miller's execution was the following day.

Since 1889, there have only been six capital cases in Scotland involving persons under twenty. All were reprieved but only one on the grounds of youth alone. It is speculation, but probably because no mitigating circumstances were found in the crime, which the trial judge described as 'vicious and sordid', and probably the view that a reprieve would be considered lenience. Perhaps also it was thought that public opinion in Glasgow required that the capital penalty be carried through.

## CHRISTINA FLANDERS

Since the pacification of clan rivalries, Hebridean islands have enjoyed a reputation for beauty and an all-pervading sense of peace. The reality can be otherwise but one of these islands seemed an unlikely place for the death, on 18 June 1961, by means of a .410 shotgun, of a young husband, for which his young wife was to be accused of murder by shooting.

The husband was Alan Flanders, an Englishman. The wife, Christina Weatherspoon or Flanders, aged thirty, was a native of the Island of Gigha. They had married in 1953 and had lived for some four years with his mother in Nottingham. They had two children but it was not a happy marriage. The husband had a drink problem, as had his mother. In about April 1960, the two came to Gigha. While there, the husband's drinking continued. The evidence of Mrs Flanders, which on this, at least, was not challenged by the prosecution, was that, on Gigha, not only had his heavy drinking continued but the husband had frequently assaulted her. On one such occasion, the evidence was that he had assaulted her by seizing her hair, hitting her head against a fireplace, and punching her. There was a fight and struggle which ended when her mother came to her rescue with a shovel, and the husband was ordered from the house. The mother confirmed this in her evidence. He then went to Grimsby to work on trawlers. In June, when the ferryman's job on Gigha became vacant, the wife told her husband about the job and that she was prepared for a reconciliation for the sake of the two children. He returned to Gigha, but the reconciliation was short-lived.

The wife's evidence, again not challenged, was of his continuing and frequent violence towards her. She said that the night before he died, he had beaten her up and threatened to kill her. The following night he died from a chest wound caused by the firing of a .410 shotgun; shot, as the Advocate Depute put it, 'through the heart'. The next day, when the wife was examined by Dr Imrie – the Glasgow police surgeon and a witness of long experience of examining injuries – he found a small bruise at the right side of the right eye, a swelling outside the eye, a bruise on the chin and multiple bruises on the arm, forearm and chest. The Crown contention was that the killing here was no accident, that his wife had shot him deliberately and, since the alleged murder was by means of a firearm, then in terms of the 1957 Homicide Act, such a murder was capital.

It was said at the time that the earlier reconciliation between the parties had been encouraged by Sir James and Lady Horlicks. Sir James was then the owner of the island and he and his wife lived there. Certainly, they both resolved to stand by Tina Flanders, to the extent of financing her defence, for which the late Manuel Kissen and I were instructed by Sir James' Scottish solicitors.

As the junior in the case, I went to Gigha to find out what I could of local circumstances, local talk, local atmosphere; to try to find anything that might be relevant to the forthcoming trial. I had cooperation from Sir James and Lady Horlicks but from the rest of the island, I was met with silence.

I have lived on a Scottish island since 1983 and have some experience of what talk on an island can be. I once heard one native of the island where I live say, 'There are no secrets on this island'. The phrase did not appear to apply to Gigha, at least not as far as the outcome of my curiosity was concerned.

The trial lasted three days, 5–7 September 1961. The whole history of the couple's married life was investigated. Evidence of the detailed actions of the victim and the accused on the night in

147

question was sought from island witnesses and from the accused herself. The prosecution's contention was that the wife not only murdered him, they also contended that, in doing so, she was carrying out a threat she had previously made to do just that. The evidence came from the district nurse, Miss Findlay. She told the court that about three months before the death Mrs Flanders had said to her, 'You will be called out one night. I will shoot him'. She reported that Mrs Flanders had added, 'It is either going to be myself and the children or him'. She testified that in February or March she had gone to the Flanders' house to see the children. Alan Flanders was downstairs looking angry so she decided to leave the house. Mrs Flanders came down and accompanied her to the gate.

> She mentioned that he had struck her that morning. She was holding her head and she had been weeping. She said she was upstairs packing to leave her husband, I gathered because of the row. I told her not to do anything in a hurry. It was then that Mrs Flanders said that she would shoot her husband.

Miss Findlay's evidence was that she was concerned at the time, but when she saw Mrs Flanders later in the day she had settled down and she dismissed it from her mind. To Mr Kissen she said she had the impression that Mrs Flanders was afraid of what her husband might do to her. There was also evidence from the local special constable that Mrs Flanders came to his door at about 5.30 a.m. on 18 June and said to him: 'I've shot Alan. Do something.' Here according to the Crown was an admission of murder. There was one little facet of evidence which was founded by the prosecution and by the bench. She was asked why it had taken her till 5.30 in the morning to go for help. Her answer was that she had not gone downstairs earlier and eventually only went 'because it was light'. More than one person who mentioned this to me was of the view that here was truth, if ever there was a truth in an answer.

The question for the jury, since there was no doubt what had caused Flanders death, was whether that gun was deliberately aimed and fired: that it was, as the depute put it, 'a cold cruel, deliberate act on the part of the wife who shot him through the heart'. That, or whether the trigger was accidentally activated in the course of a struggle.

Strong evidence for the Crown was the wife's previously evinced intention to shoot the man who made her life a misery; strong also was the area where the shot penetrated: 'a small clean circular hole in his jersey', as one witness put it. The solution lay on whether the jury accepted the Crown version or whether they accepted the accused herself, or her evidence raised a reasonable doubt in their minds. As the judge, Lord Cameron, put it in a charge that was far from favourable to the accused: 'If they accepted the evidence of Mrs Flanders, they must acquit her. Even if they were not wholly able to accept her evidence, but felt there was some reasonable doubt about what had occurred, they must still acquit.'

Mrs Flanders' evidence was taken in great detail, especially by her own counsel. She was in the witness box for three hours. She testified that the husband had threatened twice to kill her – 'I am going to shut you up once and for all, I should have done it long ago' – and that, on the night in question:

> As I walked to the window I had the feeling that my husband
> was watching me and as I turned round he was lying on the
> settee with the gun beside him. The muzzle was beside his
> face. I saw the gun and immediately thought he was going to
> shoot me. I looked at my husband and thought he was asleep.
> I approached the settee and thought I would get the gun away.
> At the same time as I reached for the gun my husband made
> a movement either to grab the gun or me, I don't know which.
> He made to get up, to bring his feet up and his body forward,
> and at the same time the gun went off.

Asked by Mr Kissen if either of her hands were on the gun, she said she reached for the barrel of the gun but whether she got hold of it or not, she could not remember. Question: 'What do you remember?' Answer: 'The gun went off and my husband called out, before or after, I don't know when. I felt I had the gun in my hand, I don't remember seeing it or what I did with it.' The Crown had another admission which they said was a confession of murder. This was from the temporary district nurse at Gigha. She said she had been wakened by a small knock on the door. It was repeated and it was Mrs Flanders who was standing there. She said to the nurse, 'Nurse, come quick. There has been an accident.' When Mrs McVicar asked what had happened, she replied, 'I have shot Alan'.

Some may have considered not proven to have been the appropriate verdict here. The defence did not agree. Mr Kissen told the jury, 'It is murder or it is nothing, there can be no verdict on any lesser charge'. His submission was that if the Crown had proved anything, it had proved that what happened had been an accident and nothing else. A verdict of not proven, he said, would give Mrs Flanders liberty, but it would not restore her good name. 'In this case, I ask you to find her not guilty so that she can return home and live with her family.' The jury took less than an hour to reach their majority verdict of not guilty.

The stress on the defence in any capital murder was intense. Here where a woman was involved, a young woman with two children, it became at times almost unbearable, not just to Manuel Kissen and myself, but to our instructing solicitor and to many of the public.

Several episodes in this case demonstrated yet again, to my mind, Manuel Kissen's thoroughness, commitment and inexhaustible energy. Our principal witness was the accused herself and her examination was a delicate and lengthy process. She had many awkward questions to answer and Manuel had to be sure that to each question there would be the answer he expected, needed and wanted. The stakes here were enormous. He wore a dark suit with the coat of a Queen's Counsel, and on top of that a silk gown. When he sat down after examining our client, his back – through shirt, coat and gown – was wet with sweat. The evidence was concluded late in the afternoon and he and I retired to the old North British Hotel at Queen Street Station to discuss the form to be taken by his speech to the jury. I left him about 6 p.m. and next met him the following morning in the High Court building, when he was looking and speaking as if he had had a sound night's sleep as he said he had. However, he had not had a sound night's sleep. He had gone out for dinner to a friend's home, returned to his own home in Glasgow about 11 p.m., and between 11 p.m. and 4 a.m., he told me, he wrote his jury speech four times. He slept from 4 until 8 a.m. and that, for him on that occasion, was sufficient.

As the court was rising after the verdict, I saw Manuel take up a sheet of paper from his papers on the table, crush it up and throw it in the wastepaper basket. I asked him what this was. His reply was that it was a draft of his plea in mitigation, which he had prepared in case our client was convicted. If the verdict had been guilty, no plea in mitigation could have altered the sentence which, since the crime was capital murder, was death. However, if there was to be a movement for reprieve in the event of the death sentence being passed, Manuel's plea in mitigation would have been of the utmost significance. This was yet another example of the thoroughness of a great pleader.

I should mention another episode. Throughout the trial, the accused knew that whatever the outcome, she had the support, moral and financial, of Sir James and Lady Horlicks. They sat in court for the whole trial, heard all the evidence and also the jury charge delivered by Lord Cameron. This was not a charge which favoured the defence. When he examined the evidence, as he did in detail, where he placed his emphases suggested that, in his view, the verdict should be a conviction. The reaction of Sir James, who was an old man, to this jury charge, in which one point against the defence was followed by another, was memorable. At the end of the charge the court adjourned for tea and Manuel and I took Sir James and Lady Horlicks to the tearoom. Sir James had been on the staff of Field Marshall Haig in the First World War, and as we sat down at the table he mopped his brow and, referring to the judge's charge, said in tones of distress: 'That was dreadful, I have never been through anything like this since the second Battle of the Somme.'[9]

He and his wife saw to the well-being of the accused to the very end and, thankfully, it was not a bitter end. They had come to Glasgow in a huge open yellow Bentley and at the end of the trial when Mrs Flanders was acquitted, she was collected by Lady Horlicks driving the Bentley, from the back entrance to the High Court buildings and so escaped the usual publicity of a press siege for her story.


# WILLIAM RODGER AND IAN RITCHIE

One of the most disturbing yet accepted of modern criminal statistics is the increasing number of crimes of violence, often apparently unmotivated, committed by the young; by children as well as by youths. Crimes, however, without precedent are indeed rare, and one of the most alarming examples of youthful violence in my experience occurred in 1962: the case of Rodger and Ritchie. This was an appalling crime and particularly so for its period. In the 1960s, Scottish society believed that the very young and the very old were, by and large, exempt from the attentions of violent criminals. On the whole that belief was justified by what came before the courts, and what was common knowledge and experience. That exemption in my experience disappeared in the last quarter of the twentieth century, and the very young and the very old now, with the rest of their contemporaries, have become the accepted victims of all forms of criminal violence.

The enormity of the Rodger and Ritchie murder is patent from the very terms of the indictment, which refers to the accused: Rodger, aged seventeen, and Ritchie, aged sixteen. The charge is that they did on 23 January 1962, in the house occupied by Emma Maria DeKuyper, or Dufour, at 429 Maryhill Road, Glasgow, assault the said woman, and did strike her on the face and head with a metal bar and other similar instrument to the prosecutor unknown, knock her down, cut her throat with a bread knife, all with intent to rob, and you did rob her of one shilling and four pence of money, and they did murder her. And such is capital murder within the meaning of the Homicide Act 1957, section 5(1) (a).

In the trial before Lord Strachan in Glasgow in May 1962, I appeared for Rodger, and the late Mr A. A. Bell, QC, for Ritchie. There was nothing novel or sophisticated about their respective defences: each of them blamed the other. Rodger giving evidence blamed Ritchie. Ritchie, by his counsel, and a witness led on his behalf, blamed Rodger. One thing was not in issue: according to the medical evidence, this old woman had been struck at least five times with an iron bar before her throat was cut with a bread knife, and she was robbed of one shilling and four pence. The victim and Rodger were neighbours in the same close. In evidence, the Crown witnesses were unshaken and conceded nothing to Rodger's defence.

The murder was on 23 January. By 31 January, the police considered they had sufficient evidence to make arrests. Detective Inspector Farmer apprehended Rodger at his house and cautioned and charged him, when Rodger's reply was he was 'saying nothing'. In the police vehicle, the police evidence was of his spontaneous and unsolicited confession of the crime. He admitted he had cut the woman's throat with a bread knife taken from a cupboard, and added that he had 'blacked out' after that. He told the police they would find his bloodied jeans in the canal at Firhill, and that he had thrown away the metal bar that he had had with him. His jeans were found where he said he had thrown them. There was evidence that hairs found on a bloodstained comb, found at the locus of the crime, could have come from Rodger. Further evidence of his guilt came from John Kilbride, a prisoner in Barlinnie Prison, who was serving a life sentence for the murder of a four-year-old girl and was adduced as the only witness on behalf of Ritchie. He testified that, in Barlinnie, Rodger, who was then in custody awaiting trial, approached the group that he, Kilbride, was in, looking for his co-accused Ritchie. He admitted then that he had committed the murder, but said he intended to blame it on Ritchie because he was the younger of the two. To blame Ritchie was exactly what Rodger did when he entered the witness box, where he claimed that he and Ritchie went to Mrs Dufour's house to commit theft if the old woman was out. He claimed that they had gone to her door, which she answered, and asked her for a shilling, and when she invited them in Ritchie attacked her with the iron bar he was carrying. He also said he saw Ritchie straightening up from the body with a knife in his hand. He denied all his alleged admissions.

Ritchie was also seen by the police and, according to their evidence, told them that he was with Rodger, but it was Rodger who was in the deceased's house while he stayed in the tenement close. Their evidence was that he admitted he had given Rodger the metal bar but said he did not think Rodger would use it. Having given what he, no doubt, thought was an exculpatory answer, he claimed that Rodger had told him he had killed the woman but that he, Ritchie, had not believed him until he read of the death in the newspapers. When cautioned and charged his reply was that he did 'not go up near the woman's house on the first floor. Rodger had gone up and had used the iron bar'.

There were, however, two witnesses concerning Ritchie of whose evidence the prosecution made surprisingly little. They testified that they had seen Ritchie on the first flight of stairs to the victim's flat, going up to the first landing, and when he saw them, they claimed he whistled and was then joined by Rodger and they both fled from the close.

The court was denied the experience of seeing and hearing Ritchie. He had apparently no intention of going into the witness box. He led, however, John Kilbride as a witness on his behalf, to whom reference has already been made. When Kilbride's evidence finished, Ritchie's defence declared the case for him to be closed.

At this point the prosecutor took what was regarded by many as an extraordinary step. He stated to the court that: 'in view of the state of the evidence as regards the panel Ritchie, he now withdrew the indictment against that panel'. The jury was then charged by the judge to find the panel Ritchie 'not guilty', which the jury unanimously did. For Ritchie there was not, nor ever would be any consequences of that fatal night. The jury had found him not guilty.

The Advocate Depute's decision, leading to this verdict of not guilty against Ritchie, did not meet with universal acceptance, and was widely criticised. There were many who took the view that the Advocate Depute should have left the question of Ritchie's guilt or innocence for the jury to decide; that on the evidence and standing the law of Scotland on murder and accession, it was not for him to pre-empt the decision.

Where a jury has been sworn to try a case, I understand the law to be that the case should only be taken from them where there is no evidence on any part of the charge, on which they would be entitled to find him guilty. The Crown prosecutor in Scotland, however, is always what is called 'Master of the Instance', and if he decides that on the evidence the circumstances are such that he cannot ask the jury for a conviction, he can then do what the Advocate Depute did here; namely, withdraw the indictment. Just why the Depute here should have considered there was not sufficient evidence against Ritchie to entitle him to ask for a conviction, was a question many raised. In the proof of any crime, the evidence may be strong, weak, plentiful or slight. The question for the prosecution is, is there enough to establish the crime if accepted by a jury? In practice, that is something which is initially decided by the prosecutor when he decides to raise an indictment against the suspect. The critics of the Advocate Depute's action here maintained that the proper and competent course would have been for him to leave the case against Ritchie to the jury, directed, as they assuredly would have been here, on the law applicable to the evidence against Ritchie that was before them.

The evidence that concerned Ritchie, and which was given at the trial, would appear to have been the same as originally convinced the Crown Office that he should be prosecuted along with Rodger on the same charge. It can be summarised as follows:

Rodger's evidence was that he and Ritchie had gone to the victim's house in the same close as Rodger's, to steal if the old woman was out.

Ritchie's statement to the police was that he was with Rodger, but that it was Rodger who went into the house while he stayed in the close.

Ritchie also told the police that he had given a metal bar to Rodger – the bar used in the attack – but that he did not think Rodger would use it, which begs the question why then did he give it to him?

Ritchie told the police he did not go up to the woman's house, but there was the evidence of the two witnesses who saw him on the first flight of stairs; he had gone up to the first landing and when he saw them he gave a whistle, and *then* was joined by Rodger, and both ran off.

There is on that admittedly thin evidence, and if the jury accepted it, evidence of a plan to steal from the victim's house: evidence that put Ritchie arming Rodger with the iron bar used on the victim; put Ritchie in the close and ostensibly keeping watch while Rodger was in the victim's house, and giving what must have been a prearranged whistle of warning when the two witnesses appeared, which brought Rodger out of the house, and then the two ran off together.

Critics of the Advocate Depute's move based their criticism on what is still the classic statement of Scots criminal law on what is called 'acting in concert'. It is found in Alison's *Principles of the Criminal Law*, where the learned author states that:

Every person shall be deemed to be present at a crime who in any shape cooperates in, facilitates or protects the actual execution of the homicide. One for instance gives notice of the person's approach by a signal from a distance, a second despatches him at a spot agreed on and a third takes post at a convenient place to prevent interruption or favour their escape, all are in one degree of guilt. By the construction of law they are all present and partakers of the murder because each of them is in his place and at the time lending effectual aid to the perpetration of the deed and but for this mutual assistance and encouragement, the attempt might not be made.'[10]

The learned author continues:

Persons may be implicated in a charge of murder, not only in consequence of a concert to kill or to do some grievous bodily harm but to commit any other felony provided the nature of the attempt imply or the behaviour of the parties indicate a unity of purpose in all concerned and a resolution to control resistance by numbers and force. Thus if several go out to rob on the highway armed and one is killed in the assault, it is murder in all those who are aiding and abetting in the robbery, whether present or not. Or if some members of a party break into a house and one of them kills, either in forcing an entry or in affecting their escape, it is murder in all those who are aiding and abetting the original felony.[11]

As regards Rodger, the jury, unanimously, found him guilty as libelled, after sixty-five minutes' deliberation. In view of his age, the sentence was that he be detained during Her Majesty's Pleasure.

# 12

# THE SHERIFF COURT

My introduction to the shrieval bench came in 1962, when I was asked if I was prepared to sit as sheriff each Monday in Stirling Sheriff Court. The Court of Session did not then meet on Mondays, and while such a commitment as Stirling might clash with criminal business, the invitation suggested that, at least, I might be being considered as a possible candidate for a shrieval appointment, and the Lord Advocates Department wanted some evidence of whether or not judicial behaviour and competence were within the individual's capacities. With that in mind, I agreed. It was a revelation and I confess a delight. Architecturally it was a civilised court. It was a dignified court, the Bar were pleasant, the business varied, and I certainly had my introduction to the variety of business that could come before a sheriff in the course of a single day. The permanent sheriff there, and there was then only one, was a man whom I considered to be a great judge worthy of far more than a Sheriff Court in which to exercise his talents. His name was Charles Murray, the son of a High Court judge. He was dignified, patient, experienced and a realist. From him came a comment I have never forgotten, and the truth of which has borne in on me with the passing of every year. These were the days when speeding charges were brought in the Sheriff Court. On Mondays, when I was in Stirling, Sheriff Murray was in Alloa, and one Monday when I arrived in the building the sheriff clerk gave me a list of the scale of fines Sheriff Murray imposed in such cases as were coming before the court that morning, and which the sheriff wanted me to see. That morning's business consisted of road traffic cases, mostly speeding charges and the list gave his basic scale of fines for the various excessive speeds: 45 mph, £10; 50 mph, £15; and so on. I saw the sheriff that day after court. He said he hoped I did not mind his having me shown his list of fines. He explained that he wanted me to see them and then he gave his reasons: 'It is important,' he said, 'for a sheriff to know his Sheriffdom. I believe it is even more important for the Sheriffdom to know its sheriff'.

These were the days when most Sheriff Courts had one or two permanent sheriffs where both Charles Murray's criteria would be met. Compare this with today where temporary sheriffs can appear in Glasgow on a Monday, Ayr on a Tuesday, and Inverness on a Wednesday, and so on. There is little consistency left on the Sheriff Court bench and, today, continuity and consistency in sentencing seems impossible. It is one of the apparently inescapable weaknesses of the present system, and has made its contribution, in my opinion, to the escalation of crime. This I refer to later.

In October 1963, the then Lord Advocate, the Rt Hon. Ian Hamilton Shearer, QC, later Lord Avonside, offered me the place on the shrieval bench in Glasgow created by the retirement of Sheriff N. M. L. Walker. I accepted and, from November 1963, became the junior sheriff substitute of Lanarkshire at Glasgow. The Lord Advocate's comment to me as I left his room, having accepted the appointment, was: 'and don't think you are God Almighty'. It was sage advice that I hope I have done my best to follow. I may add the move reduced my income by nearly two-thirds.

Glasgow Sheriff Court, to which I was appointed a sheriff, was an important court. Glasgow was no longer 'the second city of the Empire' but it was an industrial and commercial giant, which brought significant and infinitely varied civil and criminal business to its Sheriff Court. Until 1984, that court did not have jurisdiction in actions of divorce, but its domestic jurisdiction included actions of separation and aliment, affiliation and aliment, and custody and aliment of children. Its Criminal Courts were faced with a society in which crime in all its forms proliferated and its annual increasing incidence did not suggest that the courts were having much deterrent effect. Though born and brought up in Falkirk, I had known Glasgow from my earliest days, as I have

159

already described. However, probably because I travelled every day from Falkirk, I had little first-hand experience of the reality of the culture of violence in which many of its citizens lived, and in which many died or were maimed. My first introduction to this was appearing as a defence counsel in numerous High Court cases, before Glasgow sheriffs and juries. Both courts were schools where one soon learned the prevailing infinite variety of all crimes, especially crimes of violence, and the difficulty in proving these crimes faced by victims, police and prosecutor.

In the 1940s, the typical and notorious Glasgow crime had been razor-slashing. The destruction of that culture was the work of one man, the late Lord Carmont, whose customary sentence for those convicted by a jury of razor-slashing was ten years. It was called, by those who were the recipients of such sentences, 'getting a Carmont'. The decline and fall of the razor-slasher, however, was succeeded in the 1950s and '60s by a multiplicity of ways of inflicting injury against whom one had, or believed one had, a grievance, or someone who just happened to be present when the weapon, be it bottle, knife, marlinspike, poker, pool cue, or anything else that would do, was wielded. The physical integrity of the individual, and their life were things then held cheap: in 1965, seventeen people were charged with murder in Glasgow, compared with three in Birmingham and four in Liverpool.

In 1964, nearly 1,000 victims of assault were treated in city hospitals. On Friday and Saturday evenings, the casualty departments in Glasgow hospitals, especially the Royal Infirmary, offered sights and sounds that were not only horrific, they were legendary, many were unimaginable, and all expected to be, and were, treated by the medical staff as an inevitable part of the hospital week. In blood and groans, the scene was like an incident after a wartime battle. I saw it once, early on a Friday evening before the 'rush hour', when I was taken there with a suspected coronary. I could not bring myself to believe this was part of the Glasgow that Will Fife sentimentalised as 'Dear old Glasgow town' declaring it a city to which he was proud to belong.

Weekend after weekend, every form of assault practised in the city found its way to these hospital casualty departments: injuries caused by hatchets, knives, bottles, with blood everywhere; one victim with an ear cut off, offering it to the medical staff for reattachment. Whatever the nature of the assault and the extent of the injuries, nearly all the medical notes on the patient contained the polite phrase: 'drink taken', and of these casualties of city life, few were prepared to remember, or if they did remember to disclose, how, why, when and by whom their bloody condition had been caused. These were the years of the adolescent street gangs, like Tongs and Fleet, who organised and conducted their own vendettas and who painted their names – *inter alia* 'Tongs Ya Bas' and 'Fleet Ya Bas' – on every convenient wall in the territories they claimed to control, and whose sheer brutality made the giving of evidence against them an exercise which meant dicing with mutilation or death. Some crimes were connected with religious animosities, some with protection rackets, soon to be succeeded by the drug barons and their henchmen. Hard men from whom money could be borrowed were well-known to the impecunious. Repayment depended not only on solvency or the Small Debt Court, but was more frequently and effectively obtained by means of the creditor, or his men exercising their basic skills in facial surgery on the debtor. There was one case talked about where a slow payer in Govan was given an unforgettable reminder of his obligations by being nailed to the floor and then stabbed. There was another story in a newspaper of one of the dogs at Carntyne Dog Track. When the lead was taken by a dog of which a punter disapproved, the latter leapt the rails and dealt with the offending animal by means of a hatchet. Small wonder the police could expect to sustain about eighty serious assaults a year and lesser assaults daily.

Violence then was endemic and in the presence, not just of witnesses but in the presence of clouds of witnesses, which was no deterrent since it was not within the accepted or safe civic duty of such groups of witnesses to see, and if they had seen, to

161

remember, and if they remembered, to report to enquiring police anything they had seen.

In about 1966, it was reported in the press that there were 140,000 'unimproveable' slums in the city and 11,000 of them were said to be unfit for human habitation, which one newspaper described as the most catastrophic housing situation in the nation. To solve this problem, the local authorities built vast housing schemes in Castlemilk, Drumchapel and Black Hill. They built houses but the complaint was they did not there build communities. There were no cafés, pubs, cinemas and no play areas, and they became hotbeds for all forms of crime; areas in which it was even more difficult than in the city to find a witness willing to give evidence, and risk the consequences.

Few, who were familiar with Glasgow as it was then, would have disagreed with the description of it by that observant and articulate journalist, Jack Webster, who came from North-east Scotland and knew what a law-abiding community was like. 'Glasgow,' he said, 'that great conglomeration of villages, city of golden hearts and stainless steel razors, that guarantees to kill you with kindness, if not with cutlass.'

In 1963, Glasgow Sheriff Court had the reputation of being the busiest court in Europe. It had nine permanent sheriffs, with very occasional help from honorary sheriffs, such as the late James Langmuir, the retired stipendiary magistrate for Glasgow, and the late Dewar Gibb, who was Professor of Scots Law at the university.

That full-time bench may have been small, compared to its present complement of twenty-eight sheriffs (as at April 2011), supplemented by visiting temporary sheriffs, but it was an interesting, and in personalities, an infinitely varied group.

It had at its head two exceptional men: Alan Walker as Sheriff Principal, soon to be knighted (it was then the practice to knight the Sheriff Principal of Glasgow); and William J. Bryden as Senior Sheriff. The Principal had been recently appointed, and had been a sheriff substitute for many years. Indeed, he was one of the group of Glasgow sheriffs who would have distinguished themselves on any bench in Scotland, Sheriff or High Court. They were N. M. L. Walker, Jardine Dobie, Alan Walker and Bill Bryden. Sir Alan's appointment was said to be the first promotion of a serving sheriff substitute to be Sheriff Principal. Until then, the Office had been held, with the exception of Lothian and Glasgow which were full-time, on a part-time basis by a practising senior counsel from the Bar. This practice continued for a few years after 1963, but it has come to be accepted that for the future all Sheriff Principals should be appointed from the ranks of sheriffs, and Parliament removed the word 'substitute' from their title. I have little doubt that the example of what Sir Alan Walker was and did as Sheriff Principal contributed majorly to that change. Now the promotion prospects have been carried even further and a Sheriff or a Sheriff Principal is now eligible for promotion to the Supreme Court Bench.

Sir Alan's personal interest in everything that was going on in County Buildings, where Glasgow Sheriff Court sat, relied much on what his Bar Officer did. He was ex-Royal Navy and made it his business to know all that was going on in that building each day, between Bar and bench, colleagues and practitioners, instances of unnecessary delays, and incivilities between prosecutors and defence. Through him the principal was aware of everything that went on in that building. Sir Alan was a dignified, quietly spoken man and throughout his whole career much admired as a lawyer. The late Lord Macphail, who as Sheriff Ian Macphail wrote the current textbook on the Sheriff Court Practice, told me that Sir Alan's judgments on procedural matters were decisions which he regarded with the highest admiration and respect. Added to these qualities he had infinite patience.

The Senior Sheriff was W. J. Bryden, a man very like Sir Alan, imperturbable, courteous and another first-class lawyer. Everyone who appeared before him respected him. He knew how to listen, did not interrupt, always had his temper under control and wrote admirable civil judgments. When I wrote a judgment, I tried to cover every point that had been raised and the judgments were

163

accordingly lengthy – ten to fifteen pages. Bill Bryden's judgments were usually three to five pages and in them he covered everything that was necessary. When I went to Glasgow he gave me the freedom of his experience. I had a room next door to his, and each morning and at lunchtime he and I had our cup of coffee in my room, and digested the day's unfailing supply of in-house gossip, or problems that had emerged from the morning's business.

He was the son of a Perthshire farmer and a product of Oxford and Edinburgh universities. At the former he had been encouraged to read for the English Bar and he had a story of his Oxford days when he was interviewed by a distinguished tutor with the splendid and respected name of Stalybrass, who advised Bill to go to the English Bar. Bill's answer was that he did not have the means to do that. The reply was, and Bill never forgot it, 'What is your father for?'

He was held in very high regard by all his colleagues. At one meeting of the Western Sheriffs, over which Bill, as the senior sheriff present, presided, I heard Sheriff Thomas Young, who had been a successful Edinburgh solicitor and President of the Law Society before he became a sheriff, say of some suggestion Bill had made, 'Of course we shall do it that way. He is the best sheriff in Scotland'. Thomas Young was not a man, in my experience, generous of praise, admiration or compliments, but gave them all to Bill Bryden in that one phrase.

There are few limits to the variety of work, civil and criminal, that makes its way to the Scottish Sheriff Court. So wide is the civil jurisdiction of that court that only in very few disputes involving the civil law is its jurisdiction excluded. In reparation claims, the litigant frequently raises his action in the Sheriff Court rather than the Court of Session, and for a number of reasons: to save expense; to save time; and for the convenience of witnesses living in the jurisdiction. One such case raised in Glasgow's Sheriff Court (1974) for each one of these reasons was Dougan against Rangers: one of some sixty actions for damages arising from the injuries and deaths of persons involved in what was called The Ibrox Disaster (see Chapter 18). The case raised major issues of alleged negligence and involved substantial sums of money. It was described as an action unprecedented in the Sheriff Court. Its hearing lasted fourteen days, twelve of which were devoted to evidence which occupy 1,770 pages of typescript. When the action was raised in the Sheriff Court there were many who prophesised that its decision would be appealed all the way to the House of Lords. It was not. The Sheriff Court decision was accepted by both sides. Such actions, moreover, are not confined to the Sheriff Courts in the large cities. The North Sea Oil boom produced some very substantial actions in the Sheriff Courts of Orkney and Shetland, which are referred to in an earlier chapter. Where a party is disappointed with a Sheriff's decision they can appeal to the Sheriff Principal, then to the Inner House of the Court of Session, and finally to the House of Lords, and have been known to do so in the most modest of claims.

The criminal jurisdiction of the Sheriff Court is 'solemn' and 'summary': solemn where the sheriff sits with a jury; and summary where he sits alone.[12] Both jurisdictions apply the same law, but in summary jurisdictions the procedure is simpler.[13] In the solemn procedure, the sheriff's sentencing powers have now increased to five years (in my day, it was two years, and then became three) or an unlimited fine, with the result that very sophisticated and serious crimes, which a few years ago would certainly have gone to the High Court, are now tried by sheriff and jury. A jury trial in either the High or Sheriff Court generally involved days; a summary trial generally involved hours.

In the summary trials court in Glasgow in my day, nine summary trials were put down each day before a sheriff who was dealing with this business. Some accused would plead 'guilty' on the day, but if all proceeded to trial then any sheriff, whose business civil or criminal had finished, was brought in to relieve the pressure on the trial court. By and large these unending trials for theft, housebreaking, breach of the peace, assault, road traffic offences and all the minor offences that common law and, increasingly, statute created, and to which there appeared to be no end, followed a similar pattern. On the one side, the prosecution: the complainer himself, his witnesses and the police witnesses. On the other side, the accused and his witnesses, and the confrontation is adversarial in character. This is the characteristic of our criminal procedure which, in my view, does not encourage the emergence of the truth, and discourages many from admitting they have ever been witnesses. As one American court put it: 'If you have no case, abuse the other side's witnesses'. A trial conducted in this manner, as I fear some are, does not make for a relaxed and unbiased witness. One result is the commonly heard comment from prosecution and defence lawyers alike that they are 'tired of summary trials', but the tiredness does not, in my experience, militate against the forensic enthusiasm of either side while the case lasts.

The long established court day was and is 10 a.m. to 1 p.m., and 2 p.m. to 4 p.m., though frequently in criminal and, in some civil cases, late sittings were common. My personal view when I began in Glasgow Sheriff Court was that it was my duty to try to complete all the summary business put down for me, and which had remained with me, for that day. In particular, this applied to a time when summary trials were heard in a court room in the High Court building where other shrieval assistance was not readily obtained. For a time here, I would sit till 6 or 7 p.m. to finish the business. In jury trials, late sittings were very common. I recall one case when I was defending where the court sat till 8.30 p.m. to finish the case. All jury sittings involved several trials, and estimation of their individual duration was difficult but necessary, since jurors for the next trial had to return when it was hoped another trial and another jury could be commenced.

My own enthusiasm for sitting late was not popular with anyone else involved and, especially at an early stage, provoked some personal and official dissent. The first Sheriff Clerk Depute assigned to me when I went to Glasgow was Miss Moira Kemp. Moira was a Senior Sheriff Clerk Depute and a character, and had been clerk to Bill Bryden. To everyone in the building, she was known as 'Moira' but never to her face. To her face, she was always 'Miss Kemp'. Used to Bill Bryden's gentlemanly and quiet manner, she expected the same from me. Among her very strong views was her view that the courts should sit promptly at 10 a.m. and rise promptly at 4 p.m. On the latter time, she found me undisciplined. In summer, as I recollect, she played much golf and, in the winter evenings she played much bridge. She did not like interference with these commitments caused by a late-sitting court. With me, she devised a routine which, though it did not always work, at least reminded me repeatedly of what I should be doing. When she met my wife, she took the opportunity of advising her (Diana) of her husband's unnecessary predilections for sitting late. Moira rarely sat through the evidence of a criminal trial but had always to be there for the verdict. If the trial looked like going on after 4 p.m., at 3.30 p.m. she would come to the door of the court, stand there for a minute or two, look at me and her watch, shake her head and depart. At 3.45 p.m., she would approach the bench, place a note in front of me which read 'I am putting on your kettle' – this was for the tea she considered I should consume at 4 p.m. At 4 p.m., she was back with another message; this time, 'Your tea is ready'. If this did not work and this presented a crisis for her, she always obtained the help of her colleagues.

A less personal approach to this sitting late came from the late Robert MacDonald, then the Procurator Fiscal of Glasgow, a truly formidable man and a prosecutor, capable of such devastating cross-examining that I recall Lawrence Dowdall telling me of cases where the defence did not call the accused as a witness for fear of what Robert MacDonald would make of him in cross-examination. Shortly after my early phase of late sittings in the Justiciary Buildings, he stopped me in the corridor outside my room and said, among other things, 'You are exhausting some of my deputes [i.e. Depute Fiscals]. You should know that what you are doing is not necessary'. He finished with the line I have never forgotten: 'Remember this; you'll get no thanks for it'. I had the same advice from Manuel Kissen after my first heart attack, with a warning of the health risks I would incur.

Courts are the arenas for the determination of disputes between parties or between the state and individuals, and in civil and jury cases, however intense was the antipathy between litigating parties, the respective legal advisers almost invariably conducted their cases with civility and decorum, and their clients, if they had any suggestions or comments to make, made them *sotto voce,* and did not address them at the bench. This was in contrast to some of the Criminal Courts. There, too, passions might and usually did run high, but while both sides of the Bar usually retained their polite and friendly attitude to one another, the accused and their family and/or supporters, who frequently accompanied them, could be less restrained. I do not say their interventions, which were not *sotto voce,* were a daily or an inevitable occurrence but their incidence was such that while it could be said that in Civil and Jury Courts the desired atmosphere of a quiet calm prevailed all of the time, in the Criminal Courts, interruptions could be expected at least some of the time – perhaps a small part of the time – but, generally, these were incidents that tended to be remembered.

Glasgow Sheriff Court in my day was housed in County Buildings, with the High Court buildings in Jail Square, used for sheriff and jury trials when not occupied by the High Court. County Buildings was a vast Victorian purpose-built courthouse, which held a number of small, and two large courts. One of these large courts was used as the Small Debt and Ejection Court, which could seat several hundred if required, and was a court in which all the seats were frequently needed, because there was much small debt in Glasgow for the Small Debt Court, and much unpaid rent and dwellings in need of repair for the Ejection Court.

One of the common disposals in the Ejection Court was to advise the tenant who admitted arrears of rent that he should 'see their factor'; advice which according to the defenders was no use at all because when they went to see their factor he was never to be

168

found, and so when the case was next called, no progress had been made and both sides were immovable. The Ejection Court, I fear, was not one that gave anyone – parties, public, lawyers or the bench – much satisfaction.

The other large court was the Summary Criminal Court, which sat each day at two o'clock to deal with the criminal business of the previous twenty-four hours, where the police had made an arrest. It could frequently be a long court, and on Mondays, which dealt with the criminal business of the weekend, it could be very long indeed! Its scheduled starting time was two o'clock but if there had been an Old Firm football game or any major disturbance, you could have more than 100 or so individuals to deal with. The accused made their appearance and entered a plea: if 'not guilty' their trial date was fixed and the question of Bail decided; if 'guilty' they were dealt with there and then, unless the court wanted reports, when it was adjourned to a later date. The complaints – i.e. the charges, list of previous convictions, summary of the facts which the Fiscal required to describe the offence – all required preparation, and that preparation took the Fiscal's office all of Monday morning, and was frequently so voluminous that the cases in court could not start at 2 p.m. That Summary Court ended when the business was completed, which could be 7 or 8 p.m. on really busy days.

It was not a court that was easy to control. The front public benches usually held the familiar students of judicial form. The remainder were invariably filled with well-wishers of those who were in custody and, on occasion, the enthusiasm and concern they might voice for an accused, their unconcealed resentment at the police for arresting him, their indignation at a bench that locked him up, or refused bail, required the attendance of a substantial police presence if damage or injury, or something even more serious, was to be avoided. If some of those Summary Courts could be an unpredictable ordeal for all involved, characteristic of them all was the patience, resourcefulness and competence on both sides of the Bar. The Procurator Fiscal Depute had the responsibility of presenting all the cases on that day's list and, on a plea of 'guilty', narrating the facts. Two duty solicitors appeared for all who had not arranged for their own solicitors to be present, and if the Summary Court was a busy one – and it always was on a Monday, because Glasgow on Fridays and Saturdays did much to justify its reputation for violence – these duty solicitors, uncomplaining and with much patience, did their duty to their clients and to the court over long, and for them, profitless sessions. The Summary Courts which followed for the rest of the week usually appeared to be peaceful by contrast. Sunday's doings rarely provided business for the Summary Court, which in view of the substantial contribution made by Friday night and Saturdays, was undoubtedly a mercy.

The Summary Court, as well as being a living and vivid commentary on the more striking and colourful social and antisocial habits of the citizens, could produce what the newspapers called 'Scenes in Court'.

On really busy days it could erupt at any moment. To enter and sit there as sheriff on a busy Monday afternoon was like setting forth into the unknown. Some restive and positively abusive accused had to be dealt with by way of contempt of court. You certainly never knew what might happen, and the object was to try to keep not only some dignity in the court but also control it at the same time – and the demands of the latter could interface with the attempts at the former. Some accused could not have cared less where they were or why. On one occasion, I remember an accused on whom I had just passed a sentence of, I think, three months, who as he was leaving the dock, looked at me and shouted, 'You are jus' a wee f—bastard'. Neither his language nor his aspersions on the legitimacy of the bench appeared to me to be matters that could be ignored. If there had been no reaction from the bench his sentiments and language ran the risk of being repeated by everyone, who felt so inclined, appearing that afternoon. They were remarks which seemed to me to require some further discussion between the perpetrator and his object, and perhaps some

170

investigation in view of the nouns and the adjectives with which he had proved so liberal. He was brought back to the dock by the police, when I asked him to explain himself. His explanation was, 'It wasny you I was speakin' about. It was him', referring to the police officer who had him in his custody. 'It was him I meant.' My reply – which if not appreciated by him, certainly was appreciated by the assembled Bar, who never allowed me to forget it – to his suggestion that he was not referring to me but to the policeman was: 'That is a lie – of course it was me that you were referring to. I do not see anyone else in court who answers the description.'

The popularity of accused persons was demonstrated by the number of spectators who rose to leave as soon as their case had been dealt with. If they were released, spectators usually went quietly and quickly. If they were not, they let their retirement from the court and their disapproval of the decision be known in and outside the court, unless the question of finding bail arose. In my experience, the accused in Glasgow who was allowed bail by the court could nearly always find it. Funds after the weekend may have been low, but the friends could nearly always find the funds to cover bail. As one of an accused's friends advised me when I fixed bail, and he said he would pay it, 'In Glasgow, that's what friends are for'.

It was a court whose size and such dignity as it could summon, rarely inhibited the public who disagreed with what was being done. If spectators sometimes found it difficult to obtain a seat, they also found difficulty in restraining their emotions, especially if they were a parent whose offspring was in the dock. One case of this kind nearly produced a charge of breach of the peace. It was a spectator who disagreed violently with everything the Procurator Fiscal said. She was the mother of a girl who was in the dock. She shouted, swore and then accused the Procurator Fiscal of saying to other solicitors at the table, that she was – that most insulting of all Glasgow insults – 'a cow'. Support for this allegation was not forthcoming from the Bar; what was forthcoming

171

was her further abuse of the Fiscal and a demand that I deal with the Fiscal for his alleged insult. The solution gave no credit to the bench, but it worked; to adjourn the case until later in the afternoon, when thankfully all tempers had cooled.

Another occasion, which was settled by the same tactics, was when two defence solicitors each claimed they were appearing for the accused. One had been instructed by the accused's father, the other by the accused, who was I think a teenager. Neither lawyer would give way, and there was an undignified squabble, only resolved by an adjournment to enable the two to decide which of them the client wanted.

Summary Court apart, the criminal and civil business of the Sheriff Court, including children's cases (this was before *The Kilbrandon Report* which influenced the establishment of the Children's Hearing System), were all conducted in the small courts throughout the building. Most of these courts had a side room and the Sheriff went on the bench from the side room, which isolated him from the public. If, however, he went anywhere else – if he wanted to go the court library, leave the building or consult a colleague – he joined the multitudes that might be in the corridors, and hoped that he would pass through them unrecognised. For my first ten years in Glasgow, I did not have a permanent court with a side room. I had a room whence I perambulated to the destined courtroom. This could be an embarrassing, not to say a dangerous, process. One perambulated the corridors in wig and gown, clutching your notebook and preceded by your Bar Officer, and often wishing you were also accompanied by a large Alsatian. These Bar Officers were usually engaging and mild-mannered individuals, whose function when the court was sitting was to hand up productions and bring in a witness, but when they processed in the corridors, it was to get the Sheriff to his destination as quickly, uninterruptedly, smoothly and as safely as possible, which could be a daunting exercise. There were witness waiting rooms but these did not always offer the preferred space of the public corridors, where all involved in a trial, accused family and friends, frequently congregated to discuss what should happen, what could happen and what they thought was going to happen. The 'privacy' of the public corridor meant that the rest of the public could be relied on to steer clear of the assembled group. As the Bar Officer and his Sheriff approached, the volume of the conversation of the assembled group might drop or cease. They then could often become a more predatory-looking assembly than a discussion group and we hoped we could pass in peace. With the ever-present possibility of trouble as the procession proceeded, there was naturally a degree of concern in both the leader and the led. The Bar Officer, the leader, wanted no trouble because on these occasions, as one once made clear to me, he, the Bar Officer, was being paid to act as a guide dog but not as a guard dog. This was the routine until my last years in Glasgow when I had a Bar Officer, Ian Wilson, who was a retired police inspector, wholly capable of looking after himself and his Sheriff.

When he and I paraded the corridors he was known to the clients and supporters, and also to the legal advisors, as the 'pilot fish', so you will understand what they called me. They rarely tried much familiarity or banter with Mr Wilson or with me in his presence. I recall one of them leaving his friends and approaching Ian Wilson, looking up at him and with a smirk saying, 'Hey Jimmy, what time is it?'

Ian stopped, looked down at him and asked, 'How did you know my name was Jimmy?'

To which the individual replied, 'I just guessed it'.

'Well,' said Ian as we went on our way, 'just guess the time.'

He was adept at the quick comment. On another occasion, a defence solicitor put a proposition to his client who was giving evidence. The client became indignant and replied, 'No that's wrong, I never told you to say that. You are making that up.' We all heard this and as Ian Wilson passed the solicitor I heard him mutter to him, 'Oh, Mr X, a rose has fallen from your chaplet'.

In most of these small courts, the bench itself was high and lifted up, so that to an outsider its occupant seemed outwith the adversarial exchanges taking place between prosecutor and defence, or solicitors for the parties in a civil action in front of him. I underline 'seemed', because in all the Glasgow Sheriff Courts, except the one which became a Jury Court, their size and furniture made it difficult to escape from the sense of intimacy that prevailed at the Bar, however much one sought to exclude it. Some accused believed in addressing their solicitors by their first names. If you asked an unrepresented accused if he had a solicitor, and if he had, who he was, the response might frequently be Big Joe or Wee Jimmy, or whatever adjective by which the member of the Bar was known by those familiar with the court. The bench was small, the witness box was close to it: a fact which facilitated the bench hearing what was spoken there, but also provided a close and convenient position from which a witness, so minded, could readily and accurately throw at the bench the tumbler of water he had been given to sip while giving evidence. The late Professor Dewar Gibb, sitting as an Honorary Sheriff, experienced just that. Below the bench sat the Sheriff Clerk, at a table which was designed to seat prosecutor on his right and as many defence solicitors as were required on the left. The accused's position was at the end of the table, and if there were many accused, then you might have two rows of figures at the end of the table, and a corresponding number of defence solicitors. Sometimes, where an accused sat alone, his solicitor would sit with him momentarily and in this situation, there was not only no difficulty in the bench hearing what the witness was saying to his solicitor, there was also no difficulty in hearing what everyone else was saying, which might range from the accused's acid description of a witness whose evidence was unfavourable, to the remarks passed between the accused and among the Bar themselves. Occasionally, from the public benches, an interested but impatient relative of the accused or their alleged victim would offer their comment on what they thought was going on, which sometimes might even be relevant. Some of these dock conversations deserved to be preserved and collected. I regret that I did not start a collection, but I still recall some of them. Maurice Smythe, now a very successful pleader but then a young solicitor, told me this conversation between an accused and the late Willy Glen, a well-known solicitor in Glasgow and a character, which occurred, so Maurice told me, when I was delivering myself of my reasons for finding the accused, his client, guilty. The client had difficulty in understanding me, looked at his solicitor and referring to me said, 'What is he saying?'

His solicitor's reply was, 'You are getting done.'

The accused: 'Where did he get a' they big words?'

Solicitor: 'He stole them from me.'

In the early 1980s, after one particular trial, I had found an accused guilty and called for reports. On the day he came up for sentence, I was unable to be in the court, which was unusual because the practice was for the sheriff who heard the trial and found an accused guilty, to deal with the sentence. The accused certainly expected me to be there. Instead Sheriff Laura Smith, recently appointed to Glasgow, took the case and from her, he received a sentence which he considered hard. His comment was not to the bench but to the court police constable as he was leaving the dock to start his sentence. His comment was, 'It was supposed to be Irvine Smith who was to come in the day but he couldny come so he sent his f— wife!' Another incident involved a group of accused coming into the dock in the High Court building, where the cells were below the court level and the accused climbed the stairs to the dock, and only when they reached the top of the stairs did they see who was on the bench. The leader of this group saw me, turned to his fellows, and I heard him say in a voice that was heard all over the court: 'Jesus Christ, it's him!' This was not long after the time I had my heart attack and one of his companions comment on this announcement was, 'I thought that wee b—d was finished'.

The end of a trial and the Sheriff's verdict was the most popular time for a reaction to emerge from the public benches. The sentence could sometimes produce violence from the dock, with the accused struggling with the court policemen. The bench in Glasgow, at this time, considered it essential that there be a uniformed police constable in attendance at all summary trials, and they unanimously (in no way a common occurrence) and successfully opposed the proposal that to save police manpower, the Summary Trial Courts should sit with no police constable in attendance, but with one at the end of the telephone in the police department on the top floor of the building. Had effect been given to that proposition, the annual turnover on the Glasgow bench would certainly have been accelerated.

In giving reasons for a decision at the end of a summary trial it behoved the bench to use language that everyone involved, especially the accused, could understand. Spontaneity, however, may result in a word not in everyone's daily vocabulary. After one trial in which the accused had, I feared, lied repeatedly, and wanting to make it clear to him that he had lied often, freely and wildly, I described him when giving my reasons, when finding him guilty, as a 'fecund liar.' When it was all over, I had misgivings about my use of the word 'fecund' in that the accused might not have understood me. I need not have worried. When I expressed my misgivings on this when I next met his solicitor, he told me I need not worry; the accused had fully understood and appreciated my meaning. Admittedly, he did not know of the 'fecundity of nature' or the word 'fecund', but there was another word which sounded remarkably like the word 'fecund': one of the most used words in the accused's vocabulary, and his comment to his solicitor was that this was the first time in a career, which had listened to many shrieval comments, that he had heard the bench use language which he could really understand.

Some accused, of course, treat the whole proceedings with indifference. One of the most perfect examples of this attitude that I know occurred a few years ago in Greenock Sheriff Court, in a trial before Sheriff Sir Stephen Young. The accused, a man and woman, were each represented by a solicitor. The evidence had concluded and the stage of speeches reached. When the solicitor for the second accused was making his submission, the whole court heard a snap and a hiss. This sound is as familiar to Greenock as it is to anywhere else in Scotland; the sound of a ring-pull opening a can of lager. But while instantly identifiable, it is not a sound customarily heard in the course of a trial. That something unusual was happening required investigation. It was the woman who was found responsible. Doubtless considering – whether from experience or simple resourcefulness – that the ordeal or boredom of the trial might be such as to make refreshment desirable for both accused, she had brought with her a can of super lager. During the final speech – in which she did not appear to have much interest – the need for refreshment proved irresistible. Unseen, she had produced the can, opened it – hence the sound – and handed it to her co-accused, who had time to partake of its contents before the Bar staff terminated the performance.

Another example of the originality of the accused or their indifference, to what you can do without interference in a court, was an accused in Greenock Sheriff Court who, when his name was called, rose unsteadily to his feet from the back row of the court and made what seemed to me to be his uncertain way down to the front. He eventually got there and only then did I see that he was followed by his dog, a spaniel, which after he had entered the dock, and before an astonished assembly and a shaken bench, sat down in front of the dock and of him. I am an enthusiastic dog-lover but that trial did not proceed until the Bar Officer had found that dog a good home for the afternoon.

In some Sheriff Courts a disappointed and disgruntled supporter does not remain content with verbal language and will indulge in physical demonstration of their disagreement against the fabric of the court. This is rare because in my experience their vocabulary is sufficiently rich in words to convey unmistakably their emotions. Fortunately, the courts in Glasgow did not have desks whose lids might be banged. They had, however, furniture installed for the comfort of the spectators, which could be kicked, and doors which could be banged. When this happened the banger obviously knew they might be in trouble because I never experienced one of them who had banged the door shut being anywhere in sight by the time the police had got the door opened and left to look for them. In Dundee Court, where in the 1990s I occasionally sat as a Temporary Sheriff, there was one court where there was a constant course of door-banging until, to the disappointment of certain spectators this door was fitted with a device, called I understand a 'door closer', which alone controlled the opening and shutting of the door, and which was impervious to the wrathful violence of any enraged Dundonian. No doubt, it took time for this improvement and its restricting function to be appreciated. On one occasion, shortly after it was installed, a sentence I imposed so enraged an accused's supporters that the last of them on leaving attempted to indulge in what was the usual practice of banging the door. The door was open and he summoned all his strength to give the door a real bang, which might damage the door and would certainly disturb those left in the court. He seized the door and pulled but the door did not budge and the force of his pull was such as seemed to damage something in his anatomy and he grasped his groin. He did not try again and I am satisfied he would not forget that door or again try to bang it. The installment of such a device – now, I understand, a standard fitment – would have been a welcome addition to some of the courts in Glasgow in my time there.

The pronouncement of an unpopular sentence frequently produced protests, but my experience, as far as Glasgow is concerned was that, with two exceptions, the personal resentment went no further. One of the exceptions was a threat to kill me in a letter to me, smuggled from Peterhead Prison, from a man a Glasgow jury had found guilty and I had remitted to the High Court for sentence. The other was a letter to the Lord Advocate uttering death threats against several people, including myself.

In Glasgow, I never had any other such trouble. I was never inhibited from walking the city at lunchtime. When I was in Glasgow, our home never received abusive or threatening phone calls. That happened later. The Glasgow attitude, as I found it, was exampled by an incident shortly after I had left Glasgow in 1983. I was standing in the queue for a rail ticket at Central Station when I was tapped on the shoulder. I turned and the man behind me, whom I did not recognise, said, 'Are you Sheriff Irvine Smith?

I said I was, and he said, 'You gave me six months', and I had the presence of mind to say,

'And did you deserve it?' to which his astounding reply was:

'Yes and I want to shake you by the hand and take you for a drink.' He was not drunk, it was mid-morning. I certainly shook him warmly by the hand but had the excuse of catching a train when I declined his offer of a drink. The point I want to make is, he was not resentful, he was not surly, and he was not threatening.

# 13

# THE SUMMARY TRIAL

Much Summary Court business can be described as 'run of the mill' – petty assaults, theft, housebreaking, breach of the peace, road traffic and statutory offences – appropriate to the limited powers of that court, and whose consequences tend to be of interest only to the parties involved.

Some summary trials, however, can raise substantial issues of facts of law. In Glasgow, the alleged careless omission of £2 million from company accounts was decided in a summary trial, and some of these trials have features which make them, and the memory of them, of interest to more than the participants and their families. Such are cases where the alleged crime is part of a set of circumstances which are unusual, involve nice questions of law, and reveal social habits and attitudes which the sociologist in most of us finds revealing and significant. Such cases are in a class of their own and where the bench forms a verdict in these cases it is, in my view, bound to set forth in some detail, preferably in writing, the reasons which brought it to the decision, which may result in economic or social ruin or both to an accused.

One such case I tried in 1972 was The Procurator Fiscal of Glasgow against Diack and Newlands.[14] The charge against both accused was that they 'did between 20 November and 8 December 1971, both dates inclusive, at 201 Pitt Street, Glasgow, occupied by Wylie Lochhead Limited (Funeral undertakers) or elsewhere steal a funeral casket'. The trial, which lasted six days, involved unusual questions of both fact and law, and its hearing and result proved to have much more than a transient interest. One enterprising sheriff made a recording from its circumstances which won an award in a legal education context in America.

180

The facts were unusual, if not unique. The trial was conducted by two of the most experienced, effective and distinguished pleaders of the Glasgow Bar of the day. The Crown was represented by the late Leonard Lovat, one of the senior and most experienced prosecutors in Glasgow, with a rich command of language, profound common sense, a thorough mastery of tactics and a sense of humour. The accused were represented by Ross Harper who shone equally in the Civil and the Criminal Courts. In the trial that followed, both gave of their experienced best and it was conducted with the utmost decorum.

It was one of the most fascinating cases in fact and law in which I was ever involved. My written reasons for the verdicts given at its conclusion may go some way to explain its fascination for those who pled it, and for myself. My judgment was in the following terms:

On 14 November 1971, Harry B. Groom, a writer, died at Larchmont, New York, USA. He had previously expressed a wish that he be buried in Scottish waters and pursuant to this, on 18 November, Mr McFadden of Fox Funeral Home, Larchmont, New York, telephoned Wylie & Lochhead in Glasgow and spoke to Mr Diack, the manager there, to arrange for that sea burial. What precisely transpired in the telephone calls is a matter of controversy but it is undisputed that, on 20 November 1971, the body, contained in a large steel casket – referred to not inappropriately by the Procurator Fiscal as 'a very grand casket', so grand indeed that it might well have satisfied the demands of some Renaissance prince (its price certainly was princely; it cost some $634), arrived at Prestwick from New York and was there uplifted by employees of Wylie & Lochhead. Again, it is not in dispute that the following day, 21 November, in Wylie & Lochhead's premises, the body was removed from the casket on Mr Diack's instructions, and another container, this time a chipboard coffin, prepared for its burial at sea by furnishing it and by boring holes in it to admit water. On 25 November, Mr Newlands and another undertaker, Mr Johnston, accompanied the body to sea in its chipboard coffin aboard the dredger *Callatria*. After about half an hour's sailing out from Ayr, 'about three miles on the other side of Lady Isle', the coffin was committed to the sea. Members of the crew gave vivid evidence of the actual committal: the coffin on the bulwark of the ship, the engines stopping, their waiting until the ship was motionless and then the four of them lifting it and putting it over the side. 'It hit the water ... It went straight down and then shot back up again ... When it came up again white plastic stuff was hanging out ... It took seconds to fill up with water and then went down again.' This initial committal, however, intended to be final, was but the first of many experiences the late Mr Groom was to have of Scottish coffins, Scottish committals and Scottish waters. As if symbolic of the trouble that was to follow, about half a minute after the chipboard coffin disappeared, and while all were at the ship's rail contemplating the day's singular event, its lid and a bit of white plastic reappeared. If the crew of the *Callatria* were superstitious – a characteristic traditionally ascribed to seamen – no doubt the incident must have given them some misgiving. There is no doubt that it imprinted itself on their memories. The lid was recovered with some difficulty then the nameplate was removed by Mr Newlands and flung over the side to lie with the rest of the coffin. He gave the lid to some of the crew to dispose of: one of them at least suggested that this windfall might make a good coffee table. On the way back to Glasgow, Mr Johnston, the other undertaker, testified that he and Mr Newlands 'talked about a lot of things', and one assumes that the incident of the returning lid and the unusual domestic use to which it might now be being put was among them.

In less than twenty-four hours, however, it was not only the lid that had returned but the body and the remainder of the coffin. The crew of the fishing vessel *Marie*, intent on bottom trawling for prawns, hauled in their net about 11.30 a.m. to find there, not only a fair draught of prawns and fish, but also the box of the coffin with the body in it. The net was brought aboard, the coffin, because of its weight, had torn the net, and when it was being lowered to the deck, and I quote Captain Anderson: 'It fell three feet, when it hit the deck the whole thing collapsed, squashed like a matchbox ... The bottom fell away and the body came out.' The body, however, was not allowed to remain long on the *Marie*. It was decided to recommit it, this time near a wartime wreck of a tanker where Captain Anderson thought close-bottom fishing would be unlikely. Body and, separately, the various pieces of the chipboard coffin were again committed to the sea. There the body remained for some five days until, at about 4.15 p.m. on 1 December, another fishing boat, again trawling for prawns, hauled in its net and, I quote its captain: 'Once the prawns settled running, there was a head came out of the prawns and we knew we had the body that the boat lifted before.' It is perhaps appropriate that this third vessel involved with Mr Groom's remains should have been called the *Valhalla*.

This time Captain Munro decided to take the body back to Ayr. 'I did not re-commit it, it would be like passing the buck ... If we didn't get it someone else would.' At Ayr, the body was seen by the police and uplifted by Mr Newlands and taken back to Glasgow. Even there, however, it was not allowed to rest in its original casket. Chipboard having proved inadequate for the waters of the Firth of Clyde, a Paraná pine coffin was now instructed. According to Mr Gravelle, he was told by Mr Newlands that another coffin had been chosen, this time of Paraná pine, and he began to prepare this for, what all involved might by now have been forgiven for considering were, Mr Groom's very restless remains. Mr Newland's instruction to Mr Gravelle was to 'do the same as before', i.e., *inter alia*, to drill holes in the Paraná pine coffin. The weights that had been used before, iron bars tied to the deceased's legs – and used unsuccessfully to keep the body down – were to be re-used. Before this Paraná pine coffin could be used, however, there was a change of plan and Mr Newlands told Mr Gravelle that the body had to go into the original metal casket. At the stage this instruction was given – the press, as it was put, 'had the story'. The Paraná pine coffin, now useless for conventional burials, was discarded. In the report to the directors of Wylie & Lochhead by Mr Newlands and Mr Diack on the whole incident – reports characterised by much detail – neither makes any mention of this Paraná pine coffin, and if anyone was entitled to be told about that expensive and abortive incident, it was these directors. A further burial at sea was arranged for 7 December but the intervention of the CID secured its postponement until 8 December, on which date the committal took place without incident – almost indeed with a certainty and a serenity which might suggest that, at last, all was well. I quote Mr Henderson, the Harbour Master at Irvine, who was present: 'The lashings were cut and the casket went in quite easy. It was covered with a canvas substitute. I made a point of ensuring it was metal … We had to cut the canvas at both ends, to let the water in and the air out … it sank, it took eight minutes to go down; we could see it about fifteen feet under water and then it sank. We remained there, no more happened, I am certain it has not come up since … The weight didn't sink it, it only sank when big air bubbles came out … once I saw it eight feet underwater I was quite certain it would go right down.'

From all this, anyone minded to seek evidence for the folk legend that the dead comes back for its own – indeed, was here so determined to come back for its own that it was not deterred even by two iron weights tied to its legs and many fathoms of water in the Firth of Clyde – or, to seek for evidence of those superstitions that once at least exercised men who went down to the sea in ships (like the dead Frenchman in

*Captains Courageous* who came up on the fishing hook to claim his knife from the fisherman): anyone, I say, so minded to seek such evidence could be forgiven if he thought he had found it here. Not until he was committed in the casket his wife had chosen for him did Harry Groom cease, at least to date, to trouble seaman on the Firth and funeral undertakers on land. Clearly his movements would suggest, however, that, notwithstanding the existence at Wylie & Lochhead's of a Paraná pine coffin, bored and prepared for sea burial, if anyone is contemplating burial at sea, this is one thing for which the Firth of Clyde is not to be recommended.

Arising from this history Mr Diack, the manager and Mr Newlands, the assistant manager of Wylie & Lochhead, have been charged with theft of the original metal casket. That casket being unquestionably in their possession and having remained in their possession until it was committed to sea on 8 December, the parties accepted here that the critical question was if and when appropriation of the casket was made by one or other or both of the accused. It was not suggested – nor, in my view, could it have been – that the fact that the casket was finally buried at sea elided any question of theft. If the intention was formed to appropriate that casket then, at that stage, its theft took place and subsequent restitution or restoration of the casket to its original purpose is of no moment.

The evidence here occupied some 6 days and occupies 134 pages of my notes. The submissions by the Procurator Fiscal and the solicitor for the accused, neither of whom had spared any pains, and which were detailed and exhaustive on the law and on the fact, occupied a further day and a half. Their submissions may be summarised as follows:

For the Crown, it was submitted with a wealth of citation of authority, and a detailed examination of the evidence: (1) that at a given date in November the two accused accepted legitimately a metal casket and a body for one purpose and one purpose only, namely, burial at sea; (2) at a later stage, when the decision was made not to use the casket and retain it and to use a chipboard coffin, dishonest appropriation took place. The fact that their gain was only potential, he submitted, did not take away from appropriation and *mens rea*[15] nor did the fact that the casket was eventually used; (3) that circumstances here had been proved which threw the onus on the two accused to satisfy the court as to the bona fide beliefs on which they claimed to have been acting. It was for the defence in the circumstances here to exclude *mens rea* and this, said the Procurator Fiscal, they had failed to do. He asked for the conviction of both accused, and particularly Mr Diack as actor and Mr Newlands as art and part, or alternatively in respect of Mr Newlands for a conviction of reset.[16] The solicitor for the accused, again with elaborate citation for authority and examination of the evidence, submitted: (1) that if the court held that Mr Diack was genuine in his belief, albeit mistaken, that the metal casket would not allow proper burial at sea, then theft did not take place, and there was no dishonest appropriation; (2) if Mr Diack had a right to change from the metal casket to the wooden coffin then he was not guilty; (3) there must be evidence of fraudulent intention and here there was none. It was accepted that an intention to substitute a chipboard coffin for the metal casket was taken by Mr Diack but, said the accused's solicitor, there was no *mens rea* proved; (4) if, as he submitted, the theft took place when intention was formed, intention was formed by Mr Diack only, and Mr Newlands could not be art and part of the theft, since there was no accession after the event.

I deal first with the evidence of the circumstances in which the metal casket was sent to Wylie & Lochhead. At an early stage in the evidence, there was a clear suggestion that Mr McFadden of the Fox Funeral Home had failed to give adequate instruction to Mr Diack, and that the latter had not, therefore, been in a position to know that the metal casket was intended for burial at sea. Mr McFadden's evidence was also attacked as unreliable in the course of the submissions for the accused. If anything in this case is clear, however, it is that Mr Diack and Mr Newlands both appreciated when the casket arrived in Glasgow that it was intended for sea burial. Mr Diack's evidence hereon, at least in cross-examination, is quite unequivocal: 'When the casket came I thought it a very good casket, handsome. We've seen similar.' He was asked, 'Was it not obvious in the papers, that the casket was intended for burial at sea?' This question, according to my notes, was repeated some five times and he hedged in answering it on a number of these. At one stage he said, 'I do not know how to answer that'. It was then put to him:

'Was it not obvious that the casket was intended for burial at sea and that was why you used the word "worry" in your report?'

The answer was: 'I appreciated the casket was intended for burial at sea and I was worried because it was unsuitable.'

He was then asked, 'Is that correct?' and he replied:

'Yes ... I understood from the start that the metal casket was to be used.'

Not only this admission, but the time it took to obtain it, is highly significant. Mr Diack's attitude in evidence was that he was worried about using this metal casket because of its size and weight. Be that as it may, however, I have no hesitation in preferring the evidence of Mr McFadden on this matter to Mr Diack's. Apart from the fact that Mr McFadden was a very impressive witness, all the probabilities are in favour of this obvious version and against Mr Diack's. It is inconceivable, if he was asked to carry out a burial at sea and his instructions were vague, that an undertaker of Mr Diack's experience would not ask for further specification. As it is, I am satisfied he was given very precise instructions. The solicitor for the accused said the widow did not confirm that the

metal casket was to be used until after Mr McFadden telephoned Mr Diack. Mr McFadden's evidence, however, in the
course of cross-examination on this, became ever more impressive. He gave evidence of saying what he wanted done; 'That
the deceased was to be buried at sea off the coast of Scotland:
no particular place … I told him I was sending a metal casket
and he'd have to drill holes in it and add weight … I said it
was dome-shaped and needed holes on the top; if holes were
not on the top it would float. Mr Diack said hole-drilling
would be done on board the ship. He never argued about the
type of casket, a wooden coffin was not mentioned … If he
had demurred at my casket I'd have put the body in a shipping case and prepaid its return to New York … If Mr Diack
had said a metal casket was unsuitable I would have contacted
Mrs Groom … He agreed to the metal casket and that the
drilling would be done on the ship.' Later, in cross-examination, he said: 'All caskets are designed the same. It's the
material that alters the cost … It's impossible to use wood
because it does not conform to the regulations unless he's
put in a zinc-lined case. But the widow did not want that …
We were told to use metal. When I was speaking to Scotland
the relatives had not decided on the case.' It was put to him
that he did not know what type of casket was then to be
used. He replied: 'I knew, I did know. The choice had been
made as to the *type* of casket but the material; copper or steel
was not decided. The decision was as regards metal when
we decided to ship to Scotland … I told them [i.e., Mr Diack],
I'd send a metal casket and that holes were to be drilled in
it. I instructed them that I was sending a metal casket and
what to do with it … I said he was to be buried in the casket
I was sending.'

It will be noted, moreover, that Mr Diack, in evidence, testified that he had seen similar caskets, and he must have been
well aware in the course of that telephone call of the type of

article that was being sent. Moreover, that a metal casket was envisaged from the beginning is clear from the evidence of Mrs Groom, 'I wanted the body in a metal casket: I had three to choose from'. And from her evidence and that of Mr McFadden only a metal casket could be used to conform to the sanitary regulations, indeed, even without the clear evidence of Mr McFadden as to the instructions he gave, the recipients here can have been in no doubt that the metal casket was to be used for burial. It is the practice of the trade to use a returnable shell if all that is required is the transportation of a body, and no one could or did regard this metal casket as a shell. The documents that accompanied it were themselves a mandate for sea burial of body and casket and, if there was any doubt on the matter, there was abundant evidence in the case that the practice of the funeral-undertaking trade, for anyone in any doubt, is to ask instructions from the instructing undertaker or the relatives regarding what, in fact, is wanted. In short then, I have no hesitation in holding that Mr Diack was given specific instructions to bury this metal casket at sea, was advised how to do so and, if he had had any doubts at all, it would have been normal practice in the trade, of which he had a lifetime's experience, to contact Fox Funeral Home by telephone and have his doubts settled. What is clear is that there was not one word by him on the telephone to Mr McFadden that he had any doubts about using a metal casket for sea burial.

So far as Mr Diack is concerned, this finding is, to my mind, almost conclusive since, if he received a casket which he knew had come to him for burial at sea, and he did not so bury it, but instead instructed that another chipboard coffin be used, the inference of appropriation is irresistible and, on the authority of the Lord Justice-General in Dewar, that would be sufficient to end the case.[17] The Lord Justice-General, having narrated that there was misappropriation of property, continued: 'In my opinion there was misappropriation of

189

property the accused knew was sent to him merely for destruction by a prescribed method. That being so, there is no doubt that there was evidence upon which the jury were entitled to find the appellant guilty of theft, and I have very great doubt whether there was any relevance in the further contention that it was necessary to establish a guilty intent by other facts and circumstances ... The presiding judge took a lenient view when he instructed the jury to consider whether the appellant might have entertained an honest and reasonable belief, based on colourable grounds, that he was entitled to treat the coffin as 'scrap'.

In the present case, however, both sides went further, and I turn now to the two matters raised: (1) whether the Crown had proved *mens rea* in the appropriation thereby establishing theft; and (2) whether on Mr Diack's part, he was, or believed he was, justified in acting as he did. The answer to one of these questions, will largely answer the other, since, if Mr Diack was acting dishonestly or fraudulently, it is difficult to see how he can hope to convince that he was acting, or believed himself to have been acting, justifiably.

On this matter the Crown relied on numerous factors in the evidence which, it was said, led to the conclusion that *mens rea* was established. The solicitor for the accused examined each of these factors in detail and commented on the credibility of the witnesses, on whom the Crown relied, to establish them. I shall attempt to deal with the issue of credibility in respect of these items but, at this stage, this much must be said: while one fact pointing to *mens rea* may be explained away, the task becomes more difficult when the factors accumulate, and while the credibility of one witness may be successfully impugned, the task becomes still more difficult when the credibility of practically every prejudicial witness, other than the accused, must be impugned.

To my mind, one of the most significant factors in the

evidence here was the evidence of practice in the funeral profession. Mr Diack had been in that profession all his life and cannot be excused ignorance of its ways. Senior members of the profession gave evidence that, on no account, would they deviate from the instructions they had received and if for any reason they wished to do so, they would regard it as imperative that their client's instructions be taken. Here, the instructions were not fulfilled, it is alleged, because Mr Diack foresaw difficulties in using the metal casket. If difficulties were foreseen – and as it turned out any such fears were groundless – there can be no excuse for this failure to contact the Fox Funeral Home, there to obtain other instructions. His own evidence did not seek to justify his silence. He was asked: 'Did you contact Mr McFadden and tell him the casket was unsuitable?' The answer was 'No.' He was then asked: 'Why not?' To which he replied, 'I've no answer to give … when I decided to use another coffin I did not consult America. I can give no reason.' When it was put that he didn't consult them because he never meant to let them know of it, he replied, 'That's nonsense'. The accused's solicitor said that this was stupidity or commercial carelessness, but I fear the omission goes further than that. If the decision to change from a metal casket was not dishonest I can think of no reason why a telephone call could not have been made to Mr McFadden whose number was known, especially on or after 2 December, when the Ayr Police advised that contact be made. If the decision to change was dishonest the last thing to be done would be to advise New York. This matter, moreover, becomes much more sinister when it is taken along with the other evidence.

Very significant on this question is the evidence of the newspaper reporters who were involved. Mr Kerr, who was mainly responsible for the investigation here, was cross-examined and criticised in much detail by the solicitor for the accused, but I am satisfied that he was telling the truth and his evidence, in respect of the two telephone calls he had with Mr Diack, are particularly important. He testified that on 3 December he telephoned Mr Diack and told him who he was. He then asked him about the body that had come back out of the sea on the Ayrshire coast. He testified that Mr Diack admitted it was the body of Groom and *inter alia* testified that Mr Diack said: 'This was a personal matter involving himself and the family of Groom and he did not want to discuss it more …. He said it was personal to him and the family'. I asked him if the family knew what had happened and he said, 'Yes, he had been in touch with the widow'. Then he testified that Mr Diack said, 'I'm not saying anything else and hung up on me'. Two days later, Mr Kerr testified that he telephoned Mr Diack again. This time he said: 'I asked him bluntly if Groom was buried at sea in a metal casket, the same one as his body was flown in from New York'. Mr Diack said, 'Yes, it was buried in the same one.' And then, after further questions, he claimed Mr Diack said, 'I don't understand why you are taking such an interest in this'. If corroboration were needed of Mr Kerr's evidence on these matters, it came from Mr Sullivan and Mr Wilson, two of his colleagues. In short then, Mr Diack was seeking to create the impression that he had been in touch with the relatives. His own reason for not being in touch with them is wholly unconvincing, namely, that he knew the press were already involved, and the press knew more about it than he did and would have told the relatives all they wanted to know. From all this I fear there is only one conclusion to be drawn; namely, that the family and the Fox Funeral Home knew nothing about the non-use of the metal casket, knew nothing about the unsuccessful burial, and not only did they not know, but Mr Diack did not *want* them to know.

Mr Diack's instruction to use a Paraná pine coffin is a further prejudicial factor. Having failed already with a wooden coffin, only a strong determination to retain the metal casket could have justified the use of another wooden coffin, albeit Paraná pine as against chipboard. That coffin was prepared for use at sea by being drilled with holes and thereby rendered useless for conventional burials, but no mention is made of that coffin in the report to the directors of Wylie & Lochhead. And it is highly significant that its use was abandoned only at the stage when the press and police were involved in the matter. Plainly, it seems to me the accused were determined not to permit their directors to know anything about the attempt to substitute a Paraná pine coffin. If, as claimed, the whole transaction was above board, I cannot see how that is justified.

Two of the documents produced – namely, the instruction note 0/1640 and the account to the Fox Funeral Home – were founded on by the Procurator Fiscal and, in my view, rightly, and contain a number of singular features. The original terms of the instruction note would convey the impression to anyone minded to read it, and ignorant of the other facts, that this was a perfectly normal transaction relating to a polished oak coffin referred to as 'selected'. The same sheet refers to preparation of the casket for sea burial. There is no clear evidence as to when these various entries were made but, clearly, these two entries are inconsistent one with the other. The account to the Fox Funeral Home relates to preparation of body and casket for sea burial under the date 20 November 1971, but as at 21 November 1971, on the evidence here, the casket was not used for sea burial and a chipboard coffin was being substituted. There is reference in that account to the preparation of chute and ancillary equipment, but for the first burial the coffin was simply put over the side. The figures contained in the instruction note do not add up to the total figure; moreover, there is an entry, 'Account posted 30/11/71', which would confirm the impression of the clerkess that there had been an earlier account than the one produced. So far as the account produced is concerned, Mr Diack's evidence was that his $500 covered the use of the chipboard coffin, but I fear that at no stage was a satisfactory answer given to the

Procurator Fiscal's question and comment that, to charge the widow for a second coffin when she had already paid for a first, could not be described as other than dishonest.

The fact that the substitution here was done comparatively openly is not conclusive against the Crown. Openness did not preclude theft in Dewar *(supra)* where all the employees of the crematorium knew what was going on and, in any event, though the employees 'thought it all kinda unusual', they were not to know that the management did not have authority to do as they did and, in any case, the Procurator Fiscal pointed out, the people from whom this matter had to be concealed were not the Wylie & Lochhead employees but the widow and the Fox Funeral Home, and they were not in Pitt Street, but in New York.

On the evidence then, I am satisfied that as regards Mr Diack the number of factors established is such that *mens rea* in the admitted appropriation is established. There is, in my view, no acceptable evidence on which it could be said that he was justified, or believed he was justified, in acting as he did. All the evidence points the other way. If he had thought he was justified then his duty was to advise those instructing him before he acted in a way which he knew was completely contrary to his instructions. Accordingly, there is no alternative but to find the charge established against Mr Diack.

As regards Mr Newlands, the situation is, to my mind somewhat different. It is accepted for the Crown that the theft here takes place at the date the intention to appropriate is formed. There is no sufficient and satisfactory evidence in the case to warrant the conclusion that Mr Newlands was art and part of that intention being formed. There is certainly suspicion, but I do not think it goes further. Mr Diack's report, his replies to caution and charge, and his evidence were all to the effect that the decision was his and his alone. That being so, at very best for the Crown all that can be said to have been established against Mr Newlands is accession after the event, and that is not sufficient to establish guilt as libelled.

The Procurator Fiscal submitted alternatively that a verdict of reset would be appropriate but, here again, I think the difficulty that faced him on the original charge still stands. Reset requires that knowledge be established on the part of the accused that the article was stolen. Here there is no clear evidence on the part of the Crown on which it could be held established that Mr Newlands knew that the metal casket had been stolen by Mr Diack. There is no evidence that he had personally received any of the instructions from the United States, or was aware that Mr Diack was acting in complete defiance of these, or knew that these instructions had not been amended. His evidence was that he knew of no instructions about the method of burial, that it was Mr Diack who decided the various steps, and that he merely carried out Mr Diack's instructions. The Procurator Fiscal submitted that, if he was privy to the retention of stolen property, then he was guilty of reset. The critical matter, however, is proof of knowledge of the property having been stolen. I think here there are a number of suspicious circumstances, but I do not think it would be safe to hold it proved that Mr Newlands knew that the casket had been stolen, and that he was thereafter privy to the retention of stolen goods from their true owner. In his case the appropriate verdict, in my view, is not proven.

The fine of £150 imposed on Mr Diack will be regarded by today's standards, as modest if not inadequate. In 1972, however, when it was imposed, money was worth much more than today, and as his solicitor pointed out he had no criminal record and the present conviction had ruined what had been his lifetime's career.

# 14

# A SPANISH HOTEL

In May 1971, another summary trial produced unusual facts. It was the time when Britons were flooding to Spain in search of summer sun, long beaches and comfortable hotels, and the Spanish building trade was responding by creating seaside resorts with multi-storey hotels at every village beside a good beach, and at many places where there was nothing but a beach. This case can, accordingly, be described as a period piece. Three industries, British tourism, Spanish tourism and Spanish builders, occasionally encountered one another, and, in particular, they did so in the case of the Procurator Fiscal of Glasgow against the travel firm Lunn Poly, and its Glasgow manager; a case which even for Glasgow Sheriff Court contained some unusual, and for all the Scots involved, unforgettable facts.[18]

It concerned the experience of a group of Glasgow holiday-makers who between October 1969 and 19 July 1970 had found, in Lunn Poly's holiday brochure, an offer of holidays in Spain, in a 'brand new' hotel, the Victoria Playa in Pineda. When the brochure was issued in October 1969, the hotel was still being built but was described in the brochure as 'due for completion on 1 April 1970'. This indeed was one of the many examples of optimism which characterised references to this hotel in the brochure in question. In the brochure there was an artist's impression of the 'brand new hotel' and the catalogue of what patrons could expect from this new hotel was nothing if not eloquent, detailed and persuasive. Indeed, the hotel had, or rather was to have, everything a potential Glaswegian holidaymaker, in the course of the Scottish bleak midwinter when considering Spain for his family holiday, would appreciate. It was described as:

... reserved exclusively for Lunn Poly and has one of the most advantageous positions in Pineda, situated only twenty yards from the magnificent beach. The whole hotel is beautifully furnished throughout. The hotel has a large cocktail bar, spacious lounge and a bright airy dining room. A lift serves all floors. There is a large and spacious reception room. The spacious bedrooms all have private shower and toilet facilities, and the majority have private terraces. The swimming pool which is flanked by a sun terrace has a part partitioned off for children.

Here indeed, according to the brochure, was what most people would call a luxury hotel. Holidays there were advertised as starting from 17 May. It will be noted that the existence of all these attractive features is expressed in the present tense – it '*is* beautifully furnished', it '*has* a large cocktail bar', and a lift that '*serves* all floors', as if all were in existence.

On the subject of the hotel Playa Victoria, the Lunn Poly brochure remained unaltered, at least until 19 July 1970, when the Glasgow group arrived to see for themselves what the Playa Victoria had to offer. The brochure was shown and referred to prospective clients from October 1969 and, in particular, was shown to potential clients after the 1 April, as if the brochure's forecast of completion on that day was an accomplished fact. In May, Mr Jameson, who was considering holidaying in Spain, was shown the brochure and booked because of the description. Owing to his wife's physical condition a lift was necessary, and it was for this reason he accepted the hotel in question. On 16 July, Mr Ronald McDonald, himself a travel agent, phoned Lunn Poly and was told that all was well with that particular hotel. He was told that 'they'd checked and everything was all alright'. On 18 July, the day before the Glasgow party departed, Mr Jameson called at the Lunn Poly office for his tickets and there was no suggestion that the hotel was incomplete.

A day later, on 19 July, the party of Glasgow holidaymakers, who had booked their holiday in the Victoria Playa, arrived in

Spain, along with other clients of Lunn Poly booked into other hotels in the area. One can assume there would be the optimism of sunshine and promised luxury prevalent among them. For those destined for the Victoria Playa, however, the optimism was to be short-lived. The plane on which they arrived at Gerona was met by the accused's courier, allegedly a Spaniard, by the name of 'Frank'. Frank was, at least back then, an archetypal figure in tourism who if there was bad news to be given was its bringer; preferably when the intended recipients of the bad news were far from the moral support of the rest of their countrymen who had flown out with them, and were far from the airport, and thus unable to demand an immediate return flight home.

Here, after the other passengers had been delivered to their hotel, Frank advised the group for the Victoria Playa, in a master-piece of understatement, that he had 'something to tell them'. He continued, 'There were a few minor faults.' The adjectives 'few' and 'minor' suggest that Frank was not unused to having respon-sibility for giving news likely to be unpopular. He unfolded his catalogue of minor faults gradually. He stated that, 'When he left the hotel that morning there was no water in the rooms', which could suggest that by that afternoon it may have been remedied. Asked about the swimming pool, he disclosed, 'There was no water, so there was no swimming pool'. Having delivered these bomb-shells and his passengers to the site of the Victoria Playa, and while the latter were still surveying the stricken scene, and no doubt using other adjectives than Frank's 'few' and 'minor', Frank departed silently, his duty done. As one of the Scottish party put it: 'He ignored us. He did not want to know'. Here then was a situation where again the newly arrived learned the full truth of the famous saying of Robert Louis Stevenson that 'to travel hope-fully is a better thing than to arrive'. This, however, was only the beginning, for, like the Queen of Sheba when she beheld the glories of Solomon, 'the half was not told' them. It was discovered that the assistant manager could, or would, only speak Spanish. There was, in fact, no water. It was only in the second week, when the

198

hot water started to flow, that the assistant manager's English like-wise began to flow. As of 19 July, the building work on the hotel was incomplete. Its entrance was described by one of the Scottish party as 'like a bricklayer's yard; trucks, buckets everywhere'. There 'was no glass partition of any kind on the ground floor'. More importantly, however, there was no running water in the bedrooms. The Scottish party did not obtain cold water until the fourth day, and no hot water until the start of the second week: the result, I was advised in evidence, of a backhander to the plumber. There was, furthermore, no running water in the bedroom toilets for four to five days and about thirty guests were obliged to use the communal toilet on the hotel landing, or the toilet of a neigh-bouring café. There were no lights on the stairs and in consequence of this – though he admitted that the fact that the bar had at last opened, and that he had had the unaccustomed indulgence of a drink in the hotel which might have contributed – one of the Scottish party fell on the stairs and fractured his leg. In the course of the fortnight, a large crane was situated where the swimming pool was supposed to be – a crane demobilised from 14 July because of an accident but which, on that date, was still lifting building material into the unfinished hotel.

The general situation was perhaps best described in the words of some of the Scottish party: 'The place was a shambles' (Mr Jameson); 'Like a builder's yard'; 'It could be described as a fitted hotel because they built it around about us' (Mr Rough). Finally, in the course of their fortnight in Pineda, the Scottish contingent, whose experience was no doubt the talk of the British community there, met up with other Lunn Poly clients who had been booked on earlier flights for the Victoria Playa Hotel, but who had been transferred elsewhere because that hotel was not ready. The import of this evidence, in my view, was that the accused had a repre-sentative on the spot, possessed of up-to-date information on the state of the hotel, and who knew, before this particular party departed from Glasgow, that the swimming pool and lifts were not ready and the hotel not in the condition described in the brochure.

From this history, Lunn Poly (Scotland) Limited and their Scottish manager, Ronald John McNeil, were charged under the Trade Description Act 1968, between 1 October 1969 and 19 July 1970, with recklessly making statements which were false as to the provision in the course of a trade or business of certain services, accommodation and facilities; namely, the special features listed in their holiday brochure. To the charge, both accused pled 'not guilty.' There was, however, no challenge of the Crown witnesses' description of the state of this hotel when they arrived there on 19 July. The Crown case was that the phraseology of the description of the hotel was unequivocal. It stated the hotel had these facilities. It was the further contention of the Crown that the statement made by the accused was a continuing one, made throughout the period for which the brochure was current, and that there was here, what was described as a continuing offence.

There was never any suggestion by the defence that they were not the authors of the conditions described in the brochure. There was no challenge by them of the conditions described by the various Glasgow witnesses who had experienced what trying to live in a Spanish hotel, still under construction, could be like.

The defence evidence came from the second defender, the accused's Scottish manager, and from statements taken in Spain which had been agreed. It was submitted that the accused had not acted recklessly in describing the hotel as they did in their brochure in the period up to 19 July. Mr McNeil's evidence was that the parent company had entered into a contract with bed brokers in Spain, called the Viajes Llos Pages, who advised them of the progress made on the hotel. They were told originally the hotel would be ready by April. His evidence was that the parent company carried out spot checks and that Viajes Llos Pages advised them that the hotel would be ready by 19 July. Prior to that, they had accommodated their clients, who had booked in the Victoria Playa, at other hotels. In particular, he claimed that, on 15 July, the bed brokers told him that the hotel would be ready to accept his clients on the 19 July. He assumed if there were no facilities available, the bed brokers would obtain alternative accommodation. The crux of the matter, he explained, was that because July was the height of the season, no alternative accommodation could be obtained. His excuse was: 'I relied entirely on the information from Viages Llos Pages and spot checks every three to four weeks.' In passing, I think it is fair to comment that though the hotel may have been 'ready to accept' clients on 19 July, on that date it in no way measured up to the description in the brochure, and none of the clients who arrived on that date were ready to accept the hotel as the hotel they had booked.

The accused's solicitor submitted that the essence of this charge was the recklessness alleged, and when the brochure was issued there was no reason why the accused should not think that all would be well. Accordingly, the act was not a reckless one: so to act was not to act recklessly. Moreover, since they subsequently acted on information given them by Viajes Llos Pages, they again could not be held to be reckless, as they were relying on information from a reputable firm. He also made further submissions of a highly technical nature, into which this is neither the time nor the place to go. Suffice to say, none of these submissions in my view amounted to a defence to this charge. If it was certain that some of the representations made to clients calling for information were made by members of staff who did not know what the real position was, that was of no avail to the accused, because under the Trade Description Act 'a statement made regardless of whether it is true or false, shall be deemed to have been made recklessly'. The verdict, therefore, was guilty in respect of each of the accused.

The verdicts may have brought some satisfaction to the unfortunate holidaymakers. They did not, however, give them recompense for a holiday that was a disaster. The publicity which this case attracted at the time, rather than the monetary penalty imposed, may have gone some way to ensure that when a holiday is advertised as possessing particularly attractive features, not only do these features exist, so also does the hotel in which they are said to feature; and the brochure describing them is at least kept up-to-date.

# 15

# TWO CONTRASTING
# GLASGOW CHARACTERS

## WEE HUGHIE

When at the Bar I never addressed an Edinburgh jury in a criminal trial, but I had experience of juries in Stirling, Ayr, Perth and Aberdeen, and most of all in Glasgow, because it was Glasgow that, in the 1950s, had the bulk of serious criminal business in Scotland, as it still has. Drugs were not a problem then but there was everything else and, by the late mid-1950s, I was reaching the stage of most advocates attracted to criminal business: I was being instructed on behalf of clients who could afford to pay the fees of solicitor and counsel. However, frequently, the fees would be on a modified level, and if they proved inadequate in one case, because for instance it lasted longer than had been expected, the instructing solicitor would make it up by instructing one in another case. I always found the Glasgow solicitors, who instructed me, treated me with the utmost fairness and consideration. I was certainly fortunate with many not proven verdicts from juries and, as mentioned earlier, whatever else I asked for, I invariably asked them to consider a not proven verdict if I considered there was any evidence, however slight, such as to make a jury hesitate. Some of these not proven verdicts surprised me and surprised my clients even more. I reached what I do not think was a cynical but a realistic conclusion from this experience, which was that however strong a prosecution case was on paper and on the evidence that came out, there was always something, however trivial, that could be said on behalf of the client on the facts or in mitigation or both.

James Murphy, solicitor and later a sheriff in Glasgow, was a master of always being able to find something relevant in his pleas in mitigation. Time and again when he was on duty in the Summary Court, where he had only had a brief pre-appearance consultation with an accused he had never seen before, he could always find something mitigating in the circumstances of the offence or the offender. It was a resourcefulness to be envied.

Every defence criminal lawyer knows that, then and now, if they have had acquittals from a jury the fact is noted, especially among those whom the late Lawrence Dowdall referred to as 'the cognoscenti'. There were some, it was said, who ran books on such matters and no doubt there still are. If a defence pleader had a run of acquittals, the result was their services came to be wanted. I am told I had a certain reputation for persuading juries to return not proven verdicts and when I was appointed to the Sheriff Court bench in November 1963, there were some who did not attribute this to my possession of any experience, qualifications or suitability for the appointment.

One of the court officers in the Justiciary Buildings in Glasgow, where sheriff and jury trials were held when the High Court was not sitting, expressly negatived my having any qualifications or suitability for the job, or perhaps he was indulging in gentle cynicism. He was a Bar Officer known as 'Wee Hughie'. He was popular with everyone and exuded good nature. If you were a betting man, Hughie would be your agent while the trial was going on. If you wanted the latest court gossip, Hughie would not only have it, he would share it with you. If anyone in the building went off with another man's wife, Hughie had the whole story sometimes before it happened. Moreover, he did all this with a gentle sense of humour. He was a character that only Glasgow could have produced, who could and would speak in the same tongue and in the same manner to all manner and ranks of men and women. His comment to me – with a glint of a smile – when I was first appointed as Sheriff and met him in Justiciary Buildings – was that he 'had been expecting it'. Then he added, 'We a' ken why you are up there' (nodding into the court). Asked why, his reply was, 'You got far

203

ower many of them aff – ower many not provens. They had to get that stopped and they had to get you out o' there'. It was a speculation that had never entered my head.

I first got to know Hughie when I was defending in sheriff and jury trials in Glasgow. From then, and when I sat at Jail Square on jury trial, I had the benefit of his invariably fascinating comments on the passing court scene and its personalities. In his brief retirement I had from him every Christmas, a card signed simply 'Wee Hughie'.

## BARNEY NOON

One persistent offender known to police, the legal profession and the courts in Glasgow in the 1950s, '60s and '70s, and appearing less frequently in the early 1980s, was a man called Barney Noon. Barney was not given to working but he had an alcohol problem which he required to service by means of petty thefts, borrowing money which was never repaid, confidence tricks and the like, usually involving small sums and, as a consequence, frequently resulting in his appearing in court. His previous convictions did not take the form of a list of previous convictions: they took the form of a volume of many pages. In his later appearances he usually admitted the charge. He and I, when I was in Glasgow, met so often that I eventually, like the court police, came to know him as 'Barney'. Barney had been, or claimed to have been, on the convoys to Russia during the Second World War; convoys notorious for the losses they sustained, the weather and temperatures they encountered, and the miseries to which the crews were subject, and Barney was not slow to invoke his experiences there as explanatory, and therefore mitigating factors, in his varied criminal activities.

At first, I was unaware of his most unusual and remarkable interest, as opposed to his usual offences; that was, the writing of verse or as he put it, 'poetry'. He liked to address the bench himself on his appearances, and on one occasion, I think after I had sentenced him to a prison sentence, he produced and delivered himself from the dock of a verse that did not scan in the last line. He read the poem, I read the poem after him, I suggested an amendment which did make it scan, and from that momentary 'interest' on my part as he called it, he regarded me as a familiar, but he was fully aware of my attitude to his usual criminal activities. When he appeared, he usually had a new verse to recite. Sometimes, the verse was written specially for the occasion: the crime, the court, the sentence expected, would be the subjects. These verses did not always scan and there were some where the rhyme was a little far-fetched. Sheriff Rita Rae, QC, recalled one incident when she was appearing as a solicitor, where, in sentencing him to thirty days' imprisonment, I followed his approach of rhyming by using the words,

> Thirty days has September,
> April, June and Barney Noon.

Despite the many prison sentences he appeared to bear me no ill will. He was invariably polite, even when I met him on the street, as twice I did, and on each occasion he took the opportunity to touch me unsuccessfully for a fiver. At one point he sent me a handwritten collected edition of his poetry for my comment. Some of these verses were echoes, and indeed some were more than echoes, of Rupert Brooke. He had certainly read and had respect for the art of poetry, however fragile were his efforts to write it, and, while in Glasgow, non-existent in his efforts to live it.

He seemed to appreciate that I had shown an interest in his attempts at verse, and had a capacity which made him appeal to some people, if only temporarily – a capacity which facilitated his borrowing money he never repaid. Nevertheless, he called as friend the late Dr Morris, the minister of Glasgow Cathedral, who did his best to keep his admirer on a path which was too narrow for Barney to tread. However, to the very end Dr Morris showed him unfailing patience. When Barney died, it was Dr Morris who conducted his funeral service.

His latter days were spent in very pleasant places. By the efforts, I presume of the Social Work department and probably some court, he became an inmate of the Church of Scotland Home for Alcoholics, in Ronachan in Kintyre. I knew that house and its late owner, Mrs G. M. Pollock, to whom I have already referred. She had left the house to the Church of Scotland as a home for alcoholics. It was a superb Victorian mansion set in idyllic grounds and looking out on Ronachan Bay – meaning 'the place of the seals' and there were plenty of seals there. There you could not only in dreams, but in reality, behold the Hebrides in the form of the Islands of Gigha and Islay, and the panorama to the north.

When Barney found his way to Ronachan, he thought it Paradise – which it was, but he did not forget me in his new found paradise. He relished the place and wrote to me about it. One letter I received told me how readily he had taken to the country life and to country sports. On one occasion, he wrote he had been shooting with the Chief Constable, which must have been one of the few, if not the only, occasions when Barney Noon and the police saw eye to eye. I still have two of his letters, the first is undated but his reference to my 'latest illness' suggests the early 1980s, when I had some ill health. It is another indication of Barney's addiction to poetry. Here is what he wrote:

Barney Noon
c/o Ronachan House,
Clachan,
Tarbert,
Argyll

Dear Sir,
'If I have freedom in my love
And in my soul am free,
Angels alone that soar above,
Enjoy such liberty.' (Lovelace)

This letter's purpose is simply to wish you well.

In times gone by you have on occasions tempered some terms of incarceration on me with some useful judicial advice and I detected a little compassion.

Now I imagine that the Right Honourable Barney Noon has that proverbial boot on the other foot. I am using the Gaelic form of address to you when I suggest that *Mac a Ghbhainn* [Irvine] has given himself little respite from courting the blind mistress of justice with the same zeal before his latest illness.

My recent absence from the law courts has been aided and abetted by my boss, a Mr Tom McIntrye, and his delightful deputy, a Miss M. Noakes, and with that being the case surely your work pile would have diminished somewhat.

Now that this golden opportunity has arrived snub the Blind Mistress for a wee while and give yourself some rest.

If I write in a jocular mood the vein of sincerity comes in conclusion when I say I seriously hope that you will bring your powers of adjudication to your own health and well-being, so in sending you my profound regards I do hope you will be careful in keeping your body in as good a trim as what your mind is.

Yours sincerely
Barney Noon.

The other letter is again from Ronachan and is dated 2 December 1985. He had written me earlier that year asking me to sponsor him in the Glasgow Marathon which, with some hesitation, I did, by sending him a cheque for £5, and asking him to let me know to what charity he proposed to donate the money. His reply I think merits full quotation.

Dear Sir,

Please excuse me for not writing to you sooner than this. You might know that I completed the Glasgow Marathon and I am sure you will be pleased to learn that I wasn't foolish enough to think that I was not running away from 'the polis' at the fast pace that is usually exercised in such situations.

It took me about 5½ hours to complete the course and I wondered 'Was it the porridge I had supped in previous years' or was it the good living in this part of Scotland where the trees strain music from the wind that kept me in good knick?

The other day and in very informal tone I was speaking to Tom Pollock about what I reckoned to be of extreme importance in curbing vandalism. As a product of no Mean City myself, and now as I have a mentor who tries to teach me the social graces, would it surprise you to learn that I consider this factor of education, one which could be of great benefit. I myself felt some little dignity in exercising these attributes and although I am rather long in the tooth now and lack some effort of will to apply myself, the fact remains it's ever so nice – to be nice. A long time ago you started the ball rolling in giving me back the dignity I was fast losing. I don't forget that.

I very sincerely hope you are keeping well.

Yours aye

Barney Noon

He is dead now but in life he certainly knew how to pay a compliment.

Perhaps this rapport between dock and bench could and can only happen in Glasgow. Barney's two letters, when I received them, astonished and moved me. When I read the quotation from Lovelace I read verse that was new to me. When I reread the second letter recently, I had the same reaction as when I first received it, and to my astonishment and emotion I would add admiration for the very vocabulary its writer uses. The phrase 'This part of Scotland where the trees strain music from the winds', may not actually be his, it sounds like Shakespeare, but Barney Noon uses it appositely and having a vocabulary that can use words like these is difficult to associate with the sordid criminal record he undoubtedly accumulated in his younger and wilder days.

# 16

# THE STAIR SOCIETY

'Publish or perish' is, I understand, the advice given to ambitious young academics in the USA, if they hope for survival, much less success. It may be doubted if it has ever reached that stage in Scotland, but if you have even a part-time academic position and are thought to have some leisure, you are expected, especially by those who have had any place in your appointment, to write and publish something however modest, especially if you profess familiarity with a subject on which little has been written, and where the little that has been written has been written generations ago. My interest was in the History of Scots Law. I lectured on it to the Glasgow University class on the Scottish Legal System, as well as gave a class in its own right. This, as I have already mentioned, was when, for the first time, an interest was being taken by the Scottish legal profession in the history of its law. In this context the foundation of the Stair Society in 1935 is a significant date, because its ambition was to make available the historical documents which would make the writing of the History of Scots Law possible. My first acquaintance with the Society was in a second-hand bookshop in Glasgow, W. R. Holmes, which was then one of the many second-hand bookshops which flourished in the city. They had, and I purchased, a complete run of the Society's publications to 1949, representing the formidable record of almost a volume a year, including during the years of the Second World War. The first volume also printed a list of the founding members of the Society which looks and reads like a list of all that was best and distinguished in the legal profession in Scotland at the time. The Literary Director of the Society was then Hector McKechnie, advocate, who had been one of the prime moving spirits behind that Society's creation. His father had been a distinguished practising solicitor as well as a highly respected academic. He was Professor of Conveyancing at Glasgow University and, in 1914, published his book on Magna Carta, which the late Professor Mackie told me had astounded the English medieval historians of Oxford and Cambridge at the time it was published. They could not believe that such scholarship could come from a Scottish conveyancer. Austen Lane Poole, the author of Volume Three of *The Oxford History of England* which covers the period of Magna Carta, describes McKechnie's book as 'Still the most detailed and best study of the subject'.[19]

This was Hector's background. He had history in his blood and in particular an enthusiasm for the history of the law. He was a successful and busy counsel with a varied practice and was especially in demand for cases on peerage titles and questions of conveyancing. He had too an eloquent pen and in his heyday I am told an eloquent and witty tongue. By the time I went to Parliament House the older generation were talking about the fun he used to be and the laughter that usually accompanied him. He had, I was also told, every right to believe that he would be appointed to the Supreme Court Bench. He never was and his reaction to this exclusion was to make him a much demoralised man. That was the word used of him by one who knew him well. He had also the tragedy of losing his wife. It was said she unfortunately died after they had arranged their financial affairs on the basis that he would pre-decease her. His health began to deteriorate, and certainly when I came to know him, he was rarely in court and seemed indifferent to any work that was sent to him. When I was called to the Bar he came to know my historical interests and immediately encouraged me to participate in the projects of the Stair Society. In his last years, that Society was his main interest. From its beginning, he was its leading begetter and during his life he was its constant counsellor. If he had had his proper recognition it would be as the founder of the Stair Society and the scholar who initiated in Scotland the first real interest in the History of Scots Law.

Another early protagonist for the Society and all it stood for was the late Campbell Paton, a close associate of Hector. For years, he was its literary director whose duties were to try to ensure that authors and editors of proposed publications did not procrastinate and thwart the ambition of the Society to publish a volume annually. He was also a major contributor; in particular with his edition of *Baron David Hume's Lectures* on Scots law. This occupies six volumes, the last published in 1958 and each meticulously edited. He did me the compliment of inviting me to prepare the index to the six volumes which I did, and which by doing, I think, makes me one of the few living Scots who have actually read all six volumes. They are accepted as representing a massive scholarship on the parts of their original author and his modern editor.

For the twentieth volume of the Society, when Hector, now a QC and LL D, was chairman of Council and Campbell Paton was Literary Director, it was proposed that it should be 'An Introduction to Scottish Legal History', and comprise thirty-four chapters: five on the general development of the law; and twenty-nine on the history of particular branches of Scots Law and practice. I marvel at how Campbell Paton and Hector McKecknie who between them – and I speak from experience here of their determination and patience – succeeded in having that introduction volume published as projected, in 1958, because though the contributors were invariably willing, there was no sanction to compel them to produce their contributions by a specified date. All those who contributed did so without any form of remuneration from the Society: their sole aim was to contribute to the objects of the Society. I was responsible for two chapters on the formal development of the law 1532–1660 and 1660–1707, as well as the chapters on the criminal law, nominally with Ian MacDonald, later Lord Mayfield – although Ian became too busy a counsel to spend much time on the history of the criminal law. I also produced the chapter on Criminal Procedure, in which I would now like to elaborate certain matters, in particular the history of the not proven verdict; and lastly the chapter on Succession.

211

On that last chapter I had the great help of Peter McNeill who sadly died after a short illness on 22 November 2010. He became Sheriff Peter McNeill, QC, in Glasgow and then Edinburgh and was then lately come to Parliament House. I think I can claim that my going there and what advice I could give him, determined him to do likewise. He was two or three years after me as a student in the department of History at Glasgow and our professional lives have run on parallel, consecutive courses: we both took a history degree at Glasgow, went to the Bar; became sheriffs and were members of the Stair Society. We then became members of its council and, subsequently, each was its Chairman and lastly, both successively, its Vice-President. His thorough scholarship has illumined the many fields in law and history on which he has written. One suggestion I made to him he did not follow. I suggested he publish his PhD thesis on the Scottish Privy Council, which in my opinion is one of the best investigations on the machinery of government in Scotland before the union of 1707.

My other work for the Stair Society was to edit Volumes II and III of the *Selected Justiciary Cases 1624–1650*. Criminal cases from James VI had first been transcribed and published by Robert Pitcairn in his *Criminal Trials*, published between 1829 and 1833. His object, as he put it, was:

> to give publicity to the most important portions of the Ancient Records of the Supreme Criminal Tribunal of Scotland – materials of great value alike to the historian and the lawyer, and possessing no ordinary attractions for almost every class of reader. Every gleaning may elucidate some historical point or illustrate some feature of national character.

Pitcairn's reports end in 1624 and the object of the Stair Society's projected three volumes was to transcribe and publish cases selected on the same basis as Pitcairn had selected his; namely 'containing material of great value to the historian and the lawyer' for the period 1624–1650 when Oliver Cromwell imposed his own system of criminal justice on a conquered and occupied Scotland. The first volume of this selection had been published in 1953, edited by the late Sheriff Stair Gillon, whose contribution and editing were concerned with the constitution and personnel of the Justices Court, its procedure and location. What I attempted, in the introductions I wrote to Volumes II and III, was what one reviewer was kind enough to call 'a comprehensive commentary on the criminal law of the entire period'. That introduction was the result of sporadic application to the cases in question over about seventeen years while I was busy at the Bar, and later as a Glasgow Sheriff, and was designed to cover the entire period 1624–50. Some of its comments concerned what was to appear in Volume III, which was perhaps as well since before the editing of the third volume could be completed in 1974, I took the heart attack which precluded the writing of any supplementary introduction to Volume III, though the notes to individual cases there were amplified.

After Stair Gillon's first volume and his death, the manuscript of the transcribed *Selected Justiciary Cases* was passed to Hector McKechnie who asked me to cooperate with him a year or so before his death. He had collected some material, but illness compelled him to withdraw and he asked me to complete the editing. When he passed the manuscript to me in the late 1950s, it consisted of a transcript of the original records of the cases selected for publication, and in my original introduction I expressed the hope that it would be possible to have the whole of the original court books transcribed to give a complete picture of the incidents of crime and its procedure, and how it was dealt with during the period. In the late 1980s, Miss Doreen Hunter, who assisted me by preparing the indices to the three volumes, was persuaded, because she was an accomplished calligrapher and familiar with the seventeenth-century handwriting, to make a card index of all the entries in the Justiciary Cases not published in the two volumes of selections. In the early 1990s, the literary director encouraged my suggestion that these should form a supplementary volume. Detailed examination, however, of all those calendared, demonstrated that the cases

213

selected for the original project were in fact the only cases, with perhaps three exceptions, that met Pitcairn's criteria and were worth reporting in full. Repeatedly in the calendar, cases appear and then simply disappear. A case is adjourned and never appears again. It is adjourned for many reasons: because no witnesses are present or no jurors are present, or frequently to entitle parties' friends to persuade the parties to a compromise. It is difficult to resist the conclusion that in the Scotland of the period, like Ireland and France, persons who had suffered from a crime were more interested in obtaining a financial settlement from those responsible – assythment or damages – than a sentence from a Criminal Court, and where this was not so, the prosecution appears frequently to have been indifferent or ineffective, and the original complaint simply disappears. This is also the experience of Professor Geoffrey Parker in his study of sixteenth-century criminal justice in Scotland, which concluded that if so many crimes escaped the judicial process, any attempt to quantify crime could be grossly misleading.[20] Miss Hunter's calendar bears out that comment. I considered such records would not make a book of interest to the society and the project was not pursued. The calendar, however, remains available and would no doubt prove to be of interest to the genealogist, or as a record of what were initially claimed by the victims, but never proved to be crimes in the period in question.

I was a member of the Society from 1950, and latterly I had the honour of being its Vice-President, an office from which I retired on reaching my eightieth birthday in 2006, when among the many other kindnesses then shown me by the society, I was made an honorary life member.

# 17

# QUESTIONS OF LAW

## IMMORAL EARNINGS

A substantial element of the business in Glasgow Sheriff Court was trials conducted by a sheriff sitting with a jury.

The maximum sentence open to a sheriff on a jury finding an accused guilty, in my time in Glasgow, was two years and unlimited fines. It is now five years and unlimited fines. The sheriff, however, had a right to remit the accused for sentence to the High Court if, on a jury's verdict of guilty, he considered that any sentence he could competently impose would be inadequate. This right was frequently used, and could mean that often a sheriff and jury tried very serious crimes, with the prosecution relying on the sheriff exercising his power to remit if there was a conviction. I recall one case which was tried by a jury in the cramped conditions of Court 12 in the County Buildings, where a mere reading of the charges sufficed to produce the reaction, 'This should be in the High Court'. However, it was tried by a sheriff and jury and on the verdict of guilty the accused was remitted to the High Court for sentence, where Lord Johnston imposed a sentence of eight years. That case was without doubt the most serious indictment and the most sordid case I ever tried with a jury. Shortly after this sentence had been imposed – I have referred to this earlier – from the prison of Peterhead, the accused, who in that case was serving his sentence there, had a letter smuggled out of prison and posted to me which threatened to take my life. It was that sort of case.

Charges of extreme gravity then were familiar to Glasgow juries but what was not common were charges where the law in Scotland had not been defined, and the law in England in similar charges, under equivalent statutes which might have offered help, was uncertain. Only once in my experience did I encounter this situation, which meant it was for the judge in the lower court, the sheriff, to reach an opinion on what the law of Scotland was, charge the jury that the law was as he had decided it, and that they must apply it. This was done in the knowledge that if there was a conviction there would be an appeal to the High Court which would be required to decide whether the sheriff's opinion on the law was right or wrong, and issue an authoritative judgment which would be applicable to all such future cases. The case in question here was an indictment charging one Som Datt Karamchand Soni, referred to, throughout the trial in June 1969, as 'Dr Soni', with two charges of living in part on the earnings of the prostitution of a number of named prostitutes, contrary to the Immoral Traffic (Scotland) Act 1902 as amended by the Criminal Law Amendment Act 1912.

The prospect of that jury trial, when I was told it was to be before me, became a matter of extreme personal concern: the accused was a doctor and the charge was likely to and did attract much publicity. My first search for and reading of cases that might be relevant showed that there were none in Scotland, and that those in England were inconsistent. I learned, too, that both sides in the case were treating it as an important one. A senior Fiscal Depute was prosecuting. The defence solicitor was Mr Leonard Murray, whom I knew as a friend and who had long experience; a master, not only at pleading but also at the preparation of a case for others to plead. He had briefed Ian Stewart, QC, who later became Lord Allanbridge, and Donald Robertson, advocate, for the defence – both experienced and respected pleaders. There was no question that this would be, as indeed it was, a well-fought fight.

The accused was, *inter alia*, a landlord who owned and controlled about twenty-two furnished houses in Glasgow, of which he had let eight to women that he knew to be prostitutes. At the trial these ladies followed one another in the witness box. For some of them the sole reason why they came to Glasgow was to carry on their trade there, and their evidence was that the accused was aware of this and gave them priority as tenants. There was also evidence that the dominant purpose of the lets was not to provide a place to live in, but to provide a place where the prostitutes could carry on their trade. At least two of them spoke of obtaining a change of house, not because their accommodation was unsuitable for habitation, but because the new accommodation sought was more suitable for prostitution. These women had no other means of support than prostitution. In the witness box they appeared frank and open, describing their dealings with the accused, and were clearly accepted as such by the jury. They were personable, well-dressed, some with a partiality, at least in court, for large dark sunglasses, and gave the impression they were eminently capable of looking after themselves. They were an unusual collection of witnesses in a sheriff and jury trial in Glasgow. At one stage, there was discussion between bench and Bar as to what was the appropriate word to describe a plurality of prostitutes. One word suggested was 'coven', but the discussion was inconclusive. They described their introduction to the accused and further contacts with him, such that their evidence, if accepted by the jury, as it was, showed that the accused 'at a very early stage became actively involved in the prosecution of their professional activities'. One wanted another house from him as she did not like the neighbours seeing what was going on, and she got it. Another said she discussed with the landlord installing a telephone: 'and we agreed that it would be better for business if it was installed. That was the sole reason we got flats from him, because we knew we could do business there'. One of them testified that she told the accused that she wanted a ground-floor flat for prostitution and got it, although this involved a student being shifted elsewhere. They knew and testified that their landlord was concerned that they should not get involved with the police, which might have affected their ability to pay their rent. There was evidence of his witnessing the prostitutes in operation and encouraging them to get on with it.

217

There was evidence here, moreover, that the accused proposed to 'cook' the returns to the Inland Revenue, by showing the rent as being half of the rent actually charged. There was evidence that he proposed 'to tell the police that the rent was only £4 per week'. According to one of the ladies, he said to her: 'We are going to have rent books at £4 per week, but you are to pay the original sum i.e. £45 or £52 a month'. One of the prostitutes testified:

> I never paid £45 for any other flat. It was reasonable for me because he knew what I was doing and I would not get put out. I would not have paid this elsewhere if the landlord did not know what I was doing.

And another prostitute testified that the appellant had said, 'All the other girls are paying extra money'.

The Immoral Traffic (Scotland) Act 1902 makes it an offence for a male person to knowingly live wholly or in part on the earnings of prostitution. A further statute, The Criminal Law Amendment Act 1912, provides, *inter alia:*

> where a male person is proved to have exercised control, direction or influence over the movements of a prostitute in such a manner as to show that he is aiding, abetting or compelling her prostitution with any other person or generally, he shall, unless he can satisfy the court to the contrary, be deemed to be knowingly living on the earnings of prostitution.

This provision had been founded on by the Crown but at the end of the evidence, I took the view that this provision did not apply to the circumstances on which we had heard evidence in this trial and so directed the jury. I did so with some hesitation, and though the Appeal Court heard both sides and said they considered this decision correct, I still have my doubts. The question then for the court here was to define for the jury what the

Crown must prove and to entitle them, if they accepted the Crown evidence, to convict.

There was no reported Scottish case on the subject and the English cases or authorities under their equivalent statutes were uncertain and, with one exception, unhelpful. I spent much time before and during that trial considering the English cases and, in particular, did so between the closing of the Crown case and charging the jury. There was one case *Regina* v. *Silver,* where an exorbitant rent had been paid by the prostitute but the court equated this with the selling of ordinary goods and services to her, and the landlord there had been living off his own earnings.[21] He was therefore found not guilty of an offence. A wholly contrary decision was reached a year later, in *Regina* v. *Thomas,* where Mr Justice Pilcher took the view that it was for the jury to determine on the facts of each particular case whether the accused, in fact, was knowingly living in whole or in part on the earnings of prostitution.[22] He expressed his opinion thus: 'That anyone who so acts in that fashion is acting as it were as a coadjutor of the prostitute and therefore different from anyone who performs services or sells goods in the ordinary way to prostitute.' He so directed the jury in that case. There was a conviction and an appeal and his decision was upheld in the Appeal Court.

The critical question here was the terms of the charge: is the accused living in whole or in part on the earnings of prostitution? The whole decision in *Thomas* and in particular the remark of the judge on the landlord acting as a coadjutor, were in my opinion to be preferred to the line taken in the case of *Silver*. As a result, I directed the jury:

> that in law, they would be entitled to convict the accused if they held the Crown evidence proved that he was participating and assisting in the activities of the prostitutes.
> They were also entitled to convict if they held it proved that the rents charged by the accused were exorbitant.

There had been no comparative evidence on this but the evidence of the prostitutes of their discussions with the accused on money matters, in my view, made this element one which, though with some hesitation, should be left to the jury.

The jury convicted the accused unanimously, subject to certain minor amendments and he was sentenced to nine months' imprisonment. Then followed an appeal to the High Court and I awaited the decision of that body with much anxiety. I had had a situation that was new to me, as it was to the law in Scotland, and I had had the rare duty and experience of having to decide what the law of Scotland was and directing the jury accordingly. The Appeal Court's decision expressly declared the case as the first of its kind to come before the courts in Scotland, and that it had come to them for what they undoubtedly gave it; namely, an authoritative decision. Only when I read that decision did the anxieties I had felt about that case lift from me. Had I been wrong, much public money would have been wasted on that trial and much agonising personal effort.

The defence in the case, as I recall, did little to challenge the credibility of the various ladies that gave their evidence of their dealings and conversations with Dr Soni. The defence was based on what the defence considered to be the law, namely:

1.    that for a conviction here there required to be evidence of exorbitant charges for rent and here they submitted there was insufficient evidence for that; and
2.    that there was no evidence that Soni was participating and assisting in the activities of the prostitutes.

The Appeal Court repelled both these arguments and the jury's conviction and the sentence of the lower court stood.[23]

## VERBAL INJURY

In Glasgow Sheriff Court the criminal business was more spectacular and so more publicised, but its volume of civil business could contain fascinating situations and its written decisions were more complex and detailed than decisions in criminal cases. In the civil business that came my way two cases were to me exceptional: one was *Steele v. The Scottish Daily Record and Sunday Mail Limited;* the other, the case known as the Ibrox Disaster Case. The Steele case was an action by the pursuer for what the law calls 'verbal injury', averred to have resulted from an article published in the *Sunday Mail.*[246]

In the Steele case from my first reading of the pleadings and the first debate on the relevancy of the action in November 1966, I was aware that the case was one of undoubted importance, and that the law which it involved was itself the subject of some confusion. In Scots Law verbal injury is a wrong that comprehends three forms of harm: convicium; defamation (or libel or slander); and malicious or injurious falsehood. When this case first came for debate the action was founded on defamation. I found that the pursuer had failed to state a relevant case on that ground. The pleadings – the written case, for the pursuer – were then amended to a case based on convicium, a form of verbal injury which consisted of insulting, reviling or abusing a person, or holding him up to public hatred, ridicule and contempt. The proof in the action so amended went to proof over five days between 3 July and 11 December 1967, at the end of which I issued a judgment finding for the defenders and refusing the pursuer's claim. This was followed by an appeal heard before three judges in the 2nd Division of the Court of Session on 27–28 of March and 24 June 1969, with their decision on 22 July upholding my decision. This case from its beginning until the Appeal Court upheld my decision in July 1969 was a source of concern and anxiety – anxiety that notwithstanding the time I had spent preparing my final judgment, and my personal confidence in it, I might not be upheld by the Appeal Court with all the loss of confidence, disillusionment and misgivings that would follow.

The origin of this litigation were the relations between Mr G. H. Steele, a motor dealer in Glasgow, and one David MacLeod

221

who deposited with the pursuer the sum of £100 as a deposit for the purchase of a mobile shop or van. However, as he had a housebreaking and sustained loss therefrom, Macleod considered that he could not proceed with the purchase of the van, advised the pursuer accordingly, and asked him to cancel the deal. This the pursuer refused to do, and told MacLeod that he could be sued for breach of contract. MacLeod eventually asked if he could have something to the value of his deposit and eventually selected a Morris car at £110 and paid Steele the extra £10. Shortly after purchasing the car, MacLeod found a price ticket for £95 in it, and returned to the pursuer and demanded his money back. He was excited and made certain threats. Shortly thereafter he contacted a journalist who worked for the *Sunday Mail* under the name of 'the Judge'. The pursuer received some phone calls from the *Sunday Mail* on the matter and MacLeod eventually intimated to one of the pursuer's staff, and to the pursuer, that unless something was done about his £100 deposit then an article would appear in 'the Judge's' section of the *Sunday Mail*. The next episode was a phone call from a person calling himself 'the Judge' of the *Sunday Mail*, to whom the pursuer gave a description of the transaction and, in particular, what it had cost him to alter the mobile shop to MacLeod's instructions. The caller then said that unless MacLeod was repaid the £100 in full he (the pursuer) would be 'exposed' in the next issue of the *Sunday Mail*. The pursuer did not pay the money to MacLeod and the following Sunday an article appeared in the *Sunday Mail* which contained some inaccuracies and *inter alia* the following paragraph:

Tough Times – I know it would have been easy for you to win a Breach of Contract case which would probably have meant Mr MacLeod losing his entire deposit. But fair's fair – did your firm have to make him take a car he didn't want, a car he can't even afford to run? A car that he is going to find very hard to sell with the coming of winter.

You're in the big time, Mr Steele, probably you didn't know the tough times young MacLeod was going through.

Come on … let's show us that the big time has a big heart too.

The pursuer's written pleadings allege that the defenders in this article meant to represent, and did represent, the pursuer as a ruthless and unsympathetic business man, who used his vastly superior position unfairly or, in any event, without due regard for the feelings and misfortunes of his customers, in particular, David MacLeod, by using in his case a threat of legal action to induce him to purchase a motor car which the pursuer knew MacLeod neither wanted nor could afford. The statements, it was claimed, were made by the defender falsely and maliciously, and were calculated to bring the pursuer into public hatred and contempt. The pursuer further claimed *inter alia* that as a result of the article he had suffered loss, injury and damage, and his business had been prejudiced and his feelings personally hurt.

There was nothing in the pleadings, evidence and submissions in this case which could be called brief, and the word certainly has no application to the judgment that I myself produced. The whole case occupies fourteen double column pages of *The Scots Law Times Report*.[25]

My own judgment expressed the view that the account of the transaction between Steele and MacLeod given by 'the Judge' in his article was unfair, one-sided and inaccurate with regard to certain facts – words with which Lord Wheatley in the Court of Appeal agreed. These particular words, however, I considered insufficient to give the pursuer the remedy he sought here. Before the Court of Appeal both parties were agreed that the case was one of alleged verbal injury which in the twentieth century had been understood and applied, as it was here, to cases which should be properly classified as cases of convicium. The reality of the situation, however, was that parties originally agreed that the case was one of convicium, but in the appeal were agreed it should be

223

treated as verbal injury, and that the facts alleged here by the pursuer were, if proved, appropriate both to a case of verbal injury as well as one of convicium.

What precisely was required of a pursuer claiming verbal injury was given an authoritative definition in the judgment of the Appeal Court here. Such a pursuer has to prove: (1) that the action though not slanderous was false at least in some material respect; (2) that the falsity was intended to bring him to public hatred and contempt; (3) that it did so; and (4) that the falsity was intended to injure him in his business and that it did so. The pursuer's case here did not satisfy these requirements, in the decisions of both the Lower and the Appeal Courts.

The pursuer's allegation – that he was represented in the article as a ruthless and unsympathetic business man who used his vastly superior position unfairly, or in any event without regard for the feelings and misfortunes of his customers, and in particular David MacLeod by using a threat of legal action to induce him to purchase a motor car – did not, in my view, fall within the accepted meaning of convicium, nor as an element of verbal injury. I was unable to trace any case where the threat of legal action had been held to constitute convicium or verbal injury, and I took the view that I would not be entitled to extend this remedy beyond its hitherto recognised category. Besides, I did not think that the article itself justified the innuendo placed upon it by the pursuer that there was a threat of legal action. The article does not refer to such a threat – it says that MacLeod was told he *could* be sued for breach of contract, not that he *would*. Moreover, the article criticises the pursuer's business methods, but there is authority for the proposition that criticism of business methods cannot be founded on as verbal injury, if there be no imputation of dishonesty.

I further took the view that the pursuer failed to show that the article had, on a fair reading, represented him as a ruthless and unsympathetic business man and that these representations were calculated to bring him into public hatred, ridicule and contempt. These words 'hatred' and 'contempt' are strong words which import more than simple disapprobation or dislike of an individual. In Scots Law these words have been given a more positive meaning. Lord Wheatley, in the appeal, examined the phrase. His view was that the words complained of must produce more than public disapproval, adverse comment or criticism. In his opinion, something of the order of 'condemn' or 'despise' is the proper test. The innuendo the pursuer puts on the article, that it 'represents him as a ruthless and unsympathetic business man', in my view, were not relevant to infer convicium. There is no moral depravity in such a suggestion. Indeed, he would hardly be a successful business man if he was sympathetic, and I did not see how such representation was calculated to hold the pursuer up to public ridicule or contempt. If it did then anyone who insisted on the terms of his contract to the discomfort, embarrassment, loss or prejudice of the other party would be open to such an allegation. The evidence in the case, moreover, in my opinion, did not establish in fact the pursuers claim that he had been subjected to public hatred or contempt. The evidence hereon amounted at most to some disapproval of him or his firm and their methods, which might conceivably have had an adverse effect on sales. This, however, is a long way from public hatred and contempt. In short, I held that the pursuer's case failed.

A party dissatisfied with a sheriff's decision in a civil case normally appeals the decision to the Sheriff Principal – as the pursuer had done here in the 1966 appeal. Now, however, the pursuer appealed the Sheriff Court judgment to the Court of Session where a bench of three judges heard the case presented in detail as one of verbal injury, on which each of them delivered a judgment and each refused the appeal. It was the first occasion on which a Sheriff Court decision of mine in an important case had been made the subject of an appeal to the Court of Session, and that an appeal in which the Court of Session avowedly set out to give, and did give, a definitive and authoritative decision on what constituted verbal injury in Scots Law. According to the list of authorities quoted in the latest textbooks on the subject, it has been, to date, the last word on that subject.

# 18

# THE IBROX DISASTER

The most important and onerous civil case that came my way as a sheriff was one that arose from what – with entire justification – was called 'the Ibrox Disaster'. The principle issue in the case concerned the safety of spectators leaving a football ground and has been equated in many respects with the later disaster at Hillsborough. The Ibrox Disaster occurred on 2 January 1971, at the exit from the Ibrox Football ground known as Stairway 13, or the Cairnlee Drive exit, as spectators were leaving the traditional New Year game between Rangers and Celtic. In that disaster, 66 people died, including 32 teenagers, one woman and a nine-year-old boy, and more than 200 were injured. This gave rise to actions of damages against Rangers Football Club, the owners and occupiers of the stadium, and in particular of the stairway in question. Normally, such important litigations would have been raised in the Court of Session. Here, however, the pursuers raised their actions in the Sheriff Court in Glasgow on the ground that there the actions could be heard and a decision given earlier than in the Court of Session. In the Sheriff Court actions all parties eventually agreed that one of the cases should be taken as a test case, and its result on liability should be conclusive of all the others. The test case that came before me was the case raised by Mrs Margaret Dougan on her own behalf and that of her two children. She was the widow of a thirty-one-year-old boilerman's helper, Charles Dougan, who died in the accident.

Though raised and concluded in a lower court, on neither side, in its preparation and presentation, did the case conducted before me in May 1974 betray anything of its humble forensic origins. Its preparation was exhaustive and its presentation in the hands of experienced and formidable pleaders, Mr Lorne Cowie, QC, led for the pursuers, and the Dean of Faculty, Mr Kemp Davidson, QC, for the defenders. The hearing of the case occupied some fourteen days; twelve were devoted to leading the evidence which covers 1,770 typescript pages and two days were given to counsel's oral and written submissions, the latter covering a further 165 pages. The decision which I issued, in accordance with the Rules of the Sheriff Court, contained ninety-four Findings in Fact and my reasons for reaching the decision I did, and covered some thirty-nine pages. It was not appealed and is not in the printed reports. The significance of the accident was such that it led to the late Lord Wheatley – a High Court judge – reporting on *Crowd Safety at Sports Grounds* in 1972, which in its turn led to 'The Green Guide' to safety practices and, in Parliament, to the Safety of Sports Grounds Act 1975. All this will, I hope, explain and excuse the length and the detail of this present attempt to describe this case – an attempt which is based on the Findings in Fact and the judgment, and quotes extensively from both.

The history and location of Stairway 13 on 2 January was such indeed as to make the accident that happened that day inevitable, and on the whole evidence foreseeable.

The stairway in question was about 106 feet long and of uniform width of 39 feet 6 inches and, before 1962, descended a height of about 40 feet in 5 flights of stairs and 4 landings. Before 1962, it had timber risers and ash treads. In 1962, in the close season, concrete was laid over the timber risers and treads of the steps and the stairway was divided longitudinally by 7 lanes or passages, by means of 6 parallel tubular handrails. At each side of the stairway there was a strong wooden fence consisting of uprights about five feet high. The stairway served that end of the terracing frequented by Rangers supporters, where according to the evidence, their occupation of that area was traditional, if not institutional. It was approached from all parts of the terracing using a track along the top of the terracing, and it was common for spectators on the terracing to duck under the crush barriers situated there, and make for the stairway. It had been in existence for very many years and it was estimated that seventy per cent of east terracing spectators used that stairway and, apart from the four accidents which occurred between 1961 and 1971, an informed estimate was that that particular stair had been used by about 1,180,000 spectators without incident.

However, if the stairway was generally used without incident it cannot be said, at least between 1961 and 1971, that it was ever used with safety or comfort. Evidence came from a multiplicity of witnesses who used that stairway at various matches. Their experience was of densely packed conditions in which spectators anxious to leave the ground – anxiety indeed which seems frequently to have bordered on desperation – had little or no choice of the particular lane they could enter on the stairway. Their evidence was that they were swept along by a crowd, which on those occasions was so dense that a spectator might have his feet lifted from the ground at the top of the stair and be carried to the bottom, or might find himself pressed against the wooden fence at the side of the stair and turned round and round against the fence as the crowd made its slow, congested and apparently inexorable descent. When a spectator weighing sixteen stone was unable, in such a situation, to control his movements, the fate of lesser individuals can be readily appreciated.

Anxiety to leave a football ground and the density of the crowd so doing, however, were not, on the evidence, peculiar to Ibrox. There are other stairways at Ibrox which have carried a substantial number of spectators over the years. Witnesses spoke of the congestion of crowds leaving other football grounds, and of their fear when they found themselves involved with them. Spectator congestion and discomfort then was no monopoly of the Cairnlee Drive stair and while crowd conduct, or rather lack of it, was frequently referred to in evidence, I did not understand it to be suggested that such behaviour was peculiar to those using the Cairnlee Drive stair. It had other dangers. It was a fact well within judicial knowledge that games between Rangers and Celtic in

Glasgow frequently produced incidents of violence and hooliganism, and that at such games, passions – bordering frequently on hysteria – ran high. The passions of football supporters, however, did not make their appearance only when their teams were playing certain other teams and disappear when they were playing others. They were a common feature.

There is, and always will be, I fear the risk of injury inherent in descending stairs in a crowd, especially an excited one, and where some were under the influence of alcohol. What, however, stood out in the this case, in startling and irresistible colours, was that over a period of ten years there had been four accidents on Stairway 13, all similar in character, all involving someone stumbling or falling, and all involving crowd pressure continuing relentlessly downwards, producing a chain reaction so that spectators were crushed and injured and, on occasions, crushed to death – crushing which continued until such pressure was released as by the adjoining fencing or barriers breaking, or those at the top of the stairway being able or being persuaded to stop their descents. The other characteristic which the first three accidents had in common was that after each of these there was no attempt by Rangers to have a professional civil engineer, or like expert, examine the stairway and the circumstances of these accidents, and report on the possibility of their being avoided.

The first of these accidents was on 16 September 1961 at a game between Rangers and Celtic, where an equalising goal was scored towards the end of the game. When spectators were leaving the terrace, conditions on the terracing track and Stairway 13 became very congested; spectators being carried along by the crowd and having no choice as to which part of the stairway they descended. While this dense crowd was descending that stairway some one or more persons stumbled and fell. There was strong crowd pressure from the top of the staircase which continued, and, as a result, other persons on the stairway stumbled and fell. The pressure of spectators moving down the stairway caused more persons to fall and/or to be crushed against one another, and against the wooden fence until, eventually, the wooden fence at the side of the stairway broke, as did the centre handrail. It was proved on this occasion that the breaking of the side fencing relieved pressure and enabled persons to escape on to the embankment. As a result of this accident, some seventy persons were injured and two died. A jury in a subsequent Fatal Accident Enquiry held their deaths were due to their having fallen and been accidentally tramped upon and crushed by a crowd of spectators.

From about 1959, Rangers had a scheme for improving the amenities of their ground, part of which was the concreting of all terracing and stairways. After the 1961 accident, they decided this should be accelerated and employed a consulting engineer, Mr Andrew Sproull, to survey and superintend that work, and to certify the contractors' account for payment. The civil engineer involved made no recommendations as to the adequacy of the work and the defenders did not, at that stage, ask him or any other civil engineer, or such expert, to advise them on any danger from crowd pressure there might be, on this or on any of the other stairways at Ibrox.

The second accident occurred on 16 September 1967 at the end of a Rangers and Celtic match. Spectators were leaving the terracing by Stairway 13 in a crowd that was, as usual, congested as it approached the stair and while on it. As the crowd was descending, the flow was interrupted by someone stumbling or falling about the second or third landings, as a result of the continuing pressure of those descending the stairway. Other spectators fell to the ground and were crushed against one another and against the tubular handrails. As a result, part of one of the handrails was pushed out of alignment. Eleven persons were injured, at least eight of them sustaining crushing injuries and three being rendered unconscious. Like 1961, following that accident, the defenders did not consult any architect or engineer on any question of crowd safety on that particular stair.

The third accident was on 2 January 1969, when Rangers and Celtic again played their traditional New Year game at Ibrox. There was an estimated crowd of about 85,000. At the end of the game while spectators were leaving the terrace and making their way towards Stairway 13, they were again closely packed and congested and unable to go other than where the crowd took them. While descending one of the lanes of Stairway 13, and about the bottom flight of steps, someone stumbled and fell. Those following him, because of pressure from behind, were unable to stop and fell over him. The pressure generated by the said accident caused the tubular handrail to be broken and two upper posts at the lower flight of steps to be bent. As a result of that accident several spectators fell lying on top of one another or were crushed against the fence or railing, but two spectators who had climbed over the wooden fence pulled out a number of the fencing stobs, thereby allowing persons to escape through the gap. As a result, pressure at the side of the accident area was relieved, persons could escape and further casualties prevented. Despite that, however, at least twenty-nine persons sustained crushing injuries, bruising and other injuries in that accident, and were removed to hospital. Following that incident, the defenders again took no steps to consult any civil engineer or instruct any professional firm on the question of potential dangers from that stairway.

This trio of similar accidents, if it did not create concern on the part of the owners and occupiers of Stairway 13, certainly concerned Chief Superintendent Nicholson of The City of Glasgow Police; so much so that he arranged for a meeting at Ibrox to discuss the safety of the stairway after the third accident, with a view to preventing further such accidents. The meeting took place and was attended by Chief Superintendent Nicholson and Chief Inspector Johnstone, by Mr Shepherd and Mr Gow from the Master of Works Department of Glasgow Corporation, and Mr David Hope a Director of Rangers and representing the defenders. There may well have been other persons in the vicinity, but the meeting and discussion took place between these five persons. In the course of that meeting, which was variously estimated at lasting between thirty and sixty minutes, those attending moved up and down the

231

stairway discussing the happening of the accident and, in particular, the question of safety on that stair. In particular, the police and Mr Shepherd of the Master of Works Department were all of the view, which they expressed to Mr Hope, that the dangerous feature of the stairway lay in the pressure or crushing that resulted from any obstruction to the free flow of spectators. They discussed with him their various theories and suggested a number of changes. When the said meeting was concluded, Mr Hope advised the others that he would bring the matters discussed before the defenders' Board of Directors, and that if any changes were to be made they would be carried out during the off-season. I fear, however, that at the proof no evidence emerged that this meeting, its personnel, or the suggestions made at it, were ever brought to the notice of Rangers' Board. At no time did the Board discuss the particular question of safety on this stairway following the 1969 accident; a repeat of the earlier inertia.

One would have thought that attendance at a meeting of the persons who attended this one, and resulting in the suggestions that were made by them, would have made an impression upon Mr Hope, who was there in the capacity of representing Rangers. Such, however, was not the case. It was proved by the others present at that meeting that Mr Hope was there representing Rangers and was involved in the discussions they had. The defenders' version of this incident was that there was never any such meeting, which involved a straightforward issue of credibility. From the beginning of this case, neither side made any attempt to conceal their intention that the ultimate decision would not remain with the Sheriff Court. For this reason, and that any higher court should be in no doubt as to the impression created by a particular and critical witness, and the conclusions I had reached on his credibility, I considered I had to deal with this in some detail in the written judgment.

I found the whole evidence in support of the Rangers version unimpressive in the extreme. Mr Hope, in evidence, vacillated among his being unable to recollect such a meeting, his denying

232

any such meeting, his possibly of having the dates wrong, being mistaken, admitting that he could have forgotten, stating that if he had attended such a meeting he would certainly have recalled it, and so on. There was hardly any variation on the theme of equivocation – and on that theme there are many variations – to which he did not resort. The evidence here is such that it had to be read to be believed. Mr Thornton, the Assistant Manager for Rangers, who Mr Gow said was there though he took no part, similarly in giving evidence, vacillated as to whether he was at such a meeting or whether he simply could not recall having been at such a meeting. Mr White, who was then Manager, would have it believed that he met Mr Nicholson and Mr Johnstone, as well as the two representatives of the Master of Works Department, that he accompanied them to the Cairnlee Drive stairway, where they walked up and down the stair, 'various remarks were passed', and then he left. He could not recall Mr Hope being there and of the remarks, which he said were passed, he could only recollect the possibility of putting concrete in the tubular rails and removing the wooden railings. He claimed that he left that meeting feeling that no one thought that there was anything amiss with the stairway, and that there had been no discussion as to the cause of the accident. If that was his state of mind I feared his hearing, or his memory was sadly at fault. I was satisfied, however, that this was not his true state of mind because I was satisfied that he took no part in the discussion, and I doubt he was even present at the relevant time.

The impression created in evidence by Mr White became increasingly unimpressive as his cross-examination progressed. He would have had it believed that he, the Manager responsible for the ground, would 'probably' tell the Board about the meeting. The evidence of these witnesses was in striking contrast with that of the police and Messrs Gow and Shepherd, and it was their evidence that was accepted as to the personnel and events of that meeting.

Owing to the unsatisfactory nature of the evidence for the defenders on this, and on other matters, the minutes of their board meetings had a particular significance. If the verbal testimony of the defenders' witnesses, however, revealed little, their written records, produced in court, revealed even less. And if the extracts from the records produced in this case were what they purported to be, rarely can an organisation of the size and significance of Rangers Football Club have succeeded in conducting their business with records so sparse, so carelessly kept, so inaccurately written up – if indeed 'inaccuracy' is not too mild a word to describe one particular minute – and so indifferently stored. At that stage, the defenders' Board had, for many years, had meetings weekly or at least once per fortnight. In addition, they could meet on Saturdays. The defenders' contention was that minutes of these meetings were kept and should be available. It was difficult not to sympathise with Mr Frank King who had been the permanent Secretary since September 1969, and whose searches for relevant minutes produced only fragments. The minutes for the years 1960 to 1963 had disappeared. Moreover, minutes were kept in a 'minute book' form, written up allegedly after each meeting. Consequently, there was no written record of the Board of Rangers considering the 1961 accident and whether it involved the safety of the stairway. The 1969 accident was on 2 January. There must have been at least one meeting between then and 28 January, when there is the first relevant reference in the minute book. To this matter I will return. There is, however, nothing in the minutes even to suggest that the Board of Rangers discussed the cause of the accident. There is nothing in the minutes of the meeting with Mr Hope, held by the Police and Master of Works' representatives; nothing to the effect that a suggestion had been made on which professional advice might be sought. The then Chairman, Mr Lawrence, in evidence, was at pains to blame the absence of the written records on illness, death or brevity of employment of the various secretaries. It was, I fear, unconvincing. I took the view – and expressed it – that the only conclusion possible from these extracts in the minutes produced, was that the defenders never once in formal meeting applied their minds to the question of the causes of these accidents.

They never once considered that it might be desirable to take professional advice on the potential dangers of Stairway 13, and would appear – I put it no higher – to have proceeded on the view that if the problem was ignored long enough it would eventually disappear. Only when sixty-six people died in 1971 did they take the step which it was established would, in my view, have been reasonable after the 1961 or 1967 accidents, and certainly imperative after the 1969 accident and meeting. In the course of his evidence no less a figure than Rangers' Chairman, Mr Lawrence, accepted there was responsibility to seek advice after the 1967 and 1969 accidents, and admitted that if Rangers did not do so, they failed in their duty – though it may be that because of his age he did not fully appreciate the significance of the concessions he was here making.

The Hope meeting apart, other factors which brought the danger of that particular stairway to the notice of the defenders, after the 1969 accident, were the letters they received from injured spectators, but of which letters the defenders do not appear to have retained copies. The first mention of this was in the minutes produced, which narrated that the Secretary had left notes on all the developments to date regarding spectators injured on 2 January: 'All injured people who had complained were written to and their letters passed to Norwich Union Insurance Company for action'. That persons were complaining, that these persons were injured persons, and these injured persons were persons injured on the Stairway 13, was thus brought home to the Board in formal session. Furthermore, these complaints apparently created some impression on the Board since the next paragraph reads that the defenders resolved to give the injured spectators that which the defenders gave only in exceptional circumstances, namely, two complimentary tickets each, 'in an effort to appease them'. A month later, this generosity was cancelled on the ground that the club had been advised by its insurers that it was in no way liable for the accident. The use of this word 'appease' – the choice of which was either regretted or denied by those of the Board who gave evidence

– to my mind suggested that at that stage the Board were of the view that Rangers Football Club had done, or had omitted to do, something which called for a gesture of appeasement. The use of the word 'appease' was regretted by certain of the witnesses, but a perusal of their evidence on the interpretation they respectively placed upon that word demonstrated that a certain character of fiction was by no means alone in claiming that, 'When I use a word it means just what I chose it to mean, neither more nor less'. I should add that following the insurers' opinion that their insured was not to blame; the Board of Directors decided and minuted that no injured spectator would receive compensation, and it was agreed unanimously that the instruction to give two complimentary tickets to each injured party be cancelled.

After the 1969 accident, the defenders again failed to consult any firm of architects or engineers with a view to being advised on the condition of the said stairway as regards crowd safety. But in two matters they were party to what could only be described as devices to create the impression that they had taken, and were taking, appropriate precautions.

Following on the accident of 2 January 1969, the defenders' Director, Mr Ian McLaren, or one of his employees, instructed a firm, with which Mr McLaren was associated, to repair the railings and wooden fence damaged in the accident. The firm carried out these repairs, which included strengthening the wooden fencing by means of extra uprights. The details of this work were determined by Mr McLaren and the firm in question. The Master of Works Department of Glasgow Corporation did not, at any stage, specify what work was to be done, nor did they approve of the work after it had been completed. Following on this work being done, the firm's account was sent to Rangers, who submitted it to their insurance company with a letter from their Mr McLaren which stated that the work in question was carried out to the Master of Works' requirements. This was untrue.

In the course of 1968, a working party was set up under Sir John Lang on crowd behaviour at football matches; in the course of their investigation representatives of that committee visited Ibrox and met the directors. Their report was published in 1969, and a copy of this report was supplied to the defenders by the Scottish Football Association (SFA). By letter, dated 6 March 1969, the Scottish Football Association Secretary wrote to the defenders asking if their terracing, enclosures and stand were examined annually with the question of public safety in mind. The Secretary asked the defenders to advise him if such an inspection was carried out and, if so, if it was: (a) by a professional man; or (b) a local authority; or (c) a member of their own staff. That letter was considered at a meeting of the defenders' Board on 8 March 1969, when the Vice-Chairman is minuted as stating that the ground was last inspected by a professional firm in the close season of 1968. As a result, a reply, dated 10 March 1969, was sent by Rangers to the SFA stating that the defenders' entire ground was maintained regularly by their own staff, and also 'is annually inspected by a professional firm, the last time being the close season 1968'. This was blatantly untrue insofar as it relates to a professional firm. No one could or did suggest that Mr McLaren's was a professional firm in the sense of the SFA letter. In fact, the last professional firm, with whom the defenders were connected before 1971, so far as the evidence here is concerned, was that of Mr Andrew Sprowl, consulting civil engineer, and his services were dispensed with in 1967, and before then he had never carried out an annual inspection on the ground. When one witness who had attended this meeting was asked about this minute relating to annual inspection, he could only say he knew of no professional firm and had just accepted what the Chairman said. Mr Hope's comment was that 'It was left to McLaren'. Mr McLaren now being dead was not in a position to contribute his version.

In August 1970, in a further letter the SFA drew the attention of the defenders to the *Lang Report*, and, in particular, to the need for periodic inspection of ground structures by a qualified person. This letter further recommended that each club arrange for an annual inspection of the ground structure by a qualified person, and that his certificate be sent each year to the Secretary of the SFA. Accordingly, Rangers can have been in no doubt as to the importance of this matter.

The written judgment contained the following comments on the defenders recurring inactivity in the face of these accidents:

> Knowledge of the danger from crowd pressure on the Cairnlee Drive stairway then, is in my view, brought home, and brought home conclusively, to the defenders at the latest by the 1969 accident and its aftermath.

The next question, following Mr Cowie's submissions, is what would the reasonable man have done in these circumstances? There is no doubt as to what the Directors and Manager of Rangers did, since, beyond the abortive and short-lived decision to give tickets of appeasement, they did precisely nothing. Their evidence on this inactivity and their reasons for it makes what can only be charitably described as depressing reading. Indeed, it goes further than this because certain of their actions can only be interpreted as a deliberate and apparently successful attempt to deceive others that they were doing something, when in fact they were doing nothing. Mr Lawrence, the Chairman, was an old man whose evidence should perhaps, for that reason, not be judged too harshly; not so Mr Hope, who was the Director and had attended the meeting where the dangers were discussed; not so Mr White, who as Manager in 1969, was responsible for the condition of the ground. The united burden of their evidence was that they, personally, did nothing because they thought someone else was doing something. For defective or non-existent minutes, Mr Lawrence blamed dead, temporary and indisposed secretaries. For the fact that nothing was done in connection with the stairway in question, all the Rangers' witnesses were in the fortunate position of being able to lay responsibility on the shoulders of Mr Ian McLaren who, being now dead, was in no position to dispute their evidence – though, at the Fatal Accident Enquiry where he gave evidence, he in his turn demonstrated that he was not without resource. He placed responsibility on what was perhaps the only possible whipping boy available to him, namely, the Department of the Master of Works of Glasgow Corporation, for the fact that all he did was to restore the stairway to its pre-accident condition. That is, in effect, to have done nothing so far as considering remedying the danger of crowd pressure. All of the defenders' witnesses on this matter sought refuge in the fact that they considered the matter was being attended to by Mr McLaren, and Mr Hope went so far as to suggest that Mr McLaren was something of an expert on safety because of his experience in repairing tenement chimneys. Mr McLaren at the Fatal Accident Inquiry confessed to being a building contractor – though certain of his colleagues on Rangers' Board were obviously in some doubt as to the status and extent of his building activities – but he repudiated the suggestion that his firm were 'safety experts'. Mr Lawrence, who was a builder, was of the view that something 'would' be done, an expression he used repeatedly, and that engineers 'would' be consulted. He himself did not go beyond such an expression of what he appeared to accept 'ought to have been done'.

This then is the history concerning Stairway 13 in the decade or so before the tragedy of 2 January 1971. For the details of that tragedy I quote the Findings in Fact that I made in the final judgment. As mentioned earlier, Sheriff Court practice in a civil case like this required that in the final judgment on the merits of the case the sheriff shall set forth his Findings in Fact and in Law, and shall append a note setting forth the grounds on which he has reached his decision. In the final judgment here I made some ninety-four Findings in Fact, in addition to Findings in Law. Of the Findings in Fact, numbers seventy-one to eighty-five record what I considered was proved of the happenings of that afternoon by the evidence I had heard and accepted.

(71) on 2 January 1971 Rangers again played their New Year game against Celtic at Ibrox; the score was one-one, Rangers scoring the equalising goal in the last minute or so of the game;

(72) the crowd on said occasion numbered about 80,000 and included the deceased and for a Rangers and Celtic crowd was well-behaved;

(73) just before and at the end of the game, spectators in the east terracing made their way from various points of that terracing towards the Cairnlea Drive exit; the said stairway was again approached from either side by spectators using the track along the top of the terracing and directly from the terracing by spectators who used passageway 13 and who ducked under the terracing crush barriers; approaching the stairway, spectators were densely crowded together;

(74) on said occasion the end lanes at either side of the stairway were particularly crowded;

(75) as the crowd in lane l was descending, one or more persons stumbled and/or fell at about the third landing from the top; this happened when the stairway in lane 1 was closely packed with descending spectators who were being pushed downwards by the pressure of those above them and those still crowding on to the stairway from the track;

(76) this downward pressure of the crowd continued after the said person had fallen or stumbled forcing other persons to fall or collapse on those who had already fallen;

(77) the pressures so built up in lane 1 caused the tubular railing separating lanes 1 and 2 to break causing the effects of the original accident to spill over into lanes 2, 3 and 4 causing the movement of spectators there to be interrupted so that they too fell and were crushed in a similar way to those in lane 1;

(78) some persons on the stairway tried by signalling and shouting to persuade those approaching and coming on to the stairway to stop, but, initially, without effect; this was so in particular because of the continuing pressure from the track and terracing towards the stair;

(79) as a result of the downward pressure of descending spectators continuing, more and more persons were caused to be heaped upon those who had already fallen or to be pressed

240

hard against them or against the wooden railings; certain spectators were crushed to death by others lying on top of them, and others were crushed to death while still in a standing position;

(80) eventually when the pressure from the top of the stair was stopped, a pile of bodies had been formed in lanes 1, 2, 3 and 4 estimated as measuring about 25 feet to 30 feet long and by about 6 or 7 feet deep; the area occupied by this pile of bodies is approximately shown by the bent tubular railings on photograph 12D of process;

(81) by the time the pressure stopped 66 persons, including the pursuer's husband, who were part of the pile of bodies on the stairway, were dead or dying and many persons were injured;

(82) at the end of the game a warning was given over broadcast equipment to spectators as regards taking care on leaving; it is not proved that the said broadcast message could be or was heard amidst the noise on the ground of those leaving or intending to leave in the vicinity of the Cairnlea Drive stairway;

(83) in the course of the incident attempts were made by certain spectators to ease pressure by breaking the wooden fencing but, as a result of the strengthening work carried out by Mr McLaren's firm, after the 1969 accident, that wooden fence remained firmly in position;

(84) had there been a tubular rail at the side of lane 1 next to the embankment persons would have been able to escape over and under it and dangerous pressure on the stairway would not have built up;

(85) a similar result would have occurred if the wooden fencing had broken or could have been removed by spectators.

Rangers' defence here to the pursuer's claims of their negligence, was that they, the defenders, had fulfilled all the duties incumbent on them. They claimed that the 1971 accident arose not by their negligence but from a combination of unforeseen and unforeseeable circumstances. These they described as a late goal, an exceptional crush, unusually elated spectators descending the stairway, one spectator, being carried on the back of another, losing his footing and thereby causing the others to fall. Mr Davidson also made much of the fact that there was no evidence of precisely where and when Mr Dougan died and that unless these matters were established a possible link between the fall and the death could not be found. It is perhaps not surprising that there is no direct evidence of precisely where and when Mr Dougan died with the hill of bodies some seven feet high, with men standing erect yet in death because of suffocation and crushing. It would be asking the impossible of the pursuer to require that she prove the precise circumstances here of her husband's death on that stairway. The probability from the circumstances of the accident and the number of dead was, surely, that only those closest to Mr Dougan at the time he died would have known the circumstances Mr Davidson desiderates as essential, and who were themselves victims. No rescuer would be worrying about the precise identification or location of a body he was trying to remove or resuscitate from this chaos. In an accident of this kind and magnitude, with a relentless pressing crowd, with bodies piling up against and on top of one another, few would ever be able to say where and when any particular individual fell or was crushed, smothered or died. What was admitted, however, is that Mr Dougan died of traumatic asphyxia, not simple asphyxia or suffocation as did some of the victims.

As regards the defenders' claim of a man being carried on another's shoulders losing his footing, thereby causing others to fall, the evidence on this came from two sisters – one said she saw a man on another man's shoulder but then lost sight of them. This is a long way from their having fallen. Her sister who was with her at the window did not see anyone on another's shoulders but claimed she saw 'Someone ... something falling forward', a coat or a body. The significant thing is that she saw it quite high in the

242

air and thought it travelled in the air from above the first landing down to the third landing. This could not be the body of a man. Another witness saw a man on another's shoulder waving a scarf, but this was after the sequence of the accident had already begun. Even if there had been a man on the shoulders of another who fell, neither that nor the other circumstances, like the late goal founded on by the defenders, could avail them as unforeseeable. A late goal was not unusual. It had preceded one of the earlier accidents (1961) for one thing, and I assume that the football supporter of Rangers or any other club is sustained by the hope – at least – that, until the final whistle, his team can and may score a goal. In the context of a Rangers and Celtic football game at that time, there was hardly any behaviour on the part of the specta- tors which could be described as unforeseeable. We are not dealing with a subdued congregation leaving a memorial service for some deceased statesman, or an audience, satiated and silent, leaving a performance of Wagner's *Parsifal*. It was, common knowledge apart, well within the judicial knowledge of Glasgow Sheriff Court in its criminal jurisdiction, that, at that period, such games produced admitted cases of irresponsible hooliganistic and bizarre – what some described as 'insane' – behaviour on the part of certain fans. It is unnecessary to invoke such judicial knowledge, however, because in this case there was abundant evidence that there is hardly any behaviour too extreme but it has been repeatedly seen, noted, commented upon, labelled and deplored by witnesses – 'mob hysteria' 'football mania', 'hooliganism', 'selfishness', 'no thought for others', 'dancing about', 'complete strangers hugging and kissing one another', 'pushing', 'football mania of the high order', 'mass hysteria', 'wild jubilant spectators'; as one witness put it 'Chanting, raving fanatics using the stairway – you've got to see it to believe it and I'm a Rangers supporter'. On 2 January 1971, moreover, drink was a factor. Drink was not only consumed before and during the game, it would be reasonable to conclude that following the familiar saturnalia of a Scottish and Glasgow New Year holiday the average spectator's blood alcohol would be above normal. This too would inevitably add its contribution to the quality and unpredictability of the behaviour of members of the crowd. Mr Davidson's phrase for this condition was 'cerebral irritation'; a vivid, if, to a Glasgow Court, an unfamiliar description of a not unfamiliar condition. The defenders' written pleadings referred to 'unusually elated spectators' as an unforeseen circumstance. In my view on the evidence, however, elation of a high degree was usual rather than unusual, and if elation was all that had to be contended with at football games in those days, especially between Rangers and Celtic, they might have become less traumatic affairs than they were. One witness said for years he had expected such an accident as the present one to happen. Indeed elation at victory or desperation in defeat, and there was no evidence as to which was the more common among Rangers supporters, it appeared on the evidence to have made little or no material difference to the behaviour of departing supporters. However this be interpreted, either elation with victory or despondency in defeat and desperation to flee the stricken field, they alike produced the uncivilised behaviour at the end of the game to which reference was so vividly and frequently made. It does certainly not put behaviour of the crowd on the day of this tragedy into any exceptional category.

On the pursuer's contention that the defenders should have early taken advice of a civil engineer, Mr Davidson's answer was 'To whom should they have gone, and what advice would they have received?' He described the expert evidence led for the pursuer, with his characteristic vigour and wealth of language, as 'showing a pattern of hesitation, contradiction and fundamental error'. I fear that I found none of these words concerning civil engineers to be acceptable. The emphatic answer was what had been recommended and carried out by the civil engineers, whom Rangers did consult, after the Fatal Accident Enquiry into the disaster.

They then instructed Messrs Fairhurst and Partners, consulting civil and structural engineers to examine all aspects of crowd control at Ibrox and to report and make recommendations to the defenders, who undertook to carry out the recommendations that were made. As a result of the survey and research carried out by that firm, they recommended the area of access to the head of the stairway should be restricted, thereby reducing the number of people who would gain access to the stair at one time. Effect was given to this by structural work planned and supervised by these engineers, which included a baffle wall and guide rails, the removal of the wooden fencing at either side of the stairway, and its replacement by tubular handrails. The alterations deemed necessary by Fairhurst and Partners were easily and readily effected, and one informed witness could not forebear to comment on their simplicity. They called for no revolutionary research or recently discovered principles, and involved no prohibitive or exorbitant expense, and at the proof it was proved that the alterations which had been built, were working successfully. Their object and effect in practice was to reduce the area of access to the head of the stair, thereby reducing the number of persons able to gain access to it. The effect of these alterations was to eliminate congestion and turbulence at the head of and on the stairway, and as a consequence, so also the pressure of spectators descending, or attempting to descend, the stairway. After these alterations were made, persons using the stairway had room to move, and in the event of anyone falling that person could be helped up or avoided. Mr Davidson's derision of the pursuer's contention that professional advice should have been taken was, in my view, wholly unjustified.

In his written claim Mr Cowie originally tabled nine specific grounds of fault on the part of Rangers. During the hearing he added another. In his final submissions, however, he made detailed submissions on only three grounds of fault, each of which, he claimed, justified the decree for the pursuer.

1. His first submission hereon was that even after the 1961 accident a reasonable man would have taken steps to find out why the accident occurred and have taken steps to

prevent a recurrence. After each accident the defenders did nothing relevant to the question of crowd control and, in particular, they did not obtain an expert's advice on the question of safety.

2. The pursuer's case, founded on most strongly by Mr Cowie, was that the defenders should have provided means for restricting access to the top of the stairway, thereby reducing overcrowding. This, in my view, was the crux of the case and, in my opinion, it was established conclusively. The circumstances of the three earlier accidents demonstrated that it was relentless pressure on the stairway that led to the accident pressure which could only arise and operate because access to the stairway was unrestricted. I did not accept Mr Davidson's criticism of this ground as lacking in specification, or that the state of expert knowledge in 1971 was such that failure to provide a restricted means of access could not be treated as a fault on the part of the defenders. In the course of the proof, no less than three different solutions were suggested. The first, namely, that of Fairhurst and Partners – as already noted – was at the date of the proof built and in successful operation. In addition, there was expert evidence that such a scheme as was followed here could and would have been devised by a consultant engineer years before 1969.

3. They failed after the 1969 accident, and in particular after the meeting in 1969, referred to, to replace the wooden fencing at the side of the stairway with handrails.

In the 1961 accident, the wooden fence broke because of pressure thereby allowing many to escape from the crowd: 'When the fencing broke people spilled over into the banking as a way of escape'; 'Bodies were seen lying on the grass embankment where the fence had broken'. In the 1969 accident, two spectators, who had climbed over the wooden fence, pulled out a number of fencing stobs, allowing persons to escape through the gap and, as a result, pressure at the site of the accident was relieved and persons were then able to escape by the embankment and further casualties prevented.

In the course of counsel's submissions on the evidence, each side referred to reported cases and judgments which they claimed supported their respective contentions. This is not the place to rehearse these. The decision turned on the overwhelming evidence produced by the pursuer on each of the Grounds of Fault on which Mr Cowie finally founded.

In the final judgment, the conclusion relating to liability was expressed in the sentence:

> Had the defenders taken one or more or all of the said precautions the stairway would have been reasonably safe and the accident to the deceased would have been avoided, or in any event, the risk of such an accident as occurred would have been materially reduced.

The pursuer's claim therefore was held established.

On the question of damages at the date of his death, the pursuer's husband was employed as a boilerman's helper at Babcock & Wilcox Operations Limited, at Renfrew, earning a net average weekly wage of £37.97. He contributed about £27.00 per week of this to the pursuer for the maintenance of himself, the pursuer and their two children. He had been a steady worker and, as a boilerman's helper, could have continued to earn wages which would have increased. As a result, Mrs Dougan was awarded damages of £23,000 for loss of support for herself and her children, and solatium, by which the law attempts to recognise the grief at the loss of a husband and father and the disruption of family life, of £2,000 for the pursuer and £750 for each of the children. Derisory as these figures seem now they were accepted as reasonable – on the value of money then – by the pursuer's advisers.

Neither side appealed this decision on the merits, or on the sums awarded to the pursuer as damages. The question of interest and expenses were decided later in the pursuer's favour.

Of the many sequels, to individuals and institutions, of this disaster and this case, there was one which was entirely personal to me and to mine which caused an unfortunate delay in the issue of the decision.

The dates here are significant. The accident was on 2 January 1971. The proof was in May 1974 and the judgment was not issued until 23 October 1974. It was a case where the hearing and the decision could not fail to be onerous and important, and of an interest to all concerned in the conduct of football crowds. The case finished on a Friday. The following Friday, I was speaking at the Kelvinside Academicals dinner when a sudden chest pain when I was on my feet, made it clear that all was not well. With difficulty I went to Bute the next Monday, taking with me all the materials needed to write the judgment, for which I had been given a week off to prepare. The case had been taken in the Sheriff Court, I underline, as against the Court of Session, in order to obtain an early decision. I had gone to Bute on my own but my condition was such that my wife and three children, aged fourteen, eleven and eight, had to join me. By the Sunday, the local doctor decided I had to be removed to the Western Infirmary in Glasgow. I was moved by ambulance, my wife and children followed in the car and in the ambulance outside Greenock Hospital, I took a coronary infarction which put me into the intensive care in the cardiac unit for six weeks. My most moving memory of this sorry occasion was as I lay on a stretcher on the pavement, with my wife at my side, I was looking up at my three children, all now gazing down on me from the front window of the car with wide eyes. I saw this, it registered with me, I shall never forget it, before I became unconscious. At that time I did not think I was likely to see them again. The experience was such that I was in no doubt my life was in danger. I was told later that cardiac damage was done but it was the physical experience as I lay on that pavement that I remember. It was the physical equivalent of the recurrent crescendos of sound, of the climaxes in the love duet in Wagner's *Tristan and Isolde*. Then came oblivion.

The decision then that was wanted urgently had to wait until the October. It occupied the later stages of my convalescence. Rangers did not appeal that decision, but this was a case in which more than the parties were, and apparently still are, interested. The general question in the case concerned the safety of spectators leaving a football ground. The ground in question, Ibrox, belonged to one of the great and most enthusiastically supported football clubs in Scotland. The press were not ungenerous in their reports of the evidence and their quotations from the lengthy judgment. I became aware, however, on many occasions, not only at the time the judgment was issued, but over the years since – there were occasions thirty and nearly forty years after the accident – that some Rangers supporters I met were dissatisfied with the result and expressed their disapproval of it to me. They apparently could not accept that Rangers could have been at any fault. In that situation I consider it is justifiable here not just to refer to the case but to offer an account of it which is based on my original judgment and its Findings in Fact.

I wrote it such that any of those who appear to think the decision was reached on prejudice or 'disloyalty', will, if interested, be able to read and to become aware of the evidence and reasons that made the decision to me, one that was inescapable.

# 19

# AFFILIATION AND ALIMENT

The combination of the contraceptive pill and the introduction of DNA testing in the 1970s and 1980s put an end to what had been a familiar form of action in Scottish Courts, that of Affiliation and Aliment. This was the action by which the unmarried mother of a child, sought from the court a finding, called a Declarator, that the defender was the father of the child, and should be ordered to pay a sum for inlying expenses and to pay aliment for the child until it reached the age of sixteen. The willingness and the enthusiasm the male defender found to be responsible had experienced at the conception of the child, had generally disappeared by the time he was called upon to pay aliment for his child's upbringing.

Despite the former discipline of Kirk Sessions and the condemnation of illegitimacy by the Presbyterian Kirk, the ordinary Scot had never been easily deterred from extramarital sexual relations. It was so common in the eighteenth and nineteenth centuries that to make the status of marriage easy of attainment where intercourse had taken place, and to legitimise children begat prior to any formal marriage, Scots Law developed the Law of Irregular Marriage which lasted until 1940. The introduction of the contraception pill in the 1970s took from sexual intercourse, when the woman was 'on the pill', the risk of conception for the first time in human history, and is blamed for the increase in premarital intercourse.

There were, however, always women who had not taken advantage of this or any other safety precaution, and who remained at risk. Illegitimate children continued to appear. The combination of the passion of the moment and amnesia of the precautions normally taken, still occurred, and in the 1980s, actions to determine the paternity of the resulting child continued to be brought, though their frequency was diminishing. The issue for the mother was to prove that the defender was the father. The practice of determination by the court of the defender's paternity, however, was superseded in the 1980s when DNA testing became common. With the pill and DNA testing the action of Affiliation and Aliment, therefore, became part of the History of Scots Law. In its day, however, it was an action the evidence of which could produce some interesting, not to say fascinating, facets of human nature. The most common defence, in my experience, to which a defender, averse to paternity (and even more averse to paying money for the fruits of the experience) resorted, was the allegation of the mother's boundless promiscuity. This would be spoken to not only by the defender himself but also by those of his friends who appeared willing to claim having had their share in the enjoyment of the mother's favours. In the evidence of each of those Lotharios – none of whom, to me at least, ever confessed to keeping a diary – was normally a careful awareness of the importance of the date that the lady's favours had been enjoyed. The possible date of conception was usually studiously avoided. Besides this line, the evidence could sometimes produce some unorthodox facts of the romance which the pursuer claimed had resulted in her pregnancy.

In the 1960s came the incidence of the pop concert which according to some of its enthusiasts could produce on occasions more than music. I recall an early court experience of this, where the girl had attended a concert at which the pop singer was called Screaming Lord Sutch. Now, I regret I had never heard of a pop singer called Screaming Lord Sutch and when I inadvertently – and stupidly as it turned out – asked one of the first witnesses, 'Who is Screaming Lord Sutch?' it produced in the serried ranks of the youth thronging the public benches, one half supporting the pursuer and the other half the defender, a reaction which I can only describe as traumatic. They simply could not believe that anyone alive in Scotland at that time had not heard of the artist in question. Thereupon it became clear from the gossip in the court

251

and the looks cast in my direction that, in their view, this man on the bench was clearly not a man who would understand what could go on at pop concerts. He might either be senile or so divorced from the ways of the world and its youth that he was physically, socially and morally so much out of touch with reality that he could not be relied on to hear this case. I may add that never again did I ever ask the identity of a pop singer with whom I was unfamiliar, which meant most of them. It is, I understand, part of the pattern of such 'pop' occasions that they rise to a climax. I have never been to one but the tales I have been told suggests that orgiastic climaxes are not unknown. Be that as it may, the pursuer, in this particular action of Affiliation and Aliment, in the course of this 'pop' performance changed her physical condition from what it had been when she gave up her ticket at the gate. Here again there were youths willing to give evidence in favour of the defender. According to them, as I recall the evidence, the girl in question had in the course of the concert managed to fit them all in, literally and metaphorically, to the music.

Sometimes the Affiliation and Aliment case revealed unexpected considerations of and for conditions of employment. In the 1980s an unmarried girl who had borne a child raised the traditional action. The boy and the girl were both in their teens. In the evidence he was quite frank about his amorous encounters with the mother, and described them in detail. Her evidence, that they had regularly had sexual intercourse on the floor in front of the fire in the girl's house while her mother was out, was unchallenged, as unchallenged also was the evidence that the hour of the mother's return being known, their activities were regulated accordingly. In his own evidence, the defender amplified the evidence of the amorous encounters by specifying that these were many and lengthy. He put himself forward as a passionate, and it seemed on the evidence, insatiable and highly potent lover. He admitted that the two of them had for weeks been having regular sexual intercourse in front of the mother's living room fire, except for an interregnum on the relevant month when the girl conceived, for which interregnum no satisfactory explanation however was ever given. These sessions must certainly have required from him not only time but also abundant enthusiasm and fitness. He claimed that on occasions he would in the time at their disposal have four or five orgasms, and all this with no precautions taken by either party. It might have been thought well-known to them, in this age of sex education in schools, that the inevitable result of all this would have been a child. The only result which he claimed had occurred had been for the efforts to make him so tired that it frequently affected his ability to do his job, as a shelf-stacker in a local supermarket, properly. Now it is accepted that these skills might not have been demanding but if the shelf-stacker was stacking shelves when he was half asleep, here was a situation fraught with domestic and, for his employers, commercial risks. An elderly customer, who had forgotten her glasses, would certainly be much upset if taking from the normal shelf what she thought was a packet of tea, discovered when she got home that she had in fact purchased a packet of oatmeal. The pursuer here was successful in her action.

Another such case I heard in Glasgow disclosed what appeared to be a hitherto unpublished facet of retail trading in the city. Here a woman of twenty-seven, alleging the defender was the father of her illegitimate son, sued him for a Declarator that he was the father and for yearly maintenance of the boy, in what must now appear as the wholly derisory sum, of £130 per year until he was sixteen. On the face of it the case seemed a normal unexceptional action of Affiliation and Aliment. As the evidence emerged, however, particularly the evidence of the defender, his brother and a friend, the case became a local sensation. That word is not used lightly. The West of Scotland press made of this case a field day, which on the evidence, was hardly surprising. I have in front of me page 7 of the *Daily Express* for 20 January 1972 which prints its report on the case under the banner headlines, 'THE MOBILE SEX SHOP OF POLLOK'. Then in smaller print: 'In debt so the housewives paid up in other ways' and justifies these claims in the opening paragraph of the report: 'Startling claims of sexual prowess were made in court by two mobile shop operators yesterday', and they claimed 'that frequent sex with customers who could not pay their bills was something mobile shop operators came to expect'. Thereafter, the newspapers reported in detail the evidence led before the court, which concentrated principally on the evidence on which the opening lines and paragraphs of the report I have quoted were founded.

The pursuer's evidence was straightforward but if it lacked the sensational, there was abundant compensation for this in the evidence of the defence. The defender admitted he had had intercourse with the lady in the mobile shop and other places, but alleged that four other men, as well as he, had had intercourse with the lady about the time of the conception. Two of these had gone to Canada and the court was denied the experience of seeing and hearing their version of this aspect of their lives. The defender's brother, however, claimed that he too had had intercourse with the pursuer in the mobile shop while another kept watch. A photograph of the bus was shown in the report. It was an ex-Glasgow Corporation double-decker bus whose abundant space on two levels would presumably allow for the carriage and display of varied stock, as well as room for other activities that might be conducted in it. Having described in some detail what the Victorians would have described as 'indiscretions', the witness advised me that he was a married man and 'apologised' for his sexual behaviour. I must confess to some surprise at the comment the report attributes to me at this confession and apology, which is, 'There is nothing to apologise for'. I hope there was some irony in my mind when I made that remark – irony in the sense that 'apology' was not the appropriate word, some might have thought 'repentance' might have been more appropriate. He ended his explanation, 'It is hard to be confronted with 500 women when there is always one who goes off the beaten track and I am just human'. The import of his evidence was in line with the *Express* headlines and when it was suggested that he had been indulging in a form of barter, his comment was, 'If I did not get it one way, I got it another way'.

254

It was the other defence witness, however, who took his evidence of sexual promiscuity into a class of its own. It was described by the pursuer's solicitor as 'prodigious sexual athleticism' – a not unreasonable comment it might be thought on a man who claimed to have had intercourse with 300 women in one year, picked up by chance. In the course of the debate, I made the comment that the witnesses' achievements herein were reminiscent of those of the Turkish Sultan, Suleiman the Magnificent – credited with considerable sexual powers and an appropriate harem in which to exercise them. If the evidence for the defender was true, encounters such as these must have presented unusual problems for the proprietors of mobile shops when it came to their system of account-keeping. This, however, was not investigated in any detail at the proof. The extraordinary thing about all this promiscuity was that none of the male participants would admit they had ever taken any of the conventional precautions to prevent conception and indeed were not even interested in doing so. One witness's comment at that suggestion was, 'I had a car and the cash and I was out for intercourse and I never used contraceptives. I never had time to go for them'. How in such circumstances that witness had, as at that date, never found himself a defender in an action of Affiliation and Aliment borders not just on luck, but particularly at that time, on the miraculous. The case in its result did three things: firstly, it found the defender to be the father of the pursuer's child – of whom I may add, from the photograph of the child produced he was the image – and liable to maintain him; secondly, it rejected the evidence of the defender and his witnesses of the pursuer's promiscuity; and, thirdly, it disclosed facets of the retail grocery trade that had not, as far as I am aware, previously been the subject of judicial, newspaper, or popular comment.

In the district in question, Priesthill and Pollok, the reaction was considerable. The minister of the local church, the Reverend James Currie, reacted immediately: 'The ladies of Pollok are highly moral ... I have never heard the like of it in all my years as a minister here. Promiscuous is the last thing anyone can call us here'. Others took the view that the husbands of the area would not only be asking questions but they would probably be out on the streets looking for mobile shops and those operating them. One witness, traced on the night the case ended, is described in the *Express* newspaper as 'crouched down … and hid from photographers'. The pursuer's comment was that there would be murder in the scheme once the defender's claims were known.

I am unaware if any murders did result or whether any mischief was done in and to mobile shops as a result of this case, or if their future trading profits were materially prejudiced. It certainly made plenty of talk, some stories, and, in one quarter, produced commemorative verse. The wags of the district had it that the local police were inundated with complaints, some from distressed and furious menfolk, who were looking out for 'Suleiman the Magnificent', but the police could not help them because they did not know a Suleiman the Magnificent in the Priesthill or Pollok areas. He was not on the list of wanted men and they had no idea of his address. The one piece of verse produced that came my way is too scurrilous for printing in full here. Its last verse however will give its flavour:

> And so to end this story
> The world admires a trier
> But to do 300 on his run
> The man's a bloody liar.

# 20

# THE AFTER-DINNER SET

An advocate who is busy has little or no time for extramural pursuits. Each night he has his written work and preparation for the next day. As a sheriff in Glasgow, busy as life was, the work did not monopolise every evening. I had been involved in seasonal and modest after-dinner speaking from the early 1950s. The Plough Hotel Burns dinner is an example, but from the mid-1960s I found myself increasingly involved in what was called 'the After-Dinner Set'. It was so described in detail by Jack Webster in a series of articles in the *Glasgow Herald*. He gave me membership of that 'set' and I may add, did me the characteristic courtesy of coming to interview me on the subject, before the article he wrote on me was published. It was a busy and interesting scene and a varied and interesting 'set' who were involved in it. It seemed as if in Glasgow – and it is true I think of all great cities – every association, sport, trade, industry, and charity had and have an annual dinner, and in the 1960s and '70s, unlike today, they expected the speakers they invited to instruct or entertain and, if possible to do both, and to do both gratuitously. In those days, few invited to speak at these dinners expected or asked for a fee, and few were the organisers who expected to pay one. There might, solely at the discretion of the hosts, be a gift in kind, a bottle of whisky or a gift token. However, for speakers in those days, after-dinner speaking was not normally regarded as a source of income. The old practice then was for an organiser to write or phone the speaker he wanted to invite, with no mention of any reward, and frequently with no mention even of expenses – and even if expenses were agreed there were occasions, when the dinner was over, when they were forgotten. It seemed, sometimes, that any sense of obligation to the speaker on the part of the organiser disappeared once the speech had been made. One chairman, after I had spoken for him, twice invited my wife and me to dine with him at a club. The first date he had to cancel, for the second we were never offered a date.

The rewards now in this field can be substantial. I am talking of hundreds and, on occasions, thousands of pounds. I know one speaker, much in demand, who when he gave up a responsible and well-paid occupation, devoted his whole time to after-dinner speaking and found no change in the standard of living he could afford. This is a field into which I have very rarely entered though I came to always ask for the expenses incurred.

The situation changed in the 1970s and '80s. Professional speakers or stage personalities had always had their agents, but now agents appeared for most speakers. The private invitation from the dinner organiser to the speaker he wanted declined, and the practice came to be – and I understand now is almost always the case – that the organising hosts will approach an agent (and there are many) with a request for a speaker. The agent will then enquire of the speakers for whom he acts, whose interests and talents are appropriate for the proposed dinner, if they are willing to act, and they then decide on the fee required, which usually includes the agent's percentage. Thereafter, the agent submits his list of potential speakers to the dinner organisers who can then select the speaker they want. I have never had a regular agent and have only spoken at an agent's insti-gation on a very few occasions.

Though I spoke at dinners from the early 1950s, so far as making a start on the Glasgow dinner scene is concerned, I owe it to the late Lord Wallace. In the 1960s, the Glasgow dinner year really commenced, as it still does, with the dinner of the Deacon Convener of the Trades House in October, which was and is followed by the individual dinners of each of the fourteen incorporated trades – a tradition that goes back to the Middle Ages. The Deacon Convener's Dinner was and is regarded as *the* dinner in Glasgow. It was hosted by the newly elected Deacon Convener, and to it everyone of status and importance in Glasgow, if not Scotland, was and is invited. I remember at one of these dinners I sat between the Moderator of the General Assembly of the Church of Scotland and the Lord Provost of Glasgow. These Trades House dinners were held in the Banqueting Hall of the Trades House in Glasgow, which in those days was one of the most congenial and acoustically sympathetic locations for speaking in Glasgow. The Trades House is now a charitable, as well as a historical institution. Its members represent the business, trade and professional life of the city. I had the privilege of speaking at most of the craft dinners in the 1960s and '70s, and if their members accepted a speaker, he could find himself launched in Glasgow. Lord Wallace was the Deacon of the Gardeners in 1966. His dinner speakers were Lord Kissen, a Lord of Session, Herr Sichel of the German wine house, and replying for the guests, myself. That dinner was a success and after it I had many dinner invitations to speak at dinners in Glasgow and the west of Scotland, and later further afield. They became a very important part of my life. The hosts of these Scottish dinners represented the social and business life of the area. In 1971, to take but one example, I spoke at twenty-four dinners from the autumn to the spring, ranging from the Scottish Motor Trade, the High Constables of Edinburgh, the Furniture Trade Benevolent Fund and the British Pharmaceutical Conference. January was always the season of Burns suppers. One year I proposed fifteen Immortal Memories. This I may say was nothing to what was accomplished by the late Reverend James Currie. One year he told me that he had proposed the Immortal Memories at thirty-three Burns Suppers, a record made possible by presenting two or three Immortal Memories a night at different locations, one say at 8 p.m., one at 9.30 p.m. and another at 10.30 p.m. The average size of most Burns suppers I spoke at would be from 50–300, but some went up to 700, and the Lord Provost of Glasgow's Burns dinner, when I last spoke there in 1997, had a company of about 1,000. The West Sound Burns supper in 1989 had about the same.

The annual Burns celebrations, with those of St Andrew,

eventually took me to many places in the United Kingdom and abroad. I would never otherwise have spoken in Edmonton, Halifax, Winnipeg and Calgary in Canada, New York in the USA, Oman in the Persian Gulf, Bahrain in the Middle East, and Singapore in the Far East. It was at these dinners I learned the thrill of being one of a top table piped into a gathering, usually all male, all there to celebrate their Scots origins, and sometimes not just by a piper but by a full pipe band, as in Canada and Singapore.

In 1974, when I had the severe heart attack, my after-dinner speaking stopped for about twelve months, but I was fortunate enough then to be able to return to this familiar and much loved scene by late in 1975.

In my experience, the Scots at home and abroad celebrate only two national figures: their patron saint, St Andrew, and their poet, Robert Burns. The former, in my experience, is celebrated more abroad than at home. The latter is celebrated at home with such an all-embracing enthusiasm and intensity which, contrary to what is customary in such enthusiasms, continues to grow with the years.

Of these annual Burns and St Andrew's dinners, I never tired. They have given me among the greatest experiences of my life, and I have been privileged to participate in these annual celebrations for nearly seventy years, first as a performer – boy and youth – reciting 'Tam O'Shanter' and Scots verse, and later as a speaker, and with them all, for my part, I have never grown weary. They have given me memories which are among my most cherished, and the details of some of them still are fresh in my memory.

That said, it is not just the grand occasions that bring the memories, especially where Robert Burns is concerned. I have had the good fortune to have had these from many quarters. Indeed the settings have covered the whole ambit of eating places, from private houses, all sizes of hostelries, to the Great Room at Grosvenor House in Park Lane, London, which can take about 1,200 diners.

One of the oldest and most famous of Burns suppers is that held in the Burns Howff at Dumfries, where Burns himself used

260

to drink and where the speaker is given the opportunity of sleeping in the bed Burns occupied. I was there one very cold January, when the pipes had burst in the hostelry in question and Burns' bedroom, with his bed, had not quite recovered from the inundation. I wanted, however, to be able to say that I had lain on the same bed as Robert Burns and I lay symbolically on the damp bed for a few minutes. I could understand having done so, why Burns would have welcomed company there, because neither room nor bed were, at least on that occasion, warm. That night I was accommodated in more conventional accommodation.

Perhaps the most unusual venue was a Burns supper held on the ship, *The Galloway Princess,* in 1985, on a voyage from Stranraer to Larne and back, starting about 7.30 p.m. and returning to Stranraer about 2 or 3 a.m. the next morning. This was done in the depths of a Scottish January. The voyage and the dinner were televised for Border Television who gave all who were speaking time limits. which they – Border Television – varied as the dinner progressed, demanding much editing of notes by the speakers, but which at the end produced, as I recall, only half an hour of television screening. The fear that haunted us all, TV team, Chairman, speakers, artists and audience was that the crossing would encounter the traditional Scottish January weather. However, these were unfounded. We had calm seas and a prosperous voyage there and back.

I experienced one of the most memorable and moving of Burns nights – moving in its occasion, its conduct and above all in its conclusion – at the Central Hotel in Glasgow, in 1972, at the centenary dinner of the Haggis Club of Glasgow. It was a truly great occasion. Its conduct was all that was to be expected from a body who took their Burns seriously, who believed that it should be celebrated with impeccable and memorable hospitality and dignity, and with truly splendid singing. The Haggis Club knew where to find its singers, and its singers knew what was due to the Haggis Club. The company sat down at 6 p.m. on a Saturday evening. The meal, the speeches, the music, the poetry continued until about

11.50 p.m. At that point it was noted that we had not had the song 'A Fond Kiss', and the company demanded that it be sung, and sung it was. It was sung about midnight when the dinner was meant to have concluded. When the applause for that song ended, following what was obviously a tradition – a ritual – of the club, for which most of the company needed no instruction (but which to strangers like my wife and me was unprecedented) – the whole company left their chairs and stood round the walls of the dining room. The top table joined them. The Chairman named five men by their first names, some of them advanced in years, who were each allocated to sing one of the five verses of 'Auld Lang Syne': 'Peter, verse 1', 'Andrew, verse 2', and so on. When I saw this done I did not appreciate just how overwhelming the effect of it all was to be. For some of these men their voices were a shadow of what they once had been. For one or two, to sing their verse was an effort. Some were uncertain, not of the words of their verse, but if they had breath to sing it. The piano introduced the familiar tune and the first man sang the first verse, after which the whole company joined in singing the moving and universally known chorus. This happened with all five verses. Each verse and its chorus were sung as they should be, slowly and with dignity. There was no rushing at the last chorus. This was the most moving singing of 'Auld Lang Syne' I have ever not just heard, but experienced. At the end many, including myself, were in tears. Everyone including the hotel staff had forgotten that midnight had come and gone.

My wife, Diana, who is from Yorkshire, was the only one I knew who had any complaints about the dinner. Our car was parked in Central Station. About 12.30 a.m. we went to it. Since Diana was driving she had not had a drop of alcohol during the whole evening. She was probably the only member of that company to have been so deprived. Her comment when we reached the car was, 'Well, I have not had a drink all night, but I can tell you I have had enough of you and your countrymen to last me for a very long time'. This was not said in anger and was forgotten by the next morning in her reminiscences of the memorable evening.

Another night to remember was a Burn's supper held in Lord Montague of Beaulieu's Motor Museum in the New Forest. The hosts were an insurance company entertaining English clients and they certainly entertained them in style. They had Professor Robert Jack of Glasgow University to toast the lasses, and Molly Weir replying. She had been a well-known radio personality who regularly appeared on the *Beeb Daniel's and Ben Lyon's Show*. She got to that dinner late but was unflappable, and gave her admirable speech from her notes which were written on old Christmas cards. It was, after all, January, and she was quite frank with that audience that she was using old Christmas cards. I was proposing the Immortal Memory. The soloist was Moira Anderson, one of the great Scottish singers. That night she did me a great compliment. She sang the 'Star of Robbie Burns', which has and needs a rousing chorus. That English audience did not know either the chorus or the tune. I was certainly very familiar with both and sang with all the lustiness I could muster. Moira came down to me in the middle of the first chorus, got me to my feet and shared her microphone with me, and for the remainder of the song I sang each chorus with her. That is the only occasion I have ever sung with a real diva.

The Burns dinners in Canada, to me at least, demonstrated that the Scot remains a Scot, regardless of where he is or how he is governed. My first experience of this was in Edmonton in 1984. There a company of 700 men assembled. Of that 700, I was the only one there not wearing tartan, I was wearing a black dinner jacket. All the rest were either in kilts or in tartan tuxedos. Some were Scots who had emigrated to Canada just after the war in 1945, others were second- or third-generation Scots Canadians. They knew the Scots songs, they knew the tunes and they knew the traditions. (The same applies to the Scots I met in Halifax and New York on similar occasions).

The top table entered that crowded hall, not to a piper but to the city of Edmonton Police Pipe Band. It was my first experience of marching behind a pipe band and I confess 'my hair stirred as life were in it'.

And like the Scot at home, the Scot abroad retains his interest in, and where appropriate, concern for the doings of his brother Scots abroad. In 1996, I had an invitation to propose the immortal memory in New York on the Friday evening, and in Halifax, Nova Scotia, on the Saturday. This involved my flying from New York to Halifax on the Saturday. On the Thursday and Friday there was snow in New York and there was concern that the flight from New York to Halifax might be cancelled. As it turned out it did fly and I got to Nova Scotia in time for the Burns supper. The next day my journey home involved a flight from Halifax to Toronto, and from Toronto to London. No one spoke to me in Toronto Airport until we were boarding and one man in the queue behind me came forward. I knew his face although I could not place him. His opening to me was, 'Did you manage to get through to Halifax from New York?' His familiarity with my itinerary surprised me and I asked him how he knew I had been to New York and Nova Scotia, and that there had been a possible problem with the flight? His reply was that he had been proposing the Immortal Memory at the Edmonton Burns dinner on the Saturday night and they had been aware that I was speaking in Halifax and that there had been a problem with snow in New York, and were concerned that I might not get to Halifax, and that the dinner might be looking for a speaker at the last minute. I was not sitting with him on the plane and thereby lost the opportunity of making enquiries of the Edmonton club's knowledge of who the other Scots might be who were visiting Canada that year in the name of Robert Burns, because I am quite certain they would have known.

On this Burns and dinner scene, discretion as well as inspiration is sometimes required. In Glasgow, there was a dearth of hotels capable of catering for large numbers until the Albany Hotel opened in 1973. It could sit 700 and I spoke at the first public dinner held there, another Burns supper held by the licensed trade of Glasgow. It was not long, however, before most of the international hotel groups had hotels in Glasgow with seating capacity even greater than the Albany.

This new hotel capacity attracted national and international conferences of all manner of professions and institutions, and since they were in Scotland, it became the fashion to serve a haggis as one of the dinner courses, whatever the subject of the conference may have been. On these occasions, the haggis was regularly served as a dinner course. The principal haggis, the haggis that had to be piped in, was usually much larger than is the conventional haggis; indeed the haggis usually piped in bore no relation to the sheep's stomach with which the dish was originally connected. Since the audience only saw the principal haggis, there was no necessity for the principal haggis to be edible. At one prestigious international medical dinner the haggis was to be piped in but the organisers were, not surprisingly, unaware of the Scots tradition of having the haggis, once it had processed through the dining room, addressed by Burns' poem 'To a Haggis'. To those Scots with a liking for the dish, there is a view that no haggis tastes as it should unless it has been addressed by Burns' address to it. This information was new to the Chairman and when I asked if he wanted me to address the haggis, he accepted. Few of that company would understand the language of Burns' address but the Scots there were telling them it was a Scottish tradition. I joined the procession that included the chef when the large principal processional haggis was brought in. No address to the haggis had been planned and by the chef and the hotel staff none was expected. I thought I noted a look of concern on some of their faces but thought no more of it. In that poem there is a verse which begins 'His knife see rustic labour dight and cut you up with ready sleight'. The speaker at this point is brandishing a knife or a dirk and with these words he plunges it into the haggis. The next line is 'Trenching your gushing entrails bright'. I fear, however, on this occasion there was no trenching possible or desirable because the processional haggis appeared to me to be stuffed with something which had the consistency of cotton wool. The discretion necessary was to complete the poem with no further attempts to explore or display the constituents of that processional haggis.

For me one of the most polished and memorable of Burns suppers was the Supper in 1989 organised by the radio company, West Sound. The audience numbered about 1,000, many of whom had travelled a long way to the Thistle Hotel in Glasgow, to attend what even then was already recognised as a prestigious Burns supper. It was organised and directed by Mr Joe Campbell who is an enthusiastic Burnsian, with a vast experience of organising this celebration. There were no concessions to sensationalism, vulgarity or novelty. It was a night when all the traditions of such occasions were observed with dignity and decorum. The Immortal Memory was my responsibility, but I was followed by speakers with national, indeed international, reputations: Cliff Mitchelmore, in his day a radio and television icon and his wife, Jean Metcalfe, in her day the Forces' favourite on the radio, dealt respectively with the Toast and Reply to the Lassies. The music came from internationally known Scottish professional musicians, none of whom stinted in either the quality or quantity of what they offered that audience. Ian Powrie, a fiddler in the tradition of Neil Gow and Scott Skinner, demonstrated not only his skill but the beauty and variety of the fiddle music of Scotland, and gave us time to relish it. The piper was Iain MacFadyen, who won World Champion four times during his career, and his contribution on this night was not confined to playing in the top table and the haggis. We heard piping that demonstrated why he had been World Champion. Isobel Buchanan, who had sung opera with Joan Sutherland, gave her splendid voice to sing the songs of Burns. The last speaker was Edward Heath, sometime Prime Minister, who I recall got to his feet at about 11.45 p.m. and spoke to an audience who welcomed him, wanted to hear him and showed none of the restlessness that an audience might have been expected to show at that hour when he spoke. He spoke without a note. He spoke eloquently on Burns and Scotland and, when he concluded, he was given a standing ovation. We concluded the evening singing the traditional 'Auld Lang Syne' and I felt then, as I have felt on reflection since, that that night had been a civilised,

coherent and entirely relevant occasion in which I had been privileged to participate.

The proceedings were broadcast and shortly after it I was sent
cassettes of the whole evening. There, as far as I was concerned,
the matter ended until about 1995 when I received a phone call
from New York asking me to speak at a Burns supper there. I was
interested to know how the caller had found my name and my
phone number, so I asked him. His answer was 'I have got your
CD'. This was news to me because I did not know that I had a
CD, and said so. His reply was 'I bought it from Burns Cottage
in Alloway'.

I now have a copy of that CD. It is, I am told, one of a set of
three CDs, all containing excerpts from the annual West Sound
Burns supper. I have never profited by such a CD, and that matter
is not one I am concerned with. The copyright is with West Sound.
It is, however, my privilege and thrill to know that some people
have liked it, and it was certainly responsible for taking me to
many places at home and abroad to commemorate the same theme
again.

I quote below one wholly unexpected and all too kind letter on
this CD. It comes from an address in Bexley Heath, Kent, and is
dated 9 September 2002.

Dear Sir,

I trust that the person reading this is the same J. Irvine
Smith who proposed the immortal memory at the Burns
supper, now recorded on a CD.

I am writing, Sir, to express my sincere thanks to you for
your humorous, evocative and heart-rending presentation.

As a Glaswegian, but regrettably an exile, living in London
since 1959, it was all the more meaningful to me. My mode of
transport was not a boat from the port of Leith but a great
locomotive from the Central Station in Glasgow.

The words you imparted in memory of the great man are
now being listened to by a great number of people, indeed

who may never have read a word of his verse but who have had their appetite whetted. We are, as you said, a little people but we are great people and I say that without any degree of trumpetism for it is what I feel. Just last week, I was asked why I was so obviously so proud of being a Scot to which I replied, 'If you have to ask the question, you wouldn't understand my answer'.

Sir, on behalf of my many friends, Scots and English, please accept our heartfelt thanks for your words of inspiration and great good humour.

Yours sincerely

John Black.

Perhaps the most spectacular and unforgettable celebration of Saint Andrew from its start to its finish that my wife and I have ever encountered was in Singapore, in 1995, as the guest of the Caledonian Society there. Those Scots took their patriotic responsibilities very seriously indeed. For the Saturday when the celebration was to take place they organised a dinner dance in one of Singapore's largest and most prestigious hotels. The night before the function, the committee and its helpers spent the whole evening preparing and decorating the banqueting suite for dining and dancing. It was a vast area which accommodated a company of about 500 at round tables for dinner, and had as much floor space left for a full pipe band to form up and play, as well as for the company to dance. The serving staff were mostly young Singaporeans of fourteen or fifteen years of age and in case they poured red wine into the white wine glass, each white wine glass had a quarter of an inch of white wine in it when we sat down to dinner. There was to be no wine served in the wrong glass and none was. For the reception and formal part of the evening the Pipes and Drums of the Brigade of Ghurkhas provided the music. For the dancing a country dance band had been flown from Scotland. They had become regulars of that particular dinner, and regulars also a night or so later at the Saint Andrew's night in

Kuala Lumpur. The top table was a long one and when it had been assembled in couples to the playing of the pipes, it processed into the dining room, still to the Pipes and Drums, and beneath an arch of claymores held aloft by kilted men. The Pipes and Drums played throughout the meal and when the speeches were concluded the Scottish dance band took over and the whole company embarked on a night of Scottish country dances, all of which, whatever their technicalities and formalities, seemed to be second nature to all of that company. They had indeed, I was told, spent the winter practising the dances for the occasion. Their enthusiasm never flagged. They danced the night through until a breakfast of kippers was served at 6 a.m.

Having danced all night they could not choose but be tired, however, on the Sunday a goodly party of them, including my wife and myself, were able to assemble at the harbour to board a large Chinese junk which had been hired for the holding of a Scottish Ceilidh as she sailed for three or four hours round Singapore's large harbour. The Scottish dance band on the open deck again played for the dancing and accompanied those of us who were persuaded to sing Scottish songs. For me, the oppor-tunity of being able to say I had sung solo 'Oh gin I were a Baron's heir' and Stevenson's words, 'Sing me a song of a lad that is gone', to the tune of 'Over the sea to Skye', on the main deck of a Chinese junk, on a Sunday going round the harbour of Singapore was too great to be resisted. Whether I sang well or not is not for me to say, but I can say I relished the experience. There was also on board a small pipe band – about eight in all – whose Pipe Major was a mother with two or three of her teenage children among the players. They were all Singaporeans but they knew how to play the pipes and drums and they knew how to enjoy a Scots ceilidh. It will be appreciated that by the time this junk returned to its berth it was a somewhat exhausted company that disem-barked and brought that year's Saint Andrew's Festival in Singapore to an end. It had been another memorable occasion.

The traditional Scottish way of starting a formal dinner was and is to have a piper or, on great occasions, have Pipes and Drums to lead in the top table. The occasion however can, though rarely, suggest appropriate alternatives. The Tri-centenary Dinner of the Old Weavers of Paisley was one such occasion. Its opening indeed comprised a variety of incidents.

In the period from the mid eighteenth century to about the 1830s, Paisley was 'The town of the Weavers'. The shuttle of their looms was heard everywhere in the streets and it became the leading town in the country for linens, silks and cottons. The Paisley Shawl was for fifty years an essential wedding present for a Scottish bride. These weavers were an industrious, prosperous and radically minded people, and, if matters of common interest were to be discussed at a public meeting the populace was summoned to that meeting by tuck of drum; the town drummer going round the town beating the summons on the town's drum. It became a common sound when the introduction of machines for weaving cloth was introduced and the whole weaving fraternity had to debate what steps it could take to defend its livelihood. In October 1702, the local council gave the Weavers a charter and contract to regulate their doings and, in October 2002, the tricentenary of that charter was celebrated by a public dinner in Paisley Town Hall, at which it seemed every element in the community – government, industry, business, professions, commerce, kirk and university – were represented.

The pre-dinner drink was sherry but it is a strange tradition of the Old Weavers of Paisley that this should be drunk in numerous minute quantities. This they ensured by serving the sherry that evening in minute containers about the size and capacity of a dressmaker's thimble. Their size disqualified them from being called 'glasses'. Seeking explanation for the minute containers, I was advised that drinking sherry from these containers was a firm tradition at all Old Weavers functions. I confess when I went in and saw some of the company drinking an amber-coloured liquid out of minute containers and more of them standing around with empty minute containers held delicately in their fingers, it looked as if we were having not sherry but Drambuie as an aperitif. I was naturally concerned that if this dinner was being started with Drambuie, what were we going to be drinking when we got down to the more serious business of the evening, and what were we all going to be like after it? One sip of the liquid however for me did three things: it emptied its container; it convinced me we were in fact drinking sherry; and if the appetite of this company required stimulation from sherry it would need at least twenty refills of these minute glasses to produce any noticeable reaction from the consumer.

These special glasses had not been designed for sherry. I do not know nor can I guess for what liquor they had been designed. The assembled company, however, appeared to be animated. There was much movement in the hall, which I soon found was not the company moving but the large squad of waiters who were running about the hall like Olympic runners, in futile and unending efforts to keep all the rapidly emptied containers filled with sherry. As waiters they had never had to work so hard in their lives.

The next surprise of the evening occurred at about this point. We were all advised by the ringing of bells and the arrival of Paisley Fire Brigade that somebody was thought to have set fire to the Town Hall, in which we were all assembled for the dinner. At this the service of sherry stopped. The waiters went for a much needed rest. Relief was expressed that we were drinking sherry and not Drambuie which, I was advised, has a reputation for greater combustibility than sherry. We were then all put outside the Town Hall where heavy rain and a gale-force wind contended for our misery. Eventually, wet and much buffeted, we were allowed back into the hall in a condition when any enthusiasm for sherry in miniscule containers which was again on offer would have been willingly exchanged for Drambuie or whisky, in conventional sherry glasses if not in pint tumblers.

After the Fire Brigade was satisfied that there had been a false alarm, the main body made their way to the dining room, which was the town hall itself, leaving the members of the top table in

271

the foyer where they were introduced to the current Paisley Town Drum, which it had been decided was to lead in the top table, not by piper, but by tuck of that drum. The old town drum, I was told, was now in a museum but a duplicate – mark two – was to be used. It was a very large drum. I would think it would be about five feet in diameter, and certainly when the drummer strapped it on you could only really see him from the side or from behind, and there was concern about how he would see his way forward. We formed up behind him in the entrance hall for what turned out was to be a unique experience. We were to march from there down the main hall between tables, and then up a short stair on to the stage where the top table was to sit. My memory of that drum is that it produced two notes – one side I will call tenor and the other bass. They were played alternatively at slow marching pace – boom, bong, boom, bong – and at slow marching pace the top table went down the hall to the notes of that drum, through that silent, apparently stunned, standing company. Its sound and rhythm were hypnotic, its effect was frankly menacing. I realised then where Berlioz could have had his inspiration for his march to the scaffold in his *Fantastic Symphony.* A Frenchman would have seen public executions in France of which the drum was a part. The longer this repeated drumming went on the more we all came to realise why drums had been part of mankind's equipment for solemn occasions, particularly public executions, from the earliest, and the effect of it on the marching top table by this time was that all of them had apparently lost the power of speech, and were incapable of asking to be excused taking part further in this dinner, which I have no doubt some of us, including myself, felt. We had also lost our sense of time and place and were concerned that we were not at the Weavers' dinner but going to the first public execution that had been held in Paisley since the nineteenth century. That drum appeared to take upon itself a personality of its own. As we progressed slowly down that hall the reaction of the assembled company standing to receive us suggested that this was also their view. Dr Johnson's comment, I have quoted it before, was 'that the knowledge of a man that he is to be executed wonderfully concentrates the mind'. From my experience of that night I can say that to march solemnly to tuck of drum produces a like effect. I now knew what it felt like to attend a public execution where the drum was an invariable part of the procedure. This was a feeling acutely accentuated when we came to mount the steps to the platform where the top table was situated. The drum beat on remorselessly as we mounted these steps, and at one point I remembered Sidney Carton's similar experience and his saying that, 'It is a far, far better thing that I do, than I have ever done: it is a far, far better rest that I go to than I have ever known'. I can honestly say that in my history of eating and drinking I have never reached a well-set top table that I welcomed so warmly as I did the top table on the platform that night. It was only when we reached it that the drum stopped and life again returned to normal.

I have never attended a dinner so ominously and unconventionally commenced, but so successfully and joyfully continued and concluded.

In my later years, I was involved with another facet of speaking. Nineteenth-century Glasgow was a city of clubs so numerous, and with objects and interests so varied, that they justified John Strang (d. 1863) producing a famous book entitled *Glasgow and its Clubs*. Few of them survived the generation of their founders but one, known as 'The Nomads', founded in 1895, continues into the twenty-first century in robust health. It is a remarkable institution. At its beginning, its interests were musical, literary and debating. They are now wholly literary and oral. Its meetings do not depend on dining and wining for their popularity with members: this only happens twice a year at their New Year informal dinner (where the entertainment is wholly in-house) and their annual dinner. The regular fortnightly meetings depend on the willingness of three members to apply their minds to preparing, writing and delivering an address on a subject allocated to them by the club.

Today, the year's syllabus for each meeting normally sets out three topics under a list of keywords, with the names of the three members to whom each subject is allocated. Two examples of subjects from a recent syllabus are:-

**Table Talk**
  Round Table
  Turn Tables
  Table Mountain

**The Road**
  ... to Damascus
  ... to Mandalay
  ... to Perdition

But their annals, however, contain many papers by members, offering authoritative and immaculately written accounts of personalities and events, on contemporary local and national themes.

Membership of The Nomads demands an original composition, the reading of it to the club and a readiness to participate in the discussion that follows with the assembled members and a chairman. You do not become a Nomad to relax: rather for stimulation. Early shades of the schoolroom's compulsory essay have no place here.

My association with The Nomads started in 1999, with a phone call from the late James Campbell, a much respected Glasgow solicitor who was the club's incoming president, and whose first function was to find a new Honorary President in the retiral of Lord Weir from that office. He wished to nominate me for the vacancy. In the course of its existence this club had attracted many distinguished men as its Honorary Presidents. From 1955 to 1973, it had the late Sir Compton McKenzie. Later, it had the principals of two universities and, in Lord Weir, a High Court judge. This was a league into which I did not consider I had the qualifications or status to enter, and I told James so. He was, however, very persuasive and persistent and with some misgivings I accepted. It was a decision I certainly never regretted.

The duties of Honorary President are not onerous. His duty is to speak at the annual dinner and to produce a seconder for the same occasion. I had spoken at one of the dinners in the mid-1970s and I knew what the club had long expected from its speakers – as they expected from themselves; not anecdotes of crude humour but material that was original, and to which the speaker had given thought and a title, and in which some original humour was expected.

I did this duty for four annual dinners. For the first year, I was feeling my way but it taught me, I think, that from their Honorary President, the club expected an emphasis on original matter, but laced with some original humour. For the remaining three dinners, much time was spent writing new material, which I think was found acceptable, as was the reception given to the speeches each year of my seconders – of whom my son was one. I always regarded the preparation for speaking at these annual dinners as a challenge, to try and meet the standards on such matters set by that club.

It is not for me to say whether that object was attained but when, after four years, I intimated that I wished to retire, the club did me the honour of making me their second life member who continues to receive notice of all the activities of the club. I count it a privilege to have been, and still to be, one of them.

Earnest of my enthusiasm for after-dinner speaking is the fact that I have kept the menus of all the dinners I have ever spoken at. They occupy six very substantial files. In the late 1990s however the number began to decline. I was becoming old and chairmen arranging dinners, which to them are understandably always important occasions, do not want to take the risk of their speaker inconsiderately departing this life before the dinner at which he has agreed to speak. Some organisers indeed can be very blunt about this. Some five years ago, I was approached at the Burns Federation supper by the secretary of a Burns club in Fife and asked if I would return there, where I had spoken about twenty years before. When I agreed he said, 'We don't want you next year but would like you the year after'. I said, 'All being well, I am happy to come, but I should tell you my age', which I did – seventy-nine. His immediate comment was, 'Oh well, we will just leave it then.' So the invitation was never pursued. This attitude lends point to the late James Langmuir's advice to me in the 1960s, advising me, as he put it, to 'go easy' on the after-dinner scene – and he spoke from experience. His advice was:

If you are the speaker and you drop down dead after you have spoken, nobody will be very concerned, but if you drop down dead before you have spoken it will cause the Chairman and his committee untold trouble, and you'll never be asked back.

# 21

# THE DINNER SCENE

The environment of the after-dinner set is the varied and unpredictable 'dinner scene' of which I have been privileged to have had experience for some sixty years. It has been an experience of hearing and seeing the approaches and techniques of many speakers and of the psychology of many audiences. It has given also the opportunity of appreciating, if not always in practice avoiding, the risks that are inherent in undertaking such activities.

Many speakers I have heard were and are brilliant raconteurs. The late Reverend James Currie was one of them, who could successfully make a series of anecdotes the substance of his speech. If the speaker, however, is asked to propose a toast on a subject – an industry, a charity, a school, a sport – many would say there must be some reference to the subject and, if possible, at least some stories that have some connection with it. The most difficult and memorable after-dinner speech of all, in my view, to prepare and deliver is one where few or no stories are told but there is an abundance of humour drawn from the personalities, activities and objects of the subject of the toast. The most original, relevant and amusing speaker with this approach that I ever heard was the late Arthur Stepney. He had all these qualities. He was a highly articulate Englishman, an actuary by profession practising in Edinburgh. I met him when he was proposing the toast of the Insurance and Actuarial Society of Glasgow at their Annual Dinner in 1971. I was replying for the guests. He spoke first and I last, and I accordingly had the opportunity and time to appreciate the skill and originality of the speech he made, which not only impressed itself upon me, it alarmed me. He was entirely relevant, amusing and fascinating. He spoke for twenty-five minutes and everything he said was original, witty and concerned personalities and doings of the Society which was the subject of his toast. His opening was characteristic of all that followed. It was in these terms: 'The Insurance and Actuarial Society of Glasgow was founded in 1881 (pause) and accordingly (pause) it would be ninety years of age if it were still alive today'. He continued in this vein on the doings of personalities of the Insurance Society in Glasgow. As he spoke I saw and heard the enthusiasm with which he was received, and had increasing misgivings of my own abilities to maintain this atmosphere. I must however have had some success because both of us received standing ovations and he anticipated my personal congratulations to him, by his to me. We hit it off and thereafter he and I spoke at many dinners in Glasgow and Edinburgh. I recommended him to a number of chairmen who were seeking a speaker, and none were ever disappointed. He made it a rule, he told me, to speak at only four dinners a winter and for each minute he was on his feet he spent an hour's preparation. As an example of his thorough preparation, when I suggested him as a speaker to the Iron & Steel Trade, he had them send him their magazine, their literature, their history, had them meet him and had them show him round a steelworks, which we still had in those days in Scotland.

Few speakers have the temperament, patience and determination, or the time, to follow such a regime of speech preparation, especially if they are frequently asked to speak. For most of us, the speech is a compromise between humour and the subject of the toast, the humour often borrowed or repeated. On the subject of the toast, an audience expects, in my experience, to hear something but not too much. I have heard a speaker go on for forty-five minutes on the history of his company, with not one morsel of light relief. He would not stop and appeared impervious to either the restlessness or boredom of most of his audience. The temptation, in my experience, when one writes something original, which is hoped will produce laughter and does, is that its author and owner tends to use it everywhere and too much. I was certainly guilty of this with one opening I wrote, which I used again and again, until even I grew tired of it. The temptation to be a raconteur mainly, or only, invites acceptance. It is easy, and in this field timing can be adjusted by dropping or adding to the number of anecdotes. The conventional twenty-five minutes for a speech are not difficult to fill, especially if the speaker gets laughter.

When I have prepared a speech, fully written parts of it or listed headlines, I have never tried to time what had been written or compiled. My practice, almost from the start of such speaking is, before I get to my feet, to write in large figures on a place card or on the menu, the time I am instructed to sit down and place it well in front of me where I can see it readily throughout what I have to say. With this time limit clear I try on my feet to edit my notes to enable me to meet it. The editing does not always work or does not always work well, and it may be that one stops a few minutes before, or a few minutes after the time limit, but in either case the approximate time limit has been obeyed.

What can intensify the editing on one's speech is the presence or absence of laughter. If you get the laughter you hope for, this makes the timing of what is to follow the more unpredictable. I found that for me the safest way to accommodate this situation is to have each part of the proposed speech in a section of its own, the pages of each separate section held together by a paper clip. When the speech is assembled for delivery each bundle is put in its order in the file. When on your feet if you are going to use a section, you remove the paper clip holding the pages and use that section as required. If you decide you have insufficient time to use another section that whole section and others can be lifted out and laid aside.

Some speakers I know believe in using cards with individual names, stories, subjects on each card. Depending on the hospitality of the evening this can carry risks. At one Burns club supper, some thirty years ago, I was replying for the guests whom one of the club members had the duty of toasting. He believed in the

279

postcard system and had a card with notes on it for each of the guests. Unfortunately, as he went through the bundle of his cards, when he finished with one card he moved it face up to the bottom of the bundle of the other cards he was holding. He got through all the guests – and there were many of them at that dinner – with a full set of cards in his hand and in order, just as he had when he started. At this point, either through nervousness or the effects of the club's undoubtedly high standard of hospitality, he started reading the first card again and, for a second time, went through the whole bundle of cards individually, again placing each card face up after use, at the bottom of the pile he was holding. In the course of this exercise, his audience was not slow to find in it some amusement and to make apposite comment, and when, as he did, he started to read the first card again, preparatory to reading the bundle of cards for a third time there was clear evidence that the company did not think this was necessary, and at this point he was persuaded that the toast should be finally proposed. The net result of this exercise, as it will be appreciated, was not only to occupy a considerable amount of time, but to ensure that all the guests knew one another like old friends.

I have found that much preparation can be made useless by the time limit and/or bad editing by the speaker. The speaker usually has had to edit some of his speech on his feet. He frequently has to eliminate something that in retrospect he wishes he had retained and had indeed specially prepared. I had this experience once at the annual dinner of the London Egg Exchange, which really meant the egg trade in London. It was a vast dinner in the Great Hall of Grosvenor House, London, at a time when strikes and threats of strikes, and what was called 'industrial action' in all its forms, was a matter of everyday life. I prepared a whimsy, among other things, for this audience: namely, that I was happy to be able to reassure the London Egg Exchange that there was no truth in the rumour, circulating in the poultry world of the United Kingdom, that the Rhode Island Reds had called a meeting with the White Wyandotes (two species of fowl with names suggestive of political associa-

280

tions), to decide whether both breeds should have 'a sit in', and if so, whether the result would be to further their reasonable demands or would be counter-productive. The Exchange was also to be advised that also unfounded, was the rumour that the meeting was also designed to find out if the White Wyandotes could be trusted to continue to accept the leadership of the Rhode Island Reds in all matters arising from this 'sit in'. I am afraid my time ran out and I had to jettison this theme, which I thought might have amused.

The success of a public dinner, which is the anxious ambition of every Dinner Chairman I have ever met, is not guaranteed, I fear, just by well-chosen food and drink and lively, entertaining speakers. There are other prerequisites whose presence is less easy to guarantee. The well-chosen food and drink must be served timeously. I have known a top table, piped in to a seemingly prestigious and certainly historical venue of hospitality, with the whole company standing and applauding them, then the whole company sitting down, all with whetted appetites. There they sat with one another and nothing on their plates or in their glasses for forty-five minutes, at which point a bread roll was served to each diner; the first sign we had seen that the occasion was supposed to be a banquet. After serving the bread rolls, the previous invisibility of the caterers and their staff was resumed. When they eventually did return, half an hour later with the soup, it was a sullen and cigarette-smoking public that awaited them. Many of the guests, having eaten their single bread roll were now on their feet in the foyer or around the hall, smoking, complaining, abusing the caterers, debating if this would go on much longer. By the time the soup was belatedly served most of the company had lost all interest in the purpose for which they were assembled, namely to eat and drink, hear speeches and hopefully enjoy themselves. Having taken so long for the food to reach the diners, it comes as no surprise that when it came it was lukewarm. The spirit of the occasion had gone from that company, which even the belated service of some wine did not restore. No one was interested in the speakers, who were well aware they were faced with an audience which was by this time in no mood to find anything amusing.

I recall also a Burns supper in Glasgow where the company sat down and then waited some fifty minutes before any food appeared before them. They were, however, a very subdued company: they did not leave their seats or protest, they only became more subdued, their interest in the purpose of the dinner wholly numbed.

Speakers may be well-chosen, but in my experience their success can depend on some other factors than their talents. For one thing, if they have notes they must have something on which to place the notes, something that suits their height and is in a position proximate to the microphone. There is an indifference to these necessities in nearly all those who set out to cater for banquets. They will probably have one lectern which, if it suits a small speaker, will be of no use to a tall one, and the reverse. Its top may be on a slope but with an inadequate sliver of wood along its base to prevent the speaker's paper from slipping to the ground. If the papers are numerous, as mine usually were, and they do slip to the ground, the speaker must then rescue them and hold them in position to the best of his gymnastic ability. At a dinner in a very prestigious hotel in Aberdeenshire, I found on arrival that the microphone was free-standing but was designed for use only by a speaker sitting in front of it. To a standing speaker it was of no use. The hotel did not, at that time, have another microphone (they have one now), and suggested that to use the available and necessary microphone I speak standing behind a podium on which the microphone would be perched. The result was a disaster. The base of the slope of the podium was insufficient to prevent my papers from slipping off when I let them go. Not only did the papers slip off while I was speaking, the microphone began to slip down the surface of the podium. It might have been possible for a contortionist to speak, control his notes and use the microphone in that situation, but it was no use for me. I had only two hands and I needed three; one to hold the speech in place; two to hold the microphone in place; and three to turn the pages of the speech. A subsequent protest to the hotel's owner produced an apology and a promise that in any of his hotels in future I was sure to find proper public address equipment.

I have used my own solution for a lectern on the table for some thirty years, which dispenses with all the uncertainties as to shape and height of the lectern. I carry my notes in a cardboard file – and I fear I need notes – and ask a waiter at the interval before the speeches to let me have three empty wine bottles of the same size. When I have these I stand them as a triangle and the tops give me a base on which to rest my file of notes. They are then level for me, at the right height and the only thing one must do is be careful not to knock a bottle over when turning pages. I have only seen one other person do this with notes and that was no less than the late Roy Jenkins when he addressed the British Chamber of Commerce in Newcastle: he was not taking any risks with lecterns.

Audio equipment is another factor which can make or mar a speaker and a dinner. Testing it – its sensitivity, the optimum distance to be from it when speaking, the sound it can produce, and where and by whom it is being monitored if such a refinement is available – are all desirable. In the Great Room at Grosvenor House in London, there is located near the roof a cubicle in which technicians monitor each and every speaker. I saw this the first time I spoke in London and marvelled at it. Such sophistication is not common, but neither is earlier testing by intending users, who may not only be given a volume of sound and a microphone that needs adjustment to suit them, they may also hear unwanted sounds emerging from such equipment; a high penetrating whine for no apparent reason suggestive of – as one victim put it – 'the presence of uranium in the building's foundations'. Even the most careful and particular of chairmen can be unlucky here. I was told of one who tested the public address equipment the night before a conference meeting, found all to be in order. The next morning, the clear sound was gone. It was discovered that the loud speakers in the ceiling had, during the night, been painted over by the painters working there.

Another factor which I have found can affect the mood of a dinner is lighting. The top table must have sufficient light to enable the speaker to refer to his notes, and he must have sufficient light for him to see his audience and their reaction, and for them to see and identify him: bare visibility is not, to my mind, enough. The effect of a dim half-light over the whole body of the hall, before and during a dinner, seems to produce a like response in all who are subject to it. As the lighting is subdued, so also are those for whom it is meant to illuminate. Trying to speak to misty, ill-defined listeners prejudices the chance, in my view, of any positive, optimistic reaction between them and the speaker.

My excuse for all that I have written here about speaking is that public speaking has occupied a significant place in my life. It started with reciting poems and play-acting as a schoolboy and teenager. It was the medium of the profession I followed. I have had long membership of this after-dinner set and scene. I can therefore at least claim a lengthy experience of speaking in public, but it is, I am very much aware, a restricted experience. The speeches of an advocate in court are concerned with the problems of his client. They may concern questions of life and death, as well as of rights and wrongs. They attempt to articulate the arguments necessary to support a client's case. The ambitions, hopes, regrets of the client have been and are the subjects of the speeches I have there attempted. What I have never done in my after-dinner speaking, however, and never attempted to do, is to speak on those movements which poets call the 'Tides of Men' – politics, faith, national ambitions, the concerns of humanity. Mine have all been of a smaller world, concerned with simpler emotions. They have been attempts to raise a smile, perhaps a laugh, to entertain, to touch nostalgia or the personal emotions. The excuse for all this speaking was given by Thomas Mann: 'Speech is civilisation itself. The word, even the most contradictory word, preserves contact. It is silence which isolates'. And for me it has all been a source of infinite challenge, variety, experience and mostly delight.

# 22

# LEAVING GLASGOW, 1983

I left the Sheriffdom of Glasgow and Strathkelvin in May 1983 for
that of Greenock, Rothesay and Dunoon. At the time I was Senior
Sheriff in Glasgow, in a court I admired and that had an atmosphere all of its own. I had been there for twenty years and had
had what, for me, was certainly a congenial relationship with the
Bar and the Sheriff Clerk's staff and colleagues. The Bar, I know
from what was said to me, were surprised at the move, and the
farewell dinner they gave my wife and myself – from the numbers
present, its generosity, warmth and spontaneity – did not suggest
that they, at least, were happy to see me go.

The balance between the work in the Sheriff Court in Glasgow
and the class in which I lectured Glasgow University had, as I
have already said, greatly suited me, and many a time have I since
regretted that I was ever tempted to give this up for the jurisdiction and the country living that was to accompany it in North
Strathclyde. It was at one stage in these misgivings I said to Archie
MacPherson, the very wise, helpful and experienced Sheriff Clerk
in Greenock, who had known me in my early days in Glasgow,
that I thought I had made, to that date, at least two major mistakes
in my life: one was leaving the Bar when I did; and the other was
leaving Glasgow when I did. His comment was, 'Sheriff, you did
not make two mistakes. You made two blunders'. I may add he
was not alone in giving me the same depressing opinion. Just why
the former was a mistake or a blunder turns on what I had experienced in the ten years I walked the floor of Parliament House.
I was eventually busy there and in the Criminal Courts, but decided
to leave it the year before criminal legal aid was introduced –
which at once altered the financial prospects of a criminal practice

for the first time. If and why the change from Glasgow to Greenock, Rothesay and Dunoon deserved the name of either mistake or blunder turns on the unforeseen and unexpected consequences.

One of these was that in the eyes of many of my Glasgow colleagues and many of the profession, my leaving Glasgow when I was Senior Sheriff was in order to scale down and have an easier life. These were never my objectives, and, in what was the result, life was certainly not easier, but the move certainly created the impression – never intended and never eradicated – that by it I had disqualified myself for any other change; a depressing and disquieting conclusion for one who still had some fifteen years of working life before him. The fact that I left Glasgow and the life there I knew, liked and enjoyed was due to three factors: namely, the house that we owned on Bute; my doctor's advice to my wife that in the interests of my health I should leave the pressures he considered Glasgow put upon me, advice also given her by the late Willy McRae – a senior solicitor we knew well, and for whose opinion she had high regard; and thirdly, her concern at that advice.

In 1971, we purchased the house on Bute where we now live. It was acquired as a holiday home and with a view to eventual retirement but because of its character and location it has been a major influence on how we have spent the later years of our married life. It was built in 1900, by Sir William McEwen, one of the unquestionably great Scottish surgeons, who built it as a country house and as a farm, which he did in fact farm in his spare time. He purchased the farm ground from the family who had had it for centuries. He died in 1924 and his family continued to live in and work the farm until 1970, when it was sold to Bute Estate, who were interested in the land and from whom we purchased the house. As a holiday house it gave much delight to us, to our friends, our children and their many friends. We ceased for years to go on foreign holidays and were satisfied with Costa Clyde, its scenery and its country life. By the 1980s, we began to want not just to have Garrochty as a holiday house, we wanted to live there.

We were tenants in the Old Manse at Larbert and the owners would not sell to us, although they said we could remain there as long as we wished, but space in that delightful house had come to be at a premium for the whole family. I then applied for a transfer from Glasgow to that of Greenock, Rothesay and Dunoon and, in 1983, the application was granted and we confidently thought we could live on Bute and I could commute from there, as the appointment involved sitting in three courts: Rothesay on a Monday; Greenock on a Tuesday, Wednesday and Friday; and Dunoon on a Thursday.

A sheriff is not expected to be a popular figure. His functions necessarily involve decisions that some of the parties involved will resent; in all civil litigation fifty per cent of parties are likely to be dissatisfied. In criminal cases, sentences it is the court's duty to impose, will on occasions involve disposals the reverse of popular with the recipients and their friends. Unlike in the city sheriffdom, in the country, in my experience, the sheriff becomes a socially as well as a professionally isolated figure especially when, as I started at Greenock, I had no personal colleague with whom I could discuss problems. The other sheriff was at that time on sick leave and, in fact, was never able to return to the court.

The first sign that the new court was not Glasgow were the abusive phone calls to the house, usually with sounds of a busy public house in the background. These alarmed my wife. Another was having one of my car tyres slashed in Dunoon. In Rothesay, on the first day I dealt with summary trials, I found at the end of the day, my car being parked on a public street, that it was surrounded by the accused and by his witnesses and friends, who wished to give me their views on the trial and its witnesses. It looked as if I arrived just in time to prevent damage being done. In Glasgow I used, with no inhibitions, to walk the streets at lunchtime, to shop, view a forthcoming auction or simply to have exercise. In the Sheriffdom of North Strathclyde, shortly after I arrived there, I was advised not to walk the streets alone and on one early occasion when I did so in Greenock, I was followed by

287

a gang of youths who clearly knew and identified me, and whose intentions were neither friendly nor indifferent. Even after I retired from Rothesay, if I went to the Health Centre there, hostility would be displayed towards me by some of the others who were in the waiting room. I recollect two occasions in particular: one in which a man who had been sentenced repeatedly by me insisted on giving me his views in loud tones on all things connected with law, order and courts; the other was two youths indulging in snide looks and remarks towards me. It was only after I retired from Rothesay in 1998, that the feeling of isolation I had known before that began to lessen.

Leaving Glasgow meant a loss for me of what had been one of the most satisfying elements of my life. My lecturing on the History of Scots Law at Glasgow University involved meeting interested young people and lecturing on the subject for which I had enthusiasm. There was, however, no way when I was in Greenock in which I could lecture at Glasgow at 5 o'clock and get home that evening. I tried it I think for about three lectures, but it was impossible and hazardous as regards trains and boats. Indeed the question of logistics and communications was one of the major problems I found when I first left Glasgow. The thirty-five minute sail which separates Bute from the mainland imposes a change of lifestyle on those who come to live on the island. I had, until 1983, always lived in mid Scotland. My travel was a half-hour train journey to Glasgow. My friends, associations, leisure pursuits, all the lifestyle built up in twenty-five years of marriage, were on the mainland of Scotland. Now we had gone to live on an island and now, because of that, visits to friends, theatres, concerts involved overnight stays on the mainland. We could no longer entertain friends readily. Most of them baulked at the sea crossing. As one of them put it after a visit here, 'It's a good house in the wrong place'. I could no longer, unless with much travel and much arranging, walk a hill with a dog and a gun. To speak at a dinner after I retired, and I spoke at many, meant following shipping forecasts for two days before, sometimes having to travel to the mainland two days before the dinner. Latterly I was Vice-President of The Stair Society and my experiences of getting to their November meetings was such that, when I retired from that office in 2008, my farewell included what I thought was the sage suggestion that when they decided on a new Vice-President they should, to ensure his attendance at meetings, find a candidate who had an address on the mainland of Scotland.

Before 1983, I had experienced the boat journey from Wemyss Bay to Rothesay and back, but only on the occasional day in winter and encountered no problems. I knew nothing of the uncertainties of daily commuting in winter by ship. I had not discussed them with any of those who were regulars and to be my fellow travellers: therein I made a major omission. I soon learned that the sailings in winter could be unpredictable and that uncertainty added a new source of concern, because if a sheriff is sitting in a court he must get there. The first four winters I lived on Bute I learned all about the vicissitudes of island travel to and from Rothesay and Wemyss Bay.

To ship my own car off the island every day would have been prohibitively expensive and from Wemyss Bay to Greenock I relied on a car, which a friend, one of the regular travellers from Bute, kept at Wemyss Bay. At the end of the day she collected me in Greenock and we drove back to Wemyss Bay. That was the programme. Its successful accomplishment, however, depended on the weather. A morning gale could delay or cancel the sailing. The alternative then was to drive to Colintraive and cross by the short ferry there to the mainland, then to drive to Western Ferries at Dunoon, which were usually running, cross to Gourock and then have a taxi to the court at Greenock. This, of course, depended on finding a driver and a car in Rothesay that would give you a lift. If you were obliged to take that route then your car was still at Wemyss Bay and to get there for the ship in the evening, other arrangements had to be made. I recall one instance, in a July, a force 9 gale blew. No boats would sail from Rothesay. I was offered a lift by a stranger I met on Rothesay Pier who was travelling to

Glasgow Airport. We drove via Colintraive to Dunoon where we hoped to catch a Western Ferry. There we found no Western Ferry running and he then drove the whole way round, by Arrochar and Dumbarton, until I was able to find a taxi near Erskine. I was only an hour late for that court and the Sheriff Clerk had been advised of the situation. The upshot of all this was that, in 1987, a small flat in Glasgow was purchased where I lived from Tuesday to Friday.

If getting to the court had its problems, what was to be found there, particularly in the early days, was not any lesser a workload than I had known in Glasgow. Greenock was a busy court and for the first few years I had the whole of the civil workload. Indeed the workload was only made more reasonable when Sir Steven Young was appointed to Greenock and Dunoon, and later became a full-time Sheriff in Greenock. Many nights I worked in the building until 10.00 p.m. and then stayed the night in Gourock. I arranged to meet the beat policeman at 10.00 p.m. in order that he might see that I locked the building properly. It was then a train to Gourock and walking along a deserted and usually rain-drenched promenade to the hotel where I stayed. That was usually a lonely, and in winter, an eerie experience and, I came to realise, a dangerous one for me on my own.

Each of the three courtrooms were impressive, especially Rothesay. It was a spacious and dignified court, but in winter it could sometimes be uninhabitable. One Monday, early in January 1985, I arrived at the court to find that the Fiscal had arranged to have a Road Traffic Court of cases arising from road traffic offences on the island during the previous summer. There was a packed court. I also found that there had been a breakdown in the central heating system. It had not been used for two weeks and attempts to have it started that morning had failed. The place was like an icebox. With the large number of public present, most of whom had come from the mainland, I considered that the court had to get through all the business down for that day. The Fiscal wore her hat and fur coat. The public, where they could, did likewise.

I sat in a wig and gown, the only supplemental clothing being a waistcoat and cardigan. The crowd was such that I did not consider the court could be held in a small room and deal there with each case on its own. The practice is that the court must be held in public, and had there been solicitors for all accused no doubt an arrangement could have been made to take cases singly in a side room, but where many members of the public were appearing for themselves that would have been an unacceptable course. The court then sat from 10.00 a.m. till about 1.20 p.m. until the business was finished. I have never known so many cases disposed of so quickly. Everyone wanted out. When I tried to get to my feet, however, I was so cold I could hardly stand. That afternoon I found myself unable to breathe and on the Tuesday I was diagnosed with pneumonia. I had an apology from the Scottish Courts Administration for the failure of the central heating system, but it did not prevent the heating in that court breaking down on at least two other occasions, and it did not help my pneumonia from which, I may say, it took me about a year and a half to recover and be back to normal.

One of the most satisfying elements of all three courts was that I enjoyed good relations with the Bar, evidenced not least by the three farewell dinners they each gave me in 1992 when, at sixty-five, I retired from being a full-time sheriff. It is perhaps even more evidenced by the fact that members of the Greenock Bar, some eight years after I retired from temporary sheriffing, honoured me with a dinner on my eightieth Birthday. I regarded that as a very great compliment indeed.

If some of the events I have narrated suggest disillusionment on my part I should make it clear that for my wife and I living on Bute has had many compensations. She wanted to live in the house from the first time she saw it and her enthusiasm for it and the island and its ways have never faltered. She has made many friends and involved herself in the life of the island. For both of us, living there has been the privilege of living in surroundings that all who know or see them admire. It is an atmosphere akin to living in the furthest Hebrides with the constant poetry of sea, mountains and sky and an atmosphere that comes from the knowledge that we live in a valley, still unspoiled, that has been the home of humankind for thousands of years. From our situation we can see the sites of an Iron-Age fort, a Celtic monastery, a small part of a Norse longhouse and a twelfth-century chapel. Living there is to live in a valley of history.

When I submitted the above paragraphs to my wife for her comment, she scorned the suggestion of social and geographical isolation. In particular, by pointing out that we had hosted three twenty-first birthday parties – one for each of our three children – all of whom have gregarious proclivities in which they and their friends indulged on these occasions. Whatever the effect of these parties on the domestic housekeeping there was no doubt that they left me astounded at the difference in behaviour between what the younger generation do today and what my generation did at their age. There was nothing inhibited in their presence and behaviour. In addition, my wife pointed out, that following the precedent of their twenty-first birthdays we then had three of their respective weddings here, with the wedding breakfast lasting the afternoon and well into the evening, with dancing in an old stable, as most guests had found accommodation on the island. It will be appreciated that none of these functions would have been tolerable without the presence of the grape. I am in a position to state that the younger generation with whom I am familiar, are all vigorous supporters of Keats cry, 'Oh for a draught of vintage', and preferably a vintage with 'beaded bubbles winking at the brim'; an enthusiasm destructive of the budget calculations of their father. These family events past, we now, as my wife points out, have regular visits from our children and nine grandchildren who, mercifully, tend to come in shifts. On this history my wife's conclusion is that we are not and have never been lonely. I remain however of the opinion I have expressed.

# 23

# THE LAST LAPS

When I was appointed to Glasgow in 1963 the appointment was *ad vitam aut culpam* – it was for life, provided one did nothing blameworthy. Accordingly, there was no age limit at which one had to retire. Later legislation changed this and the age for retirement is now seventy-two. I knew three High Court judges appointed during the *ad vitam aut culpam* tenure who sat for long after they reached the age of seventy-two. They were Lords Carmont, Cameron and Wheatley and prior to their retirement, I never heard criticism that the powers of the latter two were failing. In 1991, I turned sixty-five and retirement being offered me, I resolved to take it. I did so hoping as I did that some part-time employment would come my way. As it turned out it did and my last seven years in harness gave me enough by way of commitments – interesting commitments – to preclude the feeling of being useless and unwanted and living a life without a purpose, which, to a large extent, has been my fate since.

A vacancy had occurred among the Chairmen of Medical Appeal Tribunals and the Lord President offered me the vacancy. These appeal tribunals consisted of two medical consultants – a consultant physician and a consultant surgeon – with a Legal Chairman. Their jurisdiction was to act as the appeal tribunal to which applicants for disablement benefit (i.e. disablement which comes from the loss of physical or mental faculty resulting from a relevant injury or prescribed disease), who were dissatisfied with the decision of the first tribunal – the adjudicating Medical Authority – on their claim, could appeal. The medical members would invariably, in private, examine the claimant and their decision was final on the medical questions. They rarely disagreed but the chairman had to consider the verbal and written evidence, listen to their conclusions and reasons before he voted and prepared the written decision. From 1992 to 1998, I sat on such tribunals, most of them in Glasgow, but some in Dumfries, Ayr and Aberdeen. To me it was a wholly new jurisdiction, its technique wholly different from what I had been used to. Its procedure was painstakingly investigatory and not adversarial like the courts.

The other appointment was as a temporary sheriff. This was the period when given the escalation in court business, particularly in criminal matters, the existing full-time personnel of the Sheriff Court were swamped. Temporary sheriffs who were advocates or solicitors in general practice were appointed to sit in those courts whose business required assistance, either regularly or in an emergency. I did not apply to become a temporary sheriff; the Scottish Courts Administration invited me to become one immediately on my retirement from North Strathclyde. This was work I enjoyed. It was mostly summary trials but there was also, on occasions, some important civil business. One, in particular, was a case I heard in Arbroath which went on for about a year. The proof involved detailed investigation into the history of the piece of ground in dispute between the parties: an investigation which involved consideration of a multitude of plans, documents and dispositions. For about fourteen days, spread over the year, counsel for the pursuer and solicitor for the defender explored the implications of these productions. So complex and numerous in law and in fact did the issues become that at the end of the evidence I invited the pleaders to let me have their submissions in writing. This was done and a day was then occupied in their amplifying and explaining these. As a result, the pursuer was successful but it took a judgment of twenty-five closely typewritten pages to explain and determine the issues. I continued to sit in Rothesay on Mondays until 1998, but I enjoyed travelling the country and in the period I was a temporary sheriff I sat in Rothesay, Ayr, Lanark, Stirling, Falkirk, Linlithgow, Alloa – all within striking distance of home and Glasgow where I had the advantage of using our flat – Perth, Dundee, Aberdeen, Forfar, Arbroath, Stornoway, Fort William, Dumfries, Stranraer and Cupar, where I became familiar with the varying accommodation and cuisine of local hotels, and the proclivities of some of the locals.

The volume of criminal business in the Sheriff Court is today, as it has been since the late 1960s, of such volume that the old system of one or two sheriffs for a sheriffdom is wholly inadequate. The employment of temporary sheriffs is the only solution that has been found but it is a solution that in my experience – and I served as one in the 1990s – is not without some disadvantages. In particular, when you have temporary sheriffs appearing in different courts all over Scotland continuity and consistency in sentencing is almost impossible, as is control of the progress of a case. One of the principal characteristics and advantages of the old shrieval system was, as the late Sheriff C. D. L. Murray put it, and I have quoted this earlier, that: 'It is important for a sheriff to know his Sheriffdom and it is even more important for the Sheriffdom to know its sheriff'. This is now impossible. The single sheriff cannot now cope with the flood of business. Another characteristic of the old system, which had gone by the 1990s, was the control which a permanent sheriff could keep over the progress of a summary criminal case. If the object of an accused is to postpone any trial that he is involved in for as long as possible, or to postpone the plea of 'guilty' he intends to make, until he finds on the bench the sheriff who has a reputation, or is believed to have a reputation, for leniency, the potential for indulging these ambitions is implicit in the present system. It is, I am told, accepted nowadays that the picking of a sheriff by an accused is not difficult, provided he is given to patience and determination. The practice is popularly known as 'sheriff shopping'. The mechanics of this include Motions for Adjournments before a trial starts, and before sentence is passed, if there has been a trial and a guilty verdict is returned. A familiar ground for seeking an adjournment of a trial or sentence before a sheriff, whose sentences were unpopular with their recipients, is that the accused is due to stand trial for another offence in the near future, and it is suggested to be desirable that all outstanding matters be dealt with at the same time. An accused that qualified for membership of what the late Lawrence Dowdall called the 'cognoscenti' of the Sheriff Court, might not only have one outstanding trial, he might have several. And if he had not, and the adjournment was granted, he might – it was not uncommon – in the interval acquire more outstanding trials which for him made the inevitable motion for adjournment increasingly desirable. If there are frequent motions for an adjournment of a trial or sentencing, a permanent sheriff will early become aware of the real objects of the motions and the weight to be placed on them. A temporary sheriff who hears a motion for an adjournment by an accused only once, even though the case history shows there have been many previously, is not in the same position. The repertoire of reasons for seeking adjournments range from what are, sometimes, valid and accepted by both sides, to the spurious. I remember one case where a solicitor, defending a two-police witness Breach of the Peace, had not been able to see one of the two witnesses. He wanted an adjournment to another day. An offer of postponing the trial till the afternoon, i.e. at least four hours later, was claimed to be inadequate for the solicitor to interview the witness. He insisted he must have an adjournment.

If reports have been called for they may contain a suggestion which indicates, according to the defence, that more information is required and a further report like a psychiatric report should be obtained and the case is again adjourned. A familiar ground, pled for an adjournment if a sentence of imprisonment was likely, was a plea that the accused had just obtained a job for the first time in many years, and had provided the new employer's name. This happened to me twice early in my period on the bench and on each occasion I continued the case for evidence of the job to be produced. On both occasions the solicitor apologised to me at the Continued Hearing for giving me wrong information. There was no job. His instructions had been as he said but the named employer knew nothing of the accused. In the last resort an adjournment can frequently be obtained by simply not turning up, or having turned up and not liking what was on the bench, departing before their case was called, accepting as part of the exercise the warrant for arrest and forfeiture of bail that would follow.

Where there have been frequent adjournments, the court seems on occasions to have lost control of the case and of the accused. I recall going as a temporary sheriff to Aberdeen when there was placed before me to deal with, a numerous collection of complaints (i.e. documents which contained the criminal charge), all, involving the same accused. My recollection is that there were nineteen complaints in all, all of different dates, all having been often adjourned for sentence, but all brought together that morning. This was a situation where I knew nothing of the facts of each case other than the fact that the accused had plead or had been found 'guilty'. The practice was that a sheriff who had tried a case should be the sheriff who sentenced, but in those days, and in particular with this accused, adjournments to a date when the trial sheriff was available had not been successful and the situation then reached, to my mind, bordered on the farcical. This was an accused the system had enabled to avoid any sentence for a very long period. Here indeed was a situation where those who were the victims of the accused's actings had every reason for wondering when – if ever – the law was going to catch up with him. After considering the charges, hearing the facts of each complaint and the defence solicitor that morning in Aberdeen, I brought an end to the process and passed sentences on each complaint. As a result I was appealed on every one of these complaints. I have no record of the result of these appeals and am now unable to obtain it.

Another case which comes to mind was one in Cupar Sheriff Court in the mid-1990s where a youth with many convictions acquired another before me. He came from Dundee but had found the amenities of the Tay Road Bridge enabled him to cross the river and continue his depredations in Fife. His favourite pastime was stealing and wrecking other people's cars. He was a youth on whom the Social Work Department had expended much effort, patience, and time. Even they, however, in their report recognised that for this accused the end of his liberty was becoming inevitable. They retained, however, the view that reformation was possible. A new scheme of intensive Social Work involvement was being started in Dundee. It was called, as I recall, 'Alternative to Custody' and the defence solicitor appearing recommended that the case be adjourned for this accused to have the opportunity of participating. The reports that were available did not encourage the view that there would be cooperation from the accused. However, the plea was made and I, wrongly as I see it now, offered him the chance of participating in this new scheme, but I did so on three conditions: (1) that if he did not cooperate to the full in this scheme, a custodial sentence would be likely to follow in the case before me; (2) that he must remain of good behaviour; and (3) that I would personally deal with the case at the end of the adjourned period. Accordingly, I indicated that I would only adjourn if the case were adjourned to a date where I would be in the court to hear how effective the cooperation of the accused had been, and what effect the Alternative to Custody process was thought to have had. What followed was on the one hand not surprising, but on the other a little perplexing.

When I returned to Cupar on the day to which the case had been adjourned I was advised that the accused had not appeared. I was advised that he was in custody in Dundee on another charge and had not been brought that morning to Cupar. Clearly someone other than the court had decided that this accused would not appear on the date the court had ordered. I was further told that arrangements could not be made to bring him that morning from Dundee to Cupar. I was never given an explanation for the failure to bring him, or who decided that he could not be brought and why. This looked to me suspicious. I made it very clear to the Crown and the defence and to anyone else in the court who was interested that I did not consider Dundee and Cupar to be separated by hostile Indian territory, said to be one of the proverbial American excuses for non-appearance in the nineteenth century, and indicated that I would remain in Cupar that day until the accused was brought and dealt with. By the afternoon he was in court. He had not cooperated in the new scheme and in that situation the sentence he had been told he would probably receive was passed. As I recall it was thereafter unsuccessfully appealed. Had I not been the sheriff who originally dealt with this accused and given him the clear warnings I had – another temporary sheriff would have known little or nothing of the warnings, their nature and their content – no doubt the accused would have remained in Dundee and not been sentenced at that time. In my original disposal I then realised I had made a mistake. I was responsible for giving this youth his liberty to attend the Social Work Department for this Alternative to Custody process, which could not be given if he was in custody. I gave him his liberty, a liberty he abused by damaging several cars and thereby causing more distress to car owners in Dundee and district.

My childhood and youth, as I have earlier described, were much occupied with learning and speaking verse and with amateur dramatics. Now, in my crepuscular years these enthusiasms have recently revived in my becoming absorbed in a long poem, much admired by the Victorians, which has given me the unique and rewarding experience of performing with Dr John Dagg. He was one of the regular consultant physicians I met on medical appeal tribunals. From his colleagues I learned that he was an accomplished pianist. Just how accomplished I was to have the opportunity and privilege of appreciating.

As a youth I had come to read and to know much of the poetry of the Victorian Poet Laureate, Alfred Lord Tennyson. About 1864, he published a long poem called 'Enoch Arden', which described situations and sentiments very much part of the Victorian ethos, which not only characterised a local phase but was a phase common to all Western Europe. 'Enoch Arden' was not only familiar and greatly admired poetry to the reading public of the United Kingdom, as the late G. M. Young put it, 'It took the heart of the

German people by storm'. There were no less than twelve translations of the poem into German before 1914. One of the German enthusiasts for the poem was the then young musician and composer, Richard Strauss, who composed a pianoforte score to accompany the public reading of the poem. He called it, 'Enoch Arden: Melodrama for Piano and Speaker'. With that melodrama, Strauss at the piano and the then Director of Munich Opera as reader, they toured Germany and their performances earned Strauss a reputation and popularity which even the early tone poems he had already composed had not given him.

Originally my knowledge of Strauss' pianoforte composition did not extend beyond simply knowing of its existence. I tried to interest a number of musical friends in the project of performing it but none showed any interest or enthusiasm until I approached Dr Dagg, who was interested. He tried to obtain the score in London and failing to find it there, traced it in Germany. I recall him saying to me when he had received it – and even to look at, it was a complex and demanding score – 'This will take me three months to master', and master it he did. Then came many protracted rehearsals made difficult for both of us, but more for Dr Dagg, by the fact that I could not read music and my speaking to the piano score largely depended on my increasing familiarity with the sound of it. By 2003, we considered we were at the stage where we could appear with it before an audience on a number of charity occasions.

Today, a melodrama which celebrates some of the virtues and values of the Victorians does not immediately appeal as a form of entertainment. The performances we have given have all been for charity; its performance with an interval occupies an evening. But if we are to judge by the reaction of the audiences at the time – and they have included all ages – and the comments they have afterwards made personally and in writing, then it would appear that the capacity of the piece to entertain, though once called an example of 'the rouge of ornate literature', has not disappeared. One letter we had, wrote:

Although I have heard many positive comments from the crowd that night I think my favourite was that of a lady who asked why there had to be a break because she just wanted the story to go on and on. I felt the same and was enchanted by the whole thing.

Another written comment contained the following:

It proved to be an epic poem and I mean by that a great story which kept the audience on the edge of their seats wondering what was going to happen next – poor Enoch Arden is a sailor and this is the classic tale of the wrecked seaman and the devastation that this does to his own life and that of his family and friends, it seems quite inconceivable that the music has remained hidden for so long. Richard Strauss currently enjoys much popularity with such pieces as the *Four Last Songs*, *The Alpine Symphony*, *Salome* and many others. This music is of similar stature and accessibility. The performance makes for a truly thrilling evening with none of the dry intellectuality I for one had expected 'in this tonal poem.'

Our last performance of it to date was in May 2008, and by that time the piece had become very much part of our respective lives, and, for both of us was the experience of knowing and performing an original and unique masterpiece which thanks to a number of recent CDs and to our efforts, is at last coming to be more generally known after nearly a century of indifference.

# EPILOGUE

I had ten years as a practising advocate, thirty-six years sitting on the Sheriff Court bench – twenty years in Glasgow, nine in Greenock, Rothesay and Dunoon, and the remainder in courts all over Scotland. If it is correct to say that the proper study of mankind is Man and, of course Woman, what I have seen and heard in these courts in these forty-six years convinces me that this admittedly proper study is one where the student will never exhaust the subject. There is early realisation that the doings of humanity are infinitely varied, and as infinitely varied are the explanations that humanity frequently offers to explain these doings.

For me, the prerequisites of this study have been the personal and domestic life that I have been privileged to experience. I have tried here to describe it. I was an only child of middle-aged parents. My mother was forty-two when she had me, and they, and especially my mother, gave me all they could of the limited resources that were theirs, and encouragement in everything in which I was interested or in which they thought I should be interested. I survived childhood indifferent to the claims of games and it was only in my mid-twenties that I discovered what I enjoyed in the way of exercise which was to become an enthusiastic walker. When you lived in Falkirk and had no car, walking the streets gave exercise but little pleasure. Then about the mid-1950s I discovered what it was to walk hills – not mountains – and then for as long as I lived on the mainland, that is until 1983, my supreme joy was to walk a small heather-topped hill known as Broadside Moor, near Carronbridge. In season I walked with a gun and later was joined by a dog: out of season with a dog and a cromack.

It started when a friend I had known from infancy showed an

302

interest in shooting rabbits. He had a car and one afternoon we stopped at the farm of North Shields near Fankerton, a few miles from Falkirk, and asked the farmer there, Alec Adam, if we could have his permission to shoot rabbits on his ground. Alec was a canny character and did not go on appearances. Our antecedents, their occupations, our history and the like were all inquired of by him and his wife, but he gave his consent. My friend's enthusiasm for shooting rabbits did not last, mine did. The next thing was to get a proper gun. First, I had an ancient hammer twelve-bore given me by a farmer which early proved to be too dangerous an implement. Then my Aunt Agnes gave me £15 to buy a second-hand box lock twelve-bore that a gamekeeper near her home in Ayrshire was selling. With that gun every Saturday I took the bus to Fankerton and walked the mile or so to the farm. I shot the very odd rabbit but I had found a sport and exercise to my liking and to my pocket; the privilege was free. I came to know that farmer and his wife very well indeed. At first myself, later my wife and our children, went weekly to that farm. He and his wife became friends such that he attended my parents' funerals and gifted me a derelict cottage and its surrounding ground on one of the best sites in Stirlingshire.

There was another character besides the farmer and his wife to be met at North Shields. Indeed the domestic situation there offered a rare if not unique variation of the normal relations between the parties to the ancient relationship of master and servant. The farm and a nearby field and hill were about 180 acres, devoted mainly to beef cattle and with one 'house cow' which supplied the house with milk. The farmer Alec Adam and his wife worked the place between them till, during the War, they were allocated an Italian prisoner of war to work with them. He was called 'Lui', although his real name was Luigi Pisani. He lived to work and on that farm he could, would and did turn his hand to any job required of him. When he was called upon to work he did so willingly and untiringly. When I knew him, he had no other interests than his work. In him the Adams had found an ideal help. In the Adams, Lui had found an ideal home.

He was one of the household. He had his bedroom. He had his board. Anything he needed the Adams supplied. When TV came in he sat with them in the evenings, as he ate with them every day. I question if he ever left the farm – except on one occasion, when he had an appendectomy in a local hospital – until eventually he left it finally, after Alec Adam died in 1977. Even in winter when the cattle were in the byre he would spend days chopping firewood into various sizes and stacking the products of his efforts against the barn wall. I remember these stacks reaching up to about eight feet high. At the end of the War, he stayed on. He had no difficulty in abandoning the lure of the macaroni, olive oil and sunshine of his native Italy for the simple fare and simple comforts of the Adam farmhouse and the uncertain climate of the Denny hills. He was eventually naturalised as a United Kingdom subject.

At the end of the War, with his decision to stay on at North Shields, Alec Adam, I was told, paid him wages, which, since he neither spent nor speculated, gradually accumulated. The story I had was that some of his family came from Italy to visit him but were more interested in his accumulated money than they were in their relative. They obtained the money and departed not to return. It was at this stage that he first refused to accept further wages from his employer, while continuing to work with the same enthusiasm as he had shown from the start. Alec, I was told, put money aside for him and then there arose the inevitable question of tax liability. To this, Lui took an uncompromising stance. He had no need to pay for the necessities of life – he had a home – he had his food regularly – he had no expensive pastimes. His attitude was he did not need money and adopted a unique and some would say enviable attitude. He point-blank refused to pay income tax and accepted that if he were to succeed in that stand his employer should not pay him any wages. In the result he continued to work with his customary energy and enthusiasm and refused to accept any wage. When Alec died in 1977 my recollection is that he had made some provision for Lui who had served him so long, so willingly and so well. From then on he lived in the locality to which he had come as prisoner of war, and lived there until he died at the age of ninety-one, having shown all the patience, industry and resilience of the peasant folk of old Calabria.

It did not take long to walk the fields of North Shields but every Saturday afternoon in the early 1950s, to do so was the high mark of the week. A few years later, through the good offices of Alec Adam, I acquired the right to shoot the farm of Broadside, part of which marched with North Shields and included a small moor – Broadside Moor. With this my shooting horizons widened and even more so when shortly after my marriage I acquired the first of many black Labrador bitches. As a child I had longed for a dog but my mother's view was that 'living upstairs' disqualified us from canine ownership.

Broadside Moor could be approached by a long slow uphill walk or by one of two very steep climbs – but what you found when you reached the top rewarded all the effort of getting there. It had on it heather and a few coveys of grouse, but walking up them was accompanied by viewing superb scenery. At first I usually went on my own, later I would occasionally have a companion or two. When I was courting Diana, who became my wife, she used to come. She even used to carry anything I shot. Her services here were not often required: the bag was never large – I should add that I never shot anything I would not eat – but her willingness was impressive. I thought here was a Diana who lived up to her name. It must, however, be stated that as from the date of our marriage any desire Diana had to emulate her namesake, the goddess, disappeared. She did not go out much with the gun again but one day she attended a shoot with me at Methven in Perthshire, where there was not only a wood heavily populated with pheasants, there was an all-male shooting party who became so excited with the number of birds that it was only by a miracle that by the end of that shoot there were the same number of shooters active and alive as had been active and alive at its start. It finished Diana with shooting. For the future she did not walk hills: she only cooked what little game her husband brought home.

That I was able to shoot over that little grouse moor at Broadside does not bespeak opulence or extravagance. The birds were few; there would be about three or four coveys in a good year, and usually the odd single bird. These grouse were not to be driven; they were walked up with a dog and they would only let a gun near them at the first or second attempts. A covey once shot at was careful not to let you or your dog near them again, but there was always the hope, and there was the exercise, the climb, the walk, and the view. I climbed that hill in the shooting season nearly every Saturday in the mid-1950s and '60s, and about nearly every second Saturday in the 1970s until 1983. On Sundays we would take the children there for a walk, but they did not then share my enthusiasm for hillwalking. They have it now. The view from the top of the moor is engraved on my memory. From the top looking west you saw the city of Glasgow, with the University easily identifiable. Looking north you saw Stirling and the Dumbarton and Perthshire Hills. To the south and east you saw the Firth of Forth with its Bridges and Arthur's Seat above Edinburgh. That view on a clear day – and in memory they nearly all seemed to have been clear days – never failed to entrance me, and when I sat and gazed on the panorama I had a habit of quoting aloud to myself A. E. Houseman's Lines:

> Into my heart an air that kills
> From yon far country blows:
> What are those blue remembered hills,
> What spires, what farms are those?
>
> That is the land of lost content,
> I see it shining plain,
> The happy highways where I went
> And cannot come again.

In the mid-1960s, a restaurant was opened in Stirling, run by a Swiss chef and a Scottish entrepreneur and his wife. Their food was ambitious and exceptional and in the area their restaurant became the fashionable place to eat. I spoke at two or three functions there and at one of them there was also a farmer by the name of David Bryce who, hearing of my interest in shooting, invited me to shoot any day I wanted over his farms in the Carse of Stirling. From that invitation a small syndicate emerged, its membership: two businessmen, a chartered accountant, a university professor (a Doctor of Civil Law of Oxford), David himself, and another farmer, Arthur Binnie. Arthur who, until his untimely death, farmed 'The Braes of Boquhapple', a place name which evokes memories of gentle braes and kindly ways which were Arthur himself. We also had in our syndicate some four or five of our younger generation, and myself. And on Saturdays when we were not at Carronbridge, we were on David's land, or on the shootings we had leased on Callendar Estate in Falkirk. David became a great friend and was one of the great characters of my life; a farmer who had his art in his blood. He was at least the fourth generation of Bryces to farm that ground and his sons and his grandsons farm it now. He loved the company of our group and every Saturday we were there, Mrs Bryce had us into the house for a plate of soup and a seat while we ate our sandwiches, talked and drank some wine. David had an aptitude for the telling comment. He characterised what he considered my incessant search for places to walk and shoot in the sentence, 'Irvine, when you're no fishing, you're mending your nets';

1974 was to be a watershed in my life. In May in my forty-seventh year, as I have already described, I was the victim of what I was told was a massive coronary infarction, from which I was lucky to escape with my life. The winter of 1973–74 had been a busy one. It ended with my trying the civil action of damages against Rangers that arose from the deaths of the people injured and killed in the Ibrox Disaster of 1971. That case is described earlier in these pages but its last episode, as far as I was concerned, was this coronary. When it seemed I had the chance of surviving, two things obsessed me; one, the preparation of the postponed judgment in the Rangers case; the other what to do to enable me to lead, what one cardiologist called 'an active life'. I was allowed to start on the judgment in September. It was issued on 23 October. The therapy by which I hoped to return to an active life was slow. The treatment for such conditions has now, I understand, changed. Then it involved slow and gentle return to physical activities. On the Island of Bute I started with very short walks going a little further each day. When we got back to the mainland I supplemented the walking with an exercise bicycle. I sat on it every evening in the corridor of the Old Manse where we lived, starting with five minutes and gradually increasing this til, when I got back to work in October, I was sitting there pedalling every night for thirty minutes. Here was an easy and a pleasant therapy because you could read while you were pedalling and it brought me back to walking hills and not too strenuous and not too successful walks with dog and gun. At last I did get back to my old and favourite pastime of 'travelling hills'. As a consequence of that, a few years ago one cardiologist described my then cardiac history as 'singular and remarkable'. The emphasis is on the word 'then.' In April 2010 I had another coronary infarction.

If I had an active life after 1974, as I think I had until 2003 – when there began to be limitations in physical effort – it was due to my wife. Her approach to the post-cardiac situation was to acquire cookery books designed for safe cardiac cooking – 'to promote a healthy heart' – and to put me on a diet they recommended. She put me on it, kept me on it and, what is more, she joined me in it, with latterly a daily modicum of red wine of whose health-giving properties I have no doubt. My recovery from that coronary and indeed every other happiness that has come my way since I married her, I owe to my wife.

Diana was the third of her parents' four children, two boys and two girls. Her father was a successful haulage contractor in Yorkshire until 1948 when he purchased what was to become a highly successful and much respected hotel; The Colonnade in Maida Vale in London, to which his two sons succeeded. Her mother who was from Lincolnshire was eleven years older than her husband and survived him for twenty-two years. They were a happy prosperous couple and came from prosperous folk. All four of their children had public school educations and Diana became a teacher in London. I met her by a circuitous route and circumstances. Her younger brother attended the Hotel School in Glasgow and became friendly with the younger son of a family who lived opposite my home in Falkirk and also attended the Hotel School. I had known him and his brother from infancy. He became friendly with Diana's brother and through him he met Diana and became her boyfriend. Then the father of that Falkirk family died leaving the mother with a large house. The younger son, Diana's boyfriend, persuaded Diana to come to Scotland to teach, and to live with his mother with a view to the two of them eventually marrying. She came and settled in with the mother and obtained a teaching appointment nearby, and when all this was completed the boyfriend took up with another girl whom he married, and added what I thought was an insult to injury, by inviting Diana to accompany his mother to his wedding. Diana tells me I was not the first to apply for the post vacated by the recently wed, but if I was not it was certainly not because I had other ideas, because I was never in any doubt about the only woman I wanted for a wife.

Marriage was in view from 1956 when we spent our first holiday together as an engaged couple in Ireland. In one important sense this was an old-fashioned marriage. The male was kept at a respectable distance until the vows had been taken. I had my misgivings about my being accepted by her family, but I was accepted by all her family and none of them ever so much as hinted to me that Diana could or should have made a better or more affluent marriage. I have no doubt she could have, but the fact that I came from a poorer social and economic level than theirs was never once hinted at. Later, when I appeared with her in Scotland people were usually curious to know how I had met her. She had what my father always called 'a touch of class'. During our honeymoon in Kintyre we were invited to the wedding of the son of the big house, Ronachan; Mrs Pollock's son. There the whole village attended and I then knew the village and the folk in that part of the world. I had holidayed there for some years. The minister was there – he was from Skye with the lilt of the West Highlands in his tongue and he said to me as I introduced my wife, 'And where did you meet your wife?' My reply was 'She comes from London. She came to Scotland to teach Scottish children'. He paused he looked down at Diana and simply said, 'What presumption'.

In the life that followed our marriage each accepted that it was a joint adventure. Diana continued teaching, I became busy at the Bar, which meant being in court during the day and preparing and drafting pleadings at nights and weekends. I used to work every night from 7 till 11 p.m., walking the dog on empty roads last thing at night. At weekends, on Friday night, we entertained or were entertained. I was usually in Parliament House on a Saturday morning and walking with a gun in the afternoon, and Saturday evenings we were again part of the social life of the Parliament House. The Bar regarded one's social responsibilities in such matters as important. On Sundays I usually worked for about ten to twelve hours. I marvelled and appreciated then, and still do, at the readiness and resilience of Diana after a week's teaching to devote the weekends to cooking for and entertaining company. She never complained. She had a reputation of being an adventuresome and successful cook. She did what I knew the wife of no other university teacher that I knew did, and have referred to this earlier; she entertained her husband's class, my class in the History of Scots Law, to dinner every year until my coronary. It was a process which since the class grew in size, no doubt because of her culinary reputation rather than the lectures delivered by her husband. One year required three dinners, although it was usually two to enable us to entertain them all, and I may add, each of those classes had us back to dinner in one of their homes, digs or a restaurant.

Diana accepted that the life we wanted to live required what resources we each could contribute, especially when it came to the

310

children born in 1960, '63 and '66 and their secondary and university education. With Richard it was more than just education. He studied medicine at Glasgow and we soon realised that in Glasgow the medical profession was a largely hereditary profession and most of Richard's friends were the sons of doctors and had cars. This started his plaints for a car which he got I think in his second year. It was a second-hand car and was constantly in need of repairs. Indeed I think he had four second-hand cars in succession until I eventually realised that it would be economical to buy him a new car and he was bought a Fiat Panda. This was one of the reasons why his mother willingly went on teaching. Indeed throughout the marriage she only gave up teaching while the children were young, returning to it thirteen years later, and taught thereafter until we came to live on Bute.

Throughout our married life of now over fifty years she has given me constant encouragement, support, balance and a home life free from stress and disagreement. I say it with every conviction; she is the nearest approach to a saint I am ever likely to meet. She is a devout and practising Christian. In her nature there can be determination but there is neither envy nor bitterness. To all with whom she is in contact she presents unwavering courtesy and inexhaustible charity. Where on my part, there may be resentment or anger, with Diana there is always patience, as well as civil, friendly, conciliatory, kind words. There is intelligence and common sense of a high order and an appreciation of what should be the response of her husband and her children, as it is hers, to the vicissitudes and challenges of life. I should add the attention she gave to her children she has continued to give to their children. She is a woman with unfailing resources of courtesy, patience and civility to all she encounters.

At the age of eighty-four I have had a long life and in it, if I have made anything of it that has been worthwhile, it is due to what two women have done for me. In my youth and early manhood, while she still had her mind, it was my mother. Of her, John Galsworthy's comment, 'A mother is in labour for her first-born son as long as she lives' would be an accurate, and to her acceptable, epitaph. The other has been my wife. Of the life I have been privileged to live with Diana I know no better appreciation than that which Robert Louis Stevenson wrote of his wife:

> Teacher, tender, comrade, wife,
> A fellow-farer true through life,
> Heart-whole and soul-free
> The august father
> Gave to me.

There has been nothing spectacular or exceptional in the life we have lived together, nothing which makes our view of what life has been to us, significant to any except ourselves and our children. It is still given to most couples – and used to be the ideal of all – to have found joy in laughter, in the love of friends and lasting happiness in the company of one another and that of our children. As, however, we look back down the arches of the years we know, as do most of our generation, that even as life has passed us by, so also have passed many of those things we in our youth and maturity believed to be worthy and of good report. It is a spectacle of which any court is daily the microcosm. What W. B. Yeats, in 'The Second Coming', described as the human situation as he saw it in the early part of the twentieth century remains, in our minds, still true of the world today. Indeed the world today has become infinitely more perilous.

> ... Things fall apart; the centre cannot hold;
> Mere anarchy is loosed upon the world,
> The blood-dimmed tide is loosed, and everywhere
> The ceremony of innocence is drowned;
> The best lack all conviction, while the worst
> Are full of passionate intensity.

Having lived long under the shadow of such a human situation and experienced its social consequences, makes pessimism to members of my generation, if not actual despair, difficult to resist. To all this I have found at least a partial palliative in the occupation and interests I have pursued and tried to recall in these pages. The interests could, I think, be described as harmless, the occupation fascinating and all-absorbing because the law and the courts are concerned in acute and personal detail with the infinite variety of the passions, challenges, ambitions and interests of humanity. Herein has been for me an experience eloquently and succinctly described in a couplet by John Buchan from a poem entitled 'From the Pentlands looking North and South'. It runs:

> Before me lie the lists of strife,
> The caravanserai of life ...

These words seem to me evocative of the life – at least until now – I have not only had the privilege but the good luck to experience.

# ENDNOTES

1   One of Aunt Chrissie's letters, whose existence and purpose I had
    forgotten, I recently found when clearing some old files. It was a
    letter she had written to me dated 1 June 1951 and from an address
    in Torquay where she was companion to the elderly lady who was
    its owner. Its occasion was my completing my Law Degree in May,
    and my having written to her with the news. She knew the hand-
    some gesture and when to make it. She had always remembered
    me at birthdays and Christmases but, on what she considered to
    be a special occasion, her marking of it took a form which only she
    of the Smith siblings had the experience and the means to make.
    Here is what she wrote:

    My Dear Irvine,

    Yesterday I must have divined the news you were then writing to
    me. I wrote to Mr Durnin at the Clydesdale Bank in Stenhousemuir
    [he as I recall was the Manager there and looked after her affairs]
    that I wanted to transfer my holding in J P Coats to you and here-
    with I send you these papers to digest . . . In October last Lever
    Company was giving their shareholders a chance to increase their
    holdings. I have 80 and thought how much better it would be to
    have 100 . . . but my luck was out he [Mr Durnin] was on holiday
    and it was too late when he applied. He then suggested J & P Coats.
    As you will see the 100 £1 Shares were rather expensive but the
    dividend is 12.5% yearly and this year a bonus was expected –
    it may happen later in the year as the Company is flourishing. I shall
    like you to have a stake in the country. Needless to say I am very
    delighted you have reached your goal.

    Love to all,
    Aunt Chrissie.

I may add, Stocks and Shares did not figure in my parents' experience. This was the first investment I had ever possessed.

2 The Phoney War lasted from September 1939 to May 1940. It was the period when Britain had declared war on Germany but there was a lack of major military operations in Europe. The Battle of France brought an end to the Phoney War.

3 Agnes Mure Mackenzie *Scottish Pageant 55 B.C. A.D. 1513*

4 Willingness to adhere means he or she would be willing to have the deserter back and continue the marriage.

5 To find that he was art and part in the murder meant that they accepted that he had been an accomplice in the commission of the crime.

6 [1991] SLT, 211.

7 Ibid., 212.

8 Ibid., 213.

9 There was a 'second' Battle of the Somme in 1918.

10 Archibald Alison, *Principles of the Criminal Law of Scotland (1832)*, p.62. Reprint with an introduction by the author of this book.

11 Ibid., p.65.

12 On a summary conviction there is a fine limit of £5,000. The limit for imprisonment for a person over twenty-one is three months, or up to six months if there is a second or subsequent offence, inferring dishonest appropriation of property or an offence inferring personal violence.

13 Summary jurisdiction is not to be confused with what is called 'summary justice'. The former refers to the constitution and procedure of the court, as contrasted with solemn procedure, which involves the jury. Summary justice refers to a court in a hurry and indifferent to the elementary rules of justice, aiming at the maximum number of convictions in the shortest possible time. Scotland, in the past, has considerable experience of such summary justice. The saying 'Jeddart justice', refers to incidents in the Borders, when James VI sought to introduce some law and order to the area, and meant, 'Hang him first and try him afterwards'. We experienced it again during the Cromwellian Union (1650–1660), which followed Cromwell's conquest of Scotland after the Battle of Dunbar. English commissioners were appointed to administer justice and earned a deserved reputation for speed. An example of their methods was the three days they spent in 1652, in the trial and fining of several

persons for adultery, were appointed to administer justice and earned a deserved reputation for speed. An example of their methods was the three days they spent in 1652, in the trial and fining of several persons for adultery, incest and fornication, for which there were over sixty persons brought before the judges in a day. This, by any standard, represents a high incidence of adultery, incest and fornication in a professedly godly and covenanted people, and a truly phenomenal expedition on the part of the court. It has been suggested that the judges would have devised a form of summary procedure which was more concerned with statistics then justice – an unfailing characteristic of summary justice, which has in my reading and experience no equivalent in post seventeenth-century Scotland.

14  [1973] SLT (Sh. Ct.), p.27.
15  *Mens rea* is having a guilty mind/ criminal intention.
16  The crime of reset consists in knowingly receiving articles taken by theft, robbery, embezzlement or fraud and feloniously retaining them or being privy to the retaining of property which has been dishonestly come by.
17  *HMA* v. *Dewar*, [1945] JC 5, 11; [1945] SLT, 114, at p. 115.
18  [1972] SLT (Sh. Ct.) p.2.
19  Austin Lane Poole, *The Oxford History of England, Volume III: From Domesday Book to Magna Carta, 1087–1216*, Oxford University Press, 1951. p. 502.
20  Geoffrey Parker, *Empire War and Faith in Early Modern Europe*, Penguin, 2003. p. 254.
21  [1956] 1WLR
22  [1957] 1WLR
23  *HMA* v. *Soni* [1970] SLT 275
24  *Steele* v. *The Scottish Daily Record and Sunday Mail Limited*, [1970] SLT 53
25  [1970] SLT 53